W9-AUY-765

Terry,

Wishing you all
the joy & love
you deserve!

♡ connie

THE OTHER SIDE OF THE BAYOU

Based on a True Story

BY CONSTANCE SCHRODER STEWART

BALBOA.
PRESS
A DIVISION OF HAY HOUSE

Copyright © 2016 Constance Schroder Stewart.

All rights reserved. No part of this book may be used or reproduced by any means, graphic, electronic, or mechanical, including photocopying, recording, taping or by any information storage retrieval system without the written permission of the author except in the case of brief quotations embodied in critical articles and reviews.

Balboa Press books may be ordered through booksellers or by contacting:

Balboa Press
A Division of Hay House
1663 Liberty Drive
Bloomington, IN 47403
www.balboapress.com
1 (877) 407-4847

Because of the dynamic nature of the Internet, any web addresses or links contained in this book may have changed since publication and may no longer be valid. The views expressed in this work are solely those of the author and do not necessarily reflect the views of the publisher, and the publisher hereby disclaims any responsibility for them.

The author of this book does not dispense medical advice or prescribe the use of any technique as a form of treatment for physical, emotional, or medical problems without the advice of a physician, either directly or indirectly. The intent of the author is only to offer information of a general nature to help you in your quest for emotional and spiritual well-being. In the event you use any of the information in this book for yourself, which is your constitutional right, the author and the publisher assume no responsibility for your actions.

Any people depicted in stock imagery provided by Thinkstock are models, and such images are being used for illustrative purposes only. Certain stock imagery © Thinkstock.

Print information available on the last page.

ISBN: 978-1-5043-5928-3 (sc)
ISBN: 978-1-5043-5963-4 (e)

Library of Congress Control Number: 2016909047

Balboa Press rev. date: 01/09/2017

Three, six, nine…
The goose drank wine;
The monkey spit tobacco on the streetcar line.
The line broke; the monkey got choked,
And they all went to heaven on a little row boat.

DEDICATION

This book is dedicated to the men in my life. You have all made a life-altering impact upon my very being. By far my most demanding teachers, you inspire me to work daily to overcome the pain of the past and to see goodness in all.

MY FATHER

Daddy, in all of your sickness, you were a most brilliant instructor – not by what you did well, but rather, by where you failed as a father. Thanks for being brave enough to live up to our soul contract, one that would cause excruciating pain throughout the course of our lives, yet offer me the opportunity to soar. May your spirit rest in knowing that you did a stellar job launching me in the direction I so yearned to fly.

MY HUSBANDS (YES, PLURAL; YOU KNOW WHO YOU ARE)

As I struggled to understand myself, you each represented – and offered - an understanding of different facets of my father. I am forever grateful for each brick you helped me place during the restoration of my being.

MY SOUL MATE

You introduced me to the closest thing to love I've known. Your gentle kindness wrapped me in a warm, safe blanket of authentic and unconditional love. I will never forget you, sweet man.

My Brothers

You all taught – and continue to teach me to appreciate family just as we are. Within the dark times, I found light because we love one another beyond screwed up family dynamics.

My Son

You walk on the edge and have taught me to let go of control. Carrying the wisdom of the Master, you have been the catalyst for a series of events that have irrevocably changed me for the better. Your kind heart, insight beyond your years and beautiful soul make me so very proud to be your mother.

APPRECIATION

My heartfelt thanks go **to Pamela Bain Jones** and **Miranda Westerman** for selflessly lending their time and valuable input to my life project. I couldn't have known how exposed I would feel the first time I allowed another to read the story of my life. Revealing long-held family secrets is no easy task; these beautiful women treated my book as they've always treated me – with much love and respect. I love you both!

Susanne Romo (susanneromo@yahoo.com), my deepest gratitude goes to you for holding my webbed writer's feet to the fire with your eagle-eye fine tooth comb. You are loved!

A very special thanks to **Tom Healcy**, for encouraging me to continue writing this book. Although we'd only just met (by phone, at that) you inspired me by sharing that you'd read every single book excerpt on my website. You not only went on to speak of my characters by name, but inquired about the book release date *and* the movie release as well! You are the reason I sat at my computer to finish *The Other Side of the Bayou*.

Undying gratitude goes to my BFF, **Alicia DeNardo**. You are always there for me, gracing me with the truest meaning of a soul sister. The miles cannot keep us apart; we connect in a space that requires no telephone or face-to-face meeting. I love you!

Darcy Divanterra, you held my hand through the "Breastcapade" experience in a way that opened my heart so much wider. I'm eternally grateful for your spiritual presence and friendship. (The Red Chair gatherings were created for your sweet sistah spirit!) Much love!

INTRODUCTION

This painful dance begins along the banks of the Mississippi River in and around a very mystical New Orleans, Louisiana. It ends in San Diego, California, when a shocking diagnosis in 2015 sent me back into the bowels of darkness, forcing me to revisit painful relationships and many of my greatest fears.

In 2002, after my third divorce, I began recording my earliest memories as a way to heal. I needed to understand more than psychology's version of my life. What had happened to me? Why had yet another relationship fallen so terribly apart? Who was I? Why had I repeated destructive patterns that caused so much pain? Was I denying an unseen truth?

Through my own epic journey, I began to slowly wake up to the truth of my past. It was far more excruciating – and exhilarating - than I could have imagined; I was driven to unveil what really happened to me - do or die. Along the way, I'd come to discover how very psychic I am and that I was born a Medium and Healer who had to begin to heal myself in order to help others. Prolific at moving energy to create mental, emotional, spiritual and physical well-being, I had to face my shadowy past before moving forward.

(I have long sensed the burden of the gifted sensitive. As a psychic medium myself, I was born to a mother who was diagnosed schizophrenic at the age of 21. She was highly psychic and had absolutely no resources or support structure growing up. As a child, I stood by in horror too many times as Mama was taken away in a strait jacket, drugged and given shock therapy. She suffered for her gifts throughout her tortured life. Sadly, Mama died without having the confirmation that she was gifted, not crazy.)

Savagely beaten by my father, I had a series of epileptic seizures that catapulted me through the crack in the earth at the age of thirteen. I felt no love from my family. Even the house, which seemed to have its own foul intentions, seemed to hate me.

Horrendously traumatic, this wasn't the first time I'd been hurled into the ethers by my vicious alcoholic father. Through years of therapy I'd come to discover that it began when I was only two years old.

I couldn't deny that my childhood had been taken away and I was forced to grow up quickly – too quickly. This life has offered me many hard lessons, at the root of which is recapturing my innocent heart.

My mind concealed from me crucial facts about my trauma and at the same time, it revealed my paranormal gifts and abilities. As a child, I "saw" and "knew" things that others didn't. I was terrified that I might be going mad like Mama.

Thirty years after the violence began and during my second marriage, I would begin to realize what I had not wanted to know - the injuries were far worse than I'd imagined.

Today, I mentor others who have been wrongly labeled. We work together to find the beauty in the gifts as the process of defining innate abilities unfolds. Along the way, grounding and self-trust is taught and gifts are defined and refined. An organic process, it's a path to genuine self-recognition. No longer defined by an in-the-box societal model, we are set free. An indelible spirit cannot be dimmed, no matter how treacherous the dark night of the soul.

FOREWORD

When our friend, Connie Stewart, almost sheepishly, asked if my wife Paula and I would be willing to share our thoughts after reading her memoir, we both said we'd be honored to do so. Little did I realize just what a privilege it would be to be let in and learn so much about Connie's alarming and troubled life. Hers was a life that burst with relentless, merciless, and remorseless trauma – including horrific abuse of all forms from her parents.

While we've learned so much from studying the impact that early inexorable abuse has on growing children and adults, including alcohol and drug problems and increased risk of serious emotional disorders, Connie's revealing, heartfelt and open look at the damage she experienced is a manifesto on how different it can all be.

Was it her near death experience, her personal healing path, her ability and need to turn inward that helped her "hear" that she was clairvoyant, a medium, an intuitive? Was the external pain, lack and abuse so great that it required her to find healing, comfort and understanding from a place above the extraordinary fear that persisted inside of her own mind? Is that what led this powerhouse teacher to find abundance, love and health over illness? Did her shouts of agony allow her to hear something else, something akin to a whisper, perhaps at a soul level? Rather than simply turn to others for answers, Connie's journey helped her find answers inside of herself in ways that opened, rather than closed, her emotional life. She did not silence her inner voice as so many victims of harsh abuse do, but rather, she turned toward - and embraced - it, learning from a deeper source than she knew existed.

This book is not an easy read – unless you are searching for mindful inspiration, motivation to improve your life regardless of external events and encouragement to find your personal strength. Looking for inner healing and a better understanding of your life's purpose? Connie's life is a testament to sealing in the notion that nothing - but nothing - ever happens TO you but rather FOR you, that in life we are never rejected, but rather redirected.

I have no doubt, that after reading this book once you will read it again. And then you will want to experience first-hand Connie's unsurpassed, unmatched and incomparable healthy spirit. When your voice tells you to reach out to Connie, and you do, know that on the other end you will find a woman whose sensitivity, deeply personal touch and spiritual gifts will advance your life in unimaginable ways.

Michael R. Mantell, Ph.D.
Author, "Don't Sweat the Small Stuff PS: It's All Small Stuff"
Transformational Behavior and Leadership Coach
Keynote Speaker

∞ ∞ ∞

From the first page, *The Other Side of the Bayou* grips your emotions in so many ways! I felt that I was bearing witness to the many unspeakable actions through which Connie lived. During the book, I was always rooting for Connie, and yet also knew, that she would come to do way more than survive. *The Other side of the Bayou* is what is considered to be compelling reading – I was not able to put it down!

Connie shares with us the inhumane deeds that her father perpetrated upon her, that were physical, emotional, and sexual, her mother's weakness, mental illness, and indifference toward her, the loss of two brothers. Even at this early time in her life, Connie shows that she will not be defeated or downtrodden!

I believe that Connie's beautiful and amazing gift came about because of the events in her life. Among these gifts are that she knows the inner emotions of others, she possesses a "sixth sense", whereby she can reach out the those no longer living on this earth, she can heal others through the hurts that she has experienced. Hers was a difficult path to arrive at where she is today, but through her infallible will, Connie is here to help others to avoid the hurts through which she lived!

Paula Mantell
Mindful-anchored Certified Personal Trainer

Author's Notes

As you swim back in time into the swampy abyss of my life, my sincere hope is that you will walk away having a deeper understanding of the insidious nature of domestic abuse, as well as the ecstasy of what saved me. The heart and soul of my message is about surviving and overcoming cruelty of the most heinous nature. It's about thriving and allowing tragedy to lead us back to our Self in an unimaginable and glorious way.

If you're reading this, we may have more in common than you know. There are pearls hidden here – I promise.

(I have tried my very best to recreate events, locales and conversations from my memories of them. In order to maintain their anonymity, in some instances I have changed the names of individuals and places. I have also changed some identifying characteristics and details such as physical properties, occupations and places of residence.)

Meet Me at the Corner of Heart & Soul...
We will sit quietly for a while as the early evening breeze
slips gently across our faces.
Our hearts will be open and nothing but love will we
share.
When we speak, it will be meaningful and kind.
We will laugh and we will cry.

We have lived full lives and just as a beautifully
weathered barn stands humbly but proudly across the field,
we are in this for the long haul.
We are friends, you and I.
The breeze blows stronger and it is time to leave.
We will return; we always do.
~ Constance Schroder Stewart

CHAPTER ONE

Breastcapade

September 16, 2015. During a preventative screening, a mass was discovered in my right breast. I'd felt the lump many months earlier but because I had fibrocystic tissue most of my adult life, I didn't have it checked out. I didn't rest easy, though, and turned to some of my old tried-and-true ways of dissolving the lump, such as increasing my iodine intake, restricted salt and caffeine, but none worked. My intuition was beginning to nag at me during the day and in my dreams.

One morning shortly after my first MRI, I awoke to a message. The voice, which I believe came from my Higher Self, clearly and firmly said, *"Oh, you have cancer all right, but you're going to be one of the very, very lucky ones."* I was both frightened and a little relieved. This would become one of the bigger challenges I'd faced as an adult.

After a series of further testing, and more anxiety, a core-needle biopsy was recommended. A radio-opaque clip was placed in my breast to mark the location. (I asked for a smiley face clip – wouldn't it be cool if the mammogram technicians were greeted with a smile?)

While I was waiting for the diagnosis, my beloved

eighteen-year-old orange tabby cat friend, Roux, crossed over. I was devastated. Traveling side-by-side in many of my dreamtime adventures and countless lifetimes, we'd been together longer than I'd been in any peer relationship. I've had cats all my life but none like Roux, whose self-appointed job was to watch over me.

Frequently helping me with clients, he was a magnificent being. Roux knew precisely who needed him; laying on the floor near the client's feet, he patiently offered his solid grounding energy as comfort. Many friends and clients understood that Roux was more than a cat; besides being large in stature, he was a huge and powerful spirit in animal form. Those closest to me saw what I saw; some days Roux took on the appearance of an Egyptian feline with elongated ears and a pointed face. He frequently mirrored my own psychic energy and, like me, enjoyed nothing better than when my dear friend visited to give us an Egyptian Reiki treatment.

Having the diagnosis delivered the same week that Roux crossed over was brutal. While on the phone with my doctor I felt suspended in time. *Invasive ductal carcinoma.* Was he speaking in slow motion or was it me? Did he have me confused with someone else? I could hardly believe what I'd heard yet my intuition told me it was true. I did my best to maintain control but my mind was reeling.

The very mention of cancer sucked me into a powerful vortex of terror, very similar to what I'd known as a child. I had to struggle to stay present. I wasn't afraid of dying; as a child I got used to thinking I would die before the age of twenty. What I was afraid of was living with a serious illness. I was also fearful of telling my son. I wanted to shield him from my fear, but I soon realized that wasn't my place. He had a right to his own perceptions and feelings; I would never wish to stand in the way of his very personal process.

Staying as calm as I could possibly manage, Ty and I sat to have "the talk". I did my very best to stay positive about what I'd learned so far from my own research. The type of carcinoma I was diagnosed with is the most common, and therefore, most researched and with highest survival rates. (I dislike the term, "survival rate". I choose to call it "thriving rate".)

His response was simply, "This won't be the thing that takes you out!" We laughed. It was just the comic relief we needed in an incredibly somber moment. From that moment on, he has been a quiet - yet strong - supporter, exhibiting a greater gentleness and kindness toward me than ever before.

Hand-picking a wonderful team of physicians, they were not only amply equipped to help me through this medical voyage but also (I strongly suspect) subscribed to beliefs that fall outside of traditional science – even if only when off duty.

Besides letting all my docs know that I am a healer and believe strongly in the power of the mind, the Universe, Spirit and naturopathic medicine, I have politely insisted that they all humor me in one particular area.

I'd recently read that 21,000 people die each day from cancer; 35,000 people are informed by doctors each day that they have cancer. Far too many people, including me, fear the mere mention of the word "Cancer". Asking each doc to refrain from using the word, I let them know that the term "frisky cells" works better for me. It's not only a description that I can wrap my head around, it also greatly reduces my fear response. I explained that I did not want to tap into the collective avalanche of fright associated with such a diagnosis. This one action alone has allowed me to face this journey less as a victim and more from a positive position of strength. (The radiologist was very interested in my philosophy and stated she'd not heard this before, further inquiring as to whether I'd be interested in becoming a patient advocate.)

The orthodox medical system at large represents the patriarchy to me and I innately understood that I had to quickly find equal footing. This was a huge opportunity to further heal lingering emotional wounds.

It was eye-opening to discover how many (all) of my doctors and nurses were unaware just how horrifying and debilitating the "C" word can be to patients. Maybe they know but can't go there. In any case, I did my best to bring them into my reality rather than get sucked fully into theirs.

While I'm on the subject, I also keep my distance from conversation such as "beat Cancer" and "the war on Cancer". Where I put my attention, energy follows. I made the decision to avoid focusing on the concept of a fight, which by its very definition indicates struggle. Instead, I prayed for Grace and Ease to accompany me on this difficult journey.

Sitting in the crowded waiting room, I tried to prepare myself to have my first Come-to-Jesus meeting with my surgeon. I planned to let him know that this adventure was far more than a physical endeavor; it was an opportunity for a transformative spiritual journey of significant impact. I'd sit back and observe his response, which would let me know if I'd chosen the best doctor.

While waiting for my name to be called, I drifted back to my early youth, recalling a day so very long ago when I was told that I had a lump on my chest (same side). I couldn't help but wonder how my deeply held and unspoken childhood fear of dying had manifested in the present. Had this terror - so deeply buried for the sake of survival - finally caught up with me? Had I not been too afraid to speak with my mom about it (in order to discover that I was not terminally ill), would I be on this daunting detour today? No matter; I believe in Divine order and a purposeful Universe.

I yearn to break the spell of old fear, in part by taking

charge in a way that I had no authority to do back then. In fact, I looked at this massive healing adventure as a tremendous opportunity for a do-over.

I would spend time with my past. To know where I'm going, I *must* know where I've been.

CHAPTER TWO

We are Family

I was two and a half years old when Mama gave me to Daddy.

We lived in one half of a shotgun duplex. It was called that because in those days taxes were based on the width of your property, so the Cajuns got wise and built long, narrow houses.

On really hot days - and there were lots of those - I loved being on the porch with its smooth, cool cement. It offered a respite; a place for drawing with stubs of colored chalk; sitting quietly while sewing Barbie doll dresses; playing jacks.

When I was still small enough I loved played under the house. It was always cool there and I loved the smell of the loose dirt. I could breathe easier even with the dust. I liked watching feet go by in the alley. Sometimes, when Mama would call me, I wouldn't answer; she never thought to look for me there. The dark, cobweb-ridden crawl space was my only safe haven. Nobody could hurt me there. Hidden silently under the house was the safest place I knew, other than the stars.

I wondered if she had secrets; she was always so tight-lipped about her childhood, other than to say her dad ran off with - and married - a "floozy". I knew how deeply it affected her as a young child because anytime Mama got upset enough to curse, she used her step-mom's name in vain.

Mama always seemed to be full of anger, but I couldn't understand why. Was it because she could sometimes see me up there, floating through the universe? When something scary was happening, like when Daddy was beating me or hugging me too tight with his hands in weird places on my body, I'd do what I called "jumping out". Jumping out was easy and I wondered why Mama and Catherine (my sis and junior by one year) didn't do it, as well. Daddy was mean to them, but not to the same extent. Maybe that was why neither of them had ever felt a need to leave.

Up among the stars I could do cartwheels, which I most certainly couldn't do on the ground. I was so clumsy on Earth. Out in space, I could twirl and spin and turn upside-down. It was always lots of fun at first – like breaking free from tight clothes – with nobody to yell at me or hurt me. But eventually, I got lonely and remembered why I had jumped out in the first place.

Did my leaving make Mama mad or jealous? Had I done something wrong? "Dear God," I prayed, "please don't let her tell Daddy." I would probably have gotten a beating for "leaving", and I surely didn't want Daddy to know where I hid.

At some point, I had to admit to myself that I had my own guilt about the whole thing. I left Mama and Catherine behind while I went off to be in the stars. But truth be known, they always seemed to like playing together without me, so I didn't think they'd mind - or even notice. It was so much fun feeling so free and not feeling threatened by Daddy. I saw so many things up there that I couldn't see from inside my body. Eventually the fun began to wear off and I would start to feel like if I didn't return soon, something bad might happen to them. It got harder and harder to have fun while worried about Mama and

Catherine. All that concern turned a good thing into bad and, like every other time I realized I was all alone, made me wish like mad that somebody - anybody - would reach out to me. I didn't want to be alone, but I had no choice. I had to face the fact that the others didn't know how to do what I could. Staying on the ground when Daddy was beating me was unbearable. Before I knew I had the ability to jump out, I fully experienced his brutality toward me, but after the first jump – or at least the first time I recall - at around age five, I knew I had found a way to keep him from hurting all of me. It was then that I developed a sense of feeling terribly isolated.

Nobody wanted to be with me. Maybe what Daddy said was true. Maybe I really was fat and ugly - and to top it off, I had to wear those gaudy glasses. Oh how I came to despise the dreaded four-eyes jokes! "Coke-bottle eyes" made me cry. Those damn pink, glittery cat-eyes used to slide down the bridge of my small nose on those miserable southern, sticky days.

Having "four eyes" led me to suppose that I wasn't much of a looker. I hated being me sometimes – truthfully, most of the time. Catherine was cute and petite and Daddy's friend Ray liked her better than he liked me. He called her his "baby girl". I was pure-dee jealous of that. Why didn't he talk to *me*, or play with *me* the way he did with her? Why couldn't *I* be his baby girl?

Being small and frail was the result of Catherine's iron-poor blood. It got her off the hook on many things. Anytime we'd fight, it was always my fault according to her and Mama and Daddy always believed her. (If they only knew that Catherine could give an Indian-brush burn like nobody's business, clawing me with her long fingernails.)

Always considered the healthy one until seven years old, I discovered a lump on the right side of my chest. I told Mama and she took me to the doctor. He poked and prodded, then took Mama aside and whispered something that sounded like, "Put a hot, wet cloth on the lump three times a day. But, she has Cancer an' will die soon." It was a horribly scary time.

Even though the mass proved non-cancerous and eventually went away on its own, that marked the time I first thought to myself, "I will never live to see the age of twenty." Of all the fears I secretly held, dying from a horrible disease was the biggest and by far the most frightening. I kept my doomsday prediction to myself; I was too afraid to say it out loud.

With no real communication or education about our bodies, we Schroder kids were left to figure things out on our own. For instance, at the time when my upper molars came in, I thought I was severely deformed. I rolled my tongue along the ridge of these new invaders and quickly decided that they felt nothing like the other teeth in my mouth. Something HAD to be wrong! I was too afraid to tell Mama and since we never went to the dentist, I had no choice but to live with this horrific secret. If I *did* live past twenty I'd never be able to open my mouth in public, that's for damn sure.

At least if I did die before twenty, my awful recurring dream would stop.

I was on a mountain summit with Catherine and Mama. There were swings, but we weren't playing on them. I was hanging off the side of the cliff with one leg and one arm dangling. My other limbs were still clinging to the peak for dear life. It was as though I was being split completely down the middle. I was yelling out to them, but they just stood there. "Don't let me fall!! HELP ME!" Expressionless, they watched me hang on by what were left of my fingernails - and my hope.

My own crying woke me each time I had the dream. I could see why Catherine would want me out of the way; she was the favored baby girl. But why on God's green earth would Mama not want to save her own little girl? And where was Daddy? Daddies were supposed to protect their little girls.

Fear and loneliness spread through me like wildfire each time I struggled back into my body after that nightmare.

Daddy (Fred to some, Fritz to others) liked his beer better than anything. New Orleans was the right kind of party place for him, all right. After all, it's the only city in the world where when your loved one dies, you book a jazz band before you call the coroner. Daddy would stop off at the bar up the street after work each day. Most afternoons he stayed there for seven or eight hours before he came stumbling home.

Oftentimes, after he neglected to come home in time to take us on a promised shopping trip, Daddy would tiptoe into my room and wake me up in the middle of the night. He'd say he was sorry that he couldn't make it and then in a slobbering voice whisper, "Look, Daddy brought ya a bag of M&M's." Sometimes, it was a dollar bill that was the grand prize for pretending to believe his lies. He'd always end the "visit" by saying, "Now, give ya Daddy a big ol' hug." He always stunk of beer and smoke so badly that I held my breath during those obligatory moments. I wasn't sure how I knew that hugging my dad wasn't supposed to make me feel the way it did, but I knew alright.

Sometimes, when Daddy was squeezing me, I'd close my eyes and picture him on the roof of our house. I'd repeat the visualization as many times as it took in order to get him off of me, but in the end, he always reappeared. If I couldn't manage to "see" him gone, then I'd go to the stars knowing they would always welcome my presence. (I wondered if being gone interfered with my ability to recall his entire visit.) I was always left with deep sadness after he left my room. Even at such a tender age I could sense that something was terribly wrong with Daddy and the way he behaved.

When I brought up the late night visits to Catherine, asking whether she got candy or money, she was a bit baffled and said that Daddy never looked in on her that way. Surely, she'd just forgotten.

Too many times I went to bed fearing Daddy would sneak up on me or do something stupid like kill somebody and be sent to prison. He was always so angry. What would happen to us if the rent wasn't paid and there was no money for food?

Catherine picked up on my fear, I'm sure of it. Between her own fear and mine, she was always afraid of something, even her own shadow. Catherine was, after all, "the little sister". Sometimes I let her cuddle up with me until she fell to sleep, quietly sucking her thumb. It felt like my job. When I convinced myself that nobody could see my own fear, I'd pluck fuzz from my stuffed teddy and softly stroke my face until I, too, could drift off to sleep. But not until I said hundreds of Jesus, Mary, Joseph's (JMJ's).

You see, the nuns who taught catechism (religious studies) taught us about Heaven and Hell. Even though Mama still proclaimed that she wasn't good enough to go to church, she insisted that her children attend religious instruction. She was adamant that we receive First Communion and Confirmation, both religious rites of passage. I figured out the religion thing pretty quickly because it was a no-brainer; if you were good you'd go to Heaven, and if you were bad, well, then Hell was where you'd receive your mail. But Purgatory, well that was a completely different story - one I just couldn't completely embrace. Apparently you'd be sent there if you weren't good enough to get through the Pearly Gates and not bad enough to be sent to eternal damnation. I could not bear the thought of a soul suspended indefinitely in a bleak, cold, gray and rumpled place. Never mind that I wasn't completely sure what a soul was - but I hated the thought just the same.

One nun, sensing my dismay over the idea of a stuck soul, taught me to say a very simple little prayer, one which she said would help release a soul from Purgatory right up into Heaven. It went like this, 'Jesus-Mary-Joseph'. That was it. Nothing fancy, but if it was good enough for the Sister, I assumed this was a big gun prayer and that it could make things happen.

Lying in my lumpy bed, I'd close my eyes and put my hand over my heart. While whispering Jesus-Mary-Joseph, I began to see soft luminous balls rising from bleakness into the light. As I fell to sleep, I knew the orb (soul) was in Heaven, safe and sound.

Because my concern was always the same - worried about the possibility that God might forget to call for someone - I continued my steadfast commitment to this thing called the soul. At a very young age I was a self-appointed soul agent. No one knew of my secret nightly ritual, not even my brother, Ricky.

Ricky was four years older than me and I simply adored him. He had All-American good looks and he was especially brave. Always trying to make money, he'd catch lizards and sell them to the local pet store, in exchange for a fistful of nickels.

∞ ∞ ∞

Every once in a while, on a Sunday we'd go visit Little Freddy at Miss Craig's house. He was two years older than me and was Mama's and Daddy's first-born son. (Ricky was two years older than Freddy, but had a different father.) Little Freddy couldn't walk, was visually impaired and severely mentally challenged. Mama said he had a stroke at birth – cerebral palsy. They didn't know anything was wrong with him until he reached the age of two and still couldn't hold his head up. Duke University Hospital diagnosed the illness while Mama, Daddy and Ricky were still living in North Carolina,

12

where Daddy had been a Marine. At the age of two, Little Freddy was placed in a special-needs home.

He hated wearing glasses as much as me and on a regular occasion threw them out the car window or flushed down the toilet. Miss Craig, who ran the foster home where Freddie lived with ten other special-needs people of varying ages, was a very special lady and never seemed to get too upset. Her wards all seemed to pitch in and help *and* torment each other at times. Little Freddy seemed happy there but it was hard to tell since I really didn't know him all that well. I often found myself wishing I lived there.

Sometimes Mama had to insist that Daddy take us to visit Little Freddy; Daddy didn't seem to care about him. He'd say a few words to him at the beginning of our visit, but usually end up smoking in the back yard.

I surely wished Little Freddy could stand up and play with us, so I prayed for him when I remembered. I'd visit my brother in my mind when Mama made us sit in the shade on the front porch at home after lunch. During our visit he'd be standing tall with a strong body, and running like the wind. He laughed out loud and adored running barefoot through the wet grass, especially at dusk.

It's a good thing Mama couldn't see Little Freddie running wild because she was paranoid about letting us play anywhere but in the backyard, which was fenced and had a locking gate. One day, she let us play in the front yard while she sat on the porch. The phone rang and she reluctantly went inside for just a moment, but not without a set of quick instructions. I didn't understand what she was so worried about, after all, wrought iron bars fenced in the whole front yard. Good God, not even a tornado could tear down that barrier.

During her short absence, a tall African American man walked by. He held a folded newspaper over his midsection.

13

When he was in clear sight of Catherine and me, he lifted the paper to expose his genitals. Normally, this would have been quite upsetting to little girls, but the truth is that I wasn't sure what I saw and thought it was a stick of chili! Chili was not scary; I'd seen Mama cutting pieces from the sticks many times. But I did think something was fishy about how he kept chili in his pants. And THAT is why I ran inside yelling.

Daddy went bursting through the front door like a superhero. He charged down the steps and flew over the gate. He was out of sight in no time flat. Sweet Jesus, I'd never seen Daddy move like that! When he returned, he had only to report that he had lost the guy in the chase. "It's a good Goddamn thing I didn't catch his black ass," Daddy snapped. "I'da killed that son of a bitch!"

The very next day, a woman stopped to say hello to Catherine and me. We were playing with our new Patty Play Pal dolls (plastic life-sized best friends) in the front yard. (Oddly, once again Mama was momentarily inside the house.) The lady was holding a face cloth, folded in fourths. She unfolded it ever so slightly to reveal a diamond ring. I'd never seen such a ring; Mama had only a gold band (well, maybe it was gold).

"My daughter is sick an' I'm on the way to see her in the hospital. Can I borrow one of ya dolls to go show my 'lil girl?" Hesitantly, we said yes. As soon as my blonde Patty Play Pal was over the fence, she took off running. This time, I yelled for Ricky. He was out of the yard like a streak of lightening. Wow, for the second time in two days I'd seen the males in my family demonstrate unusual speed and heroism.

Daddy lost what little faith he had in Mama's ability to watch over us after that day and sequestered us indefinitely to the back yard. That made me sad; I could see the world from the front yard. So many different kinds of people, all colors and shapes stepped through my imaginary (or, so I thought)

"X-ray machine". I didn't have to interact with them to know their story. Much of the time, I could somehow "see" who they were just by studying them for a few seconds.

∞ ∞ ∞

Mama was frequently unwell. Prior to an emotional outbreak, she spent a lot of time in her rocking chair singing the same song about country roads over and over. The line about taking her back to a place where she belonged made her cry, but she kept belting it out. She seemed to want to be anywhere but with us.

That scared me so I tried to do things to cheer her up. My best jokes were frail attempts at best, but I never stopped trying.

I didn't know what was wrong, but I knew it probably wasn't normal. After a few months of off-balance behavior, Daddy called the doctor, who sent an ambulance. Two men came into our house and whispered to Daddy. Mama didn't like them one teeny-tiny bit and she let them know that right off the bat.

"Get the hell outta this house!" she'd scream. They'd ask her politely to go to the hospital with them. When she adamantly refused, they'd force her into a long-sleeved, white jacket that tied in the back. She hated that jacket. I didn't like the way her arms and hands were stuck in the sleeves. Eventually the two men would grab her arms and drag her out of the house and off the porch into the van with the glaring red and orange lights. Even though she was acting goofy and it scared me, I didn't want Mama to go away.

Catherine screamed at the top of her lungs as fear gripped her little body. I didn't want her to see me scared because I knew it would frighten her even more. Ricky was much more composed than me - that was his style. He tried to console

Catherine and me, but even this courageous young boy - whom I so totally adored - could not shield us.

I felt so incredibly sad when Mama went away. Our fears and insecurities grew each time. Daddy found someone to take care of us during the day but were we in his care at night. Because we were too afraid to sleep alone, we slept in the same bed with him.

Daddy was always so knocked out from the booze that he slept as heavy as a log. He'd roll over in his sleep and throw his dense arm over me, trapping me for the entire night. I did my best to release myself from under his weight, but it took more strength than I could muster. Somehow, Catherine always got to sleep on the outside of the bed while I got harnessed in the middle. I hated sleeping with him. I continued to cringe when he said, "Come on now, an' cuddle up with ya Daddy."

During those times, I was more thankful than ever for Ricky, who was very loving in his own boyish way. He'd try to reassure us, but his words paled against the tall bar-laden windows at the state mental hospital where we visited Mama.

The first few visits were the best *and* the worst. We were so happy to see Mama, but at the same time afraid of the surroundings. She moved about like a zombie. She was too thin and had an odd color to her face, which caved in, revealing an eerily frail skeletal frame. Almost no recognition shown in Mama's eyes and Daddy never let us stay long enough to comfort her. She succeeded at only the slightest conversation and it seemed her primary concern was only whether I was looking after Catherine.

(Because of seeing Mama in that awful place and the long drives across the Lake Pontchartrain bridge, I began having reoccurring nightmares. *Our family was in the car driving across the bridge when we suddenly came upon a missing section. With no warning, we plummeted into the six hundred and thirty square-mile lake. As the car began to sink, water quickly filled the inner compartment. I was acutely aware that I'd die as soon as we ran out of air if I didn't drown first!*

The nightmares were also stoked by the fact that Daddy frequently fell to sleep behind the wheel on that twenty-four-mile bridge. Eventually the car would begin to swerve out of the lane and I'd have to yell out to wake him. I frequently had to steer while he pulled himself from the edge of full-on sleep. I also turned the radio volume as loud as possible, sang at the top of my lungs and tried to keep him engaged in conversation.)

After a while, life came back into Mama, but she paid a huge price. "Shock treatments," we overheard Daddy tell someone. We figured someone would stand behind a door, then jump out and scare the hell out of Mama. I was all for whatever it took to get her better and home with us - at least until the next time.

Several months after Mama's breakdown, we moved to Harahan, a suburb of New Orleans, where we lived across the street from the levee. The fifteen or twenty-foot earthen barrier was built around the City of New Orleans and its surrounding towns to protect the parishioners from the rising waters of the Mississippi River. Since the city actually sits below sea level, the levee is vital to safety. Of course, none of that mattered to us kids. The levee was really more like an extended backyard.

We could actually see the levee from Ricky's bedroom, which was at the very back of the house. His was a small room, made so because of the sloped ceiling; I could only stand up in certain spots. This didn't stop it from being the best room in the house, since it was the furthest away from Mama's and Daddy's room.

And, then this happened. Gazing out his bedroom window, full moon a' blazin', Ricky saw an old blue car driving slowly on the levee. Already very quiet out, most people in our neighborhood had likely just eaten supper and were still letting their food go down in front of the television.

There was a law against driving on the levee; only parish workers were allowed. Right away, Ricky smelled trouble. Sitting hunched in his rickety bed so as not to be seen by the strangers in the car, he staked-out the levee intruders. He noticed what appeared to be bags being tossed out of the driver's side window. Now he KNEW something was up. Nobody took an evening ride on top of the levee just to toss out garbage.

When Catherine and I came around to the backdoor after school the next day, Mama was waiting for us. "Get in the house, right now!" What did we do now? We really were innocent this time, no matter what she thought!

"Hurry, I said - get inside this minute, dammit!" She continued to glare worriedly across the street and over toward the levee where several men wearing bright orange vests raked the ground. Big deal. So they finally cut the grass. Mama certainly was prone to the screaming meemies.

Once inside, Ricky began to excitedly share with us what he'd seen the night before - and what the local TV station had reported that day. Mama yelled at him to shut up. "RICKY, STOP IT, ya gonna scare the girls!" Eventually, however, Catherine and I begged so hard that Mama let Ricky spill the beans.

It seems that somebody had reported finding several brown paper bags (like the kind we got at Schwegmann's grocery store) strewn across the levee and stuffed with human body parts! Jesus H. Christ, that must've been pure-dee hell for the guy who got chopped up! Wonder if the cockroaches got to him? (Roaches were always in the grocery bags because they liked to eat the glue. Eventually, you just learned to ignore them because you knew the only ones you could kill were the weak and it would only serve to strengthen the breed.)

Once again, it was a long time before we were permitted to

play in the backyard. But sure as the sun rises, the first day that we were allowed out back something else happened.

Catherine and I were playing cheerleader when a tall, thin man approached. This was odd in itself, since we lived at the end of the street near the levee; nobody came down this far but the neighbors.

"What y'all doin'?" he asked. Hesitantly, I muttered, "Aw, just playin'." All of a sudden, I became aware of our little dog Mitzi in a compromising position with a terrier from up the street. It immediately embarrassed me, especially because this stranger was now watching, too.

He asked, "Know what they doin'?" Christ, how do you answer a question like that? You don't want to appear stupid, but you sure don't want to talk about S-E-X with an adult. That would be pure-dee hell!

He said it again. "You girls know what those dogs are doin'?" I muttered something; he then moved a little closer and said he had something to show us. Lord have mercy, not a chili stick again! "But," he said, "I can't show y'all 'till after dark. Why don't y'all meet me up on Thibodeaux Street, at the corner of Purnell, say 'bout seven-thirty."

My body was telling me loud and clear that this tall, skinny man with greasy hair was up to no good. If he had something to show us, why couldn't he show us right there and then?

Looking at the man I said, "Sure, we'll be there." I felt I needed to say something – anything - to get him to leave.

As soon as he headed back up the street, we ran inside to tell. Daddy was spittin' fire and Mama became panicky. Daddy said *he'd* have something for that man at seven-thirty, all right. "Flo, I'll lay one on that fuckin' bastard that he'll never forget!"

"Oh Jesus, Mary, Joseph help us!" Mama chanted. (*That's what I said to release the souls from Purgatory!*) I felt all turned upside down; even though nothing ever came of Daddy and the stranger, it struck me as really odd how protective Daddy could be *sometimes*.

∞ ∞ ∞

One day our dog, Cathy, who lived in a pen in the backyard, was yelping more than usual. Daddy came home drunk and really angry about something (or maybe nothing). He kept yelling at the dog to "shut the fuck up". Finally, he screamed at Ricky to get his BB gun and shoot the "Goddamn dawg". Did Daddy actually want Ricky to shoot his own pet? What a living nightmare! Mama was crying and screaming. "No Freddy! Pleeeeze don't do that, Freddy! For God's Sake, Freddy, *NO!*" Ricky was crying hard, too. I hadn't seen him cry very many times - maybe never before that night.

I hated Daddy! He was a horrible man! Ricky pumped the gun once, then twice. POP! The BB went whirring along its path to the dog pen. He was a good shot so when he missed Cathy I could tell he purposely aimed high. He was probably hoping that Daddy wouldn't notice in his drunken stupor. Oh, but he did, all right.

"SHOOT AGAIN, GOD DAMMIT!" Through his tears, my almost-perfect brother pumped the gun once more. This time he knew he had to hit Cathy to keep Daddy from doing something awful to him - or to all of us. *POP!* More speeding BBs. But this time was different. Cathy let out a yelp that was surely heard six blocks over. I felt as if the BBs had hit me in the heart.

"I HATE YA!" I yelled at Daddy. "YOU MADE RICKY KILL CATHY, YA MURDERER! I HATE YA!" I wished I were dead instead of Cathy. I despised that son-of-a-bitch daddy of mine. "WHAT DID CATHY EVER DO TO YA!?" I demanded. "SHE'S A POOR HELPLESS DOG. *I HATE YA!*"

It took extra teddy fuzz to get me to sleep that night.

CHAPTER THREE

When God Gave Out Brains

Even though Mama didn't go to church herself, she sometimes sent us with relatives.

My least favorite thing about going to mass was Holy Communion, where we were given a sacred host (symbolic of Christ's body). It was really just an uncooked wafer of bread which we were supposed to let slowly dissolve on the tongue. I figured you'd go to Hell if you chewed rather than dissolved it. Or maybe that was only a Purgatory-worthy sin, like not wearing a doily on your head – I wasn't quite sure. What I did know was that when it came time to take communion at the altar, that raw dough invariably got stuck to the roof of my mouth, getting all gooey and caused me to gag. I'd pretend to be coughing, cover my mouth with one hand, then as discreetly as possible, reach in and start scraping it off the roof of my mouth. I tried convincing Ricky to eat it, but he flat out refused. Lord have mercy on my soul!

I frequently saw Miss Fahan in church. She lived across the street from us with her husband, who owned a local bar and restaurant, which Daddy religiously supported. (Yes, alcohol was *his* religion. He and his friend, Pete hung out there a lot. I liked Mr. Pete. Sometimes when he called for Daddy, he'd sing a song. "Three, six, nine/The goose drank wine/The monkey spit tobacco on the streetcar line/The line broke/The monkey got choked/And they all went to heaven on a little row boat." Mr. Pete was so wonderfully different from our family; he was always happy.)

Mr. Fahan invited us over to his yard once when his wife was away. He was pretty old and seemed like a nice man. His shirt was always pressed and tucked into his pants, and he often wore a clean straw hat.

Suddenly, Mr. Fahan quietly stood behind me and slipped his hand down inside my blouse, rubbing my chest in a way that made me feel funny inside. I gently pulled away so as not to insult him; I wasn't completely sure what was going on.

During supper that evening, I told Daddy and Mama about Mr. Fahan's earlier display of affection. Daddy jumped up from the table, knocked over his chair nearly tossing his plate and zoomed out of the house. He returned with a warning. "Ya girls stay away from them from now on, ya hear me!" That was the end of our friendship with the Fahans.

As our spaghetti supper resumed I fiddled with the long, bloody snakes on my plate. I was starving, but I could not - would not - eat that slimy stuff. Earlier that afternoon I had asked Mama for a snack, but all she said was, "Eat one hand an' save the other for later." What in the hell did that mean?! God, I hated it when she spoke/sang those sarcastic responses.

After everyone else had finished eating but were still sitting at the table, Daddy looked over at me angrily, reached out his heavy arm, and with one swift motion, slammed my face down into the plate. "Ya just sit there 'till ya eat every last bite, God dammit!" The bridge of my pink, glittery cat-eye glasses sliced into my nose and drew blood, which of course was undetectable because of the spaghetti sauce. I was trapped in a kid's body with absolutely no human rights.

Within minutes, everyone got up and left the table. Daddy went off to bed and Mama left the room; she knew Daddy wouldn't permit her to sit with me. And me? Well, I sat there for at least four hours, until I decided that I'd had enough. Who in the hell did he think he was?! Drunkard! I got up from the table and tiptoed to the garbage pail. As soon as I began scraping my plate I heard Daddy get out of bed. I froze. Should I run? Oh God, he's gonna KILL ME! In the few seconds it took those terrified thoughts to fly around the inside of my brain, Daddy appeared at the kitchen door. My last thoughts just before every ounce of blood drained from every part of my body were that I wondered if he'd heard my angry thoughts about him, followed quickly by suspecting I'd never make it to the age of twenty.

Daddy gave me a look that would have melted steel. I tried not to cry but tears fell anyway; I didn't want him to see my fear. Our eyes were glued to one another for what seemed like hours though it may have been just a few seconds. Instead of hitting me, for which I hurriedly tried to brace myself, he just turned with a disgusted grunt and left the room.

The flight-or-fight response appeared to cause the same adrenaline rush as actually being hit. It seemed like I was always in a state of high anxiety around Daddy. I figured I had to be; after all, I never knew what was coming next. Spaghetti still makes me gag.

Life wasn't all bad in those days, just mostly bad. I met my soon-to-be best friend, Carol Kotter, not long after we moved to the shotgun house. She lived with her family at the opposite end of Brody Street. Carol was fair-skinned and blonde, with lots of freckles and a broad smile full of big, white teeth. We hit it off right away, mainly because we could relate to each other

23

so well. Even though I was a city girl from the Crescent City and she was a bumpkin from rural Mississippi, we understood one another. I think some of that could be attributed to our fathers, who both were way too mean when they drank. She knew what it meant to be scared, to be beaten by her dad and to have to know how and when to humor him to stay safe. Her mom was a second-class citizen just like Mama, so they also got along. Carol had a bunch of brothers and sisters of all ages and sizes. Seems like country people always have a wagonload of kids running around the farm. Guess they figure somebody has to feed the chickens and slop the hogs.

Some days, we'd ride our bikes for hours on Brody Street - up one side and down the other. When we reached the end opposite my house, we rode slowly so that we could check out old Mr. McFarland's home, which was directly across the street from Carol's house. That place was haunted and we all knew it. It was two-story with a tall crawl space below. Most days I was too afraid to get very close, seeing as how I'd heard rumors that Mr. McFarland had murdered several people and buried them there. The magnetic pull of his house was so great, however, that we knew we could not keep from investigating. It was undoubtedly a force greater than us. YA-YA!

When we finally gathered up enough guts to go up onto the porch, we waited until he was inside (presumably napping) and tiptoed quietly up the endless flight of stairs. My heart was beating so hard I thought it was going to cut a flip. We crouched down like men on military maneuvers and waddled close to the door. I took the lead and stood up, gently grabbing the doorknob, turning it ever so slowly. AH-EE, it wasn't locked. My mojo was up and the juju was working in my favor! The door swung open in a wide, sweeping motion, making awful noises.

There, on the kitchen table within three feet of me, was

a beautiful plate laced with a round white doily and loaded with homemade coconut pralines. JACKPOT! I crept up to the table ever so gingerly. Just as my hand was about to reach the fattest praline, I heard a noise. "DAMMIT TO HELL! RUN!", I screamed. We took off faster than a hot knife through butter, and didn't stop running until we fell in a heap on my front porch.

"We made it out alive," Carol gasped. "Yeah," I said, "but we left our bikes down there." "Jesus, Mary, Joseph! What we gonna do? We CAN'T go back!" We plotted and schemed for a while, but no other conclusion could be drawn. The fact of the matter was we had to go back and it had to be soon. No way would we approach that place after dark. Too many weird things happened to kids venturing out to Mr. McFarland's after sunset. For all we knew, one or two of our very own friends might even be buried in that under-house graveyard. Bobbie Fotche "moved" suddenly the previous summer, leaving no forwarding address. Nevertheless, brave twosome that we were, we slowly made our way back down the street. As we approached the house we could see Mr. McFarland sitting on his porch swing. We didn't really know a thing about this old man, but maybe we could work this to our advantage. When we were finally standing at the base of the stairs we decided that I would go up to greet him. I was always a pretty good talker, even as a kid. Carol's talent was that she could move fast; man could she run. (Country girls are good at stuff like that. I was the brains and she was the brawn.)

Reaching the top of the stairs, I greeted Mr. McFarland. "HOW ARE YA TODAY, MISTAH MCFARLAND?" He was very hard of hearing and usually his response had nothing whatsoever to do with the question. "Nah, I'm not hungry sugah', thank ya, though," he replied. As we chatted, I noticed his pants were wet near the zipper. "Go inside an' get yaself a prawleen," he said. Jesus! I was starting to feel bad. Maybe Mr. McFarland wasn't a murderer after all. Looking at him - old, hard of hearing, peed in his pants and offered pralines to the neighborhood kids - I didn't see a bad guy. I was confused. Did we paint an ugly face on a sweet, lonely old man? Maybe. I had to admit that a kind old man just didn't have the same lure as a murderer dwelling in a crickety, haunted house. I'd give it more thought later.

Mr. McFarland died before I had a chance to come to any firm conclusions about his true nature. His family left his belongings in the house for a long time, which really made it seem haunted. That end of the street never felt the same again. Sometimes, when I rode my bike past his house, the porch swing would start swinging. When I looked close enough, I saw a shadowy figure looking back. I figured Mr. McFarland liked the place so much he didn't want to leave.

With the haunted house mystery somewhat behind us, I needed another cause, so I began caring for neighborhood wounded cats. I liked the feeling of making a difference and being needed. Young and old, cats found their way to our house, beat up from fighting with that big old gray tom who lurked through the neighborhood. I'd get my homemade first-aid kit and dab away the dirt, blood, and pain with hydrogen peroxide and tender strokes. I'd gently speak to each animal, telling it that it would be safe at my house and that I would love and care for it. I kept as much of that bargain as I could, but Daddy frequently undermined my good intentions.

I swear, Daddy seemed to know just when we'd become really attached to a particular animal and then declare it was time to take it for a "ride". I never knew exactly where that ride led, but the cat would be gone the next day. The only thing Daddy would tell us is that cats and horses got along. That always broke my heart in a million pieces. I cried quietly and alone, feeling a deep, excruciating pain in my gut each time Daddy took something away. I was in pain a lot. It's then that I learned that I should try to never let on when I really cared, never. I asked God to help me camouflage my desires for my own safety.

Even though Daddy clearly didn't believe in God, Mama insisted that Catherine and I make our First Communion. (First Communion is the colloquial term for a person's first reception of the sacrament of the Holy Eucharist, occurring typically at age seven.)

As was custom, we picked out our saint names. Mine was Elizabeth and Catherine's was Ann. It was fun adding an extra name: Constance Marie Elizabeth Schroder. It had a ring to it, all right. It'd look pretty damn good on my tombstone, though they'd have to etch the letters teeny-tiny to make them all fit. Aunt Marian, Mama's older sister, gave us each a shimmering crystal rosary. It was the most beautiful thing I'd ever seen in all my life! I was sure it was made of diamonds because Aunt Marian and Uncle Joe seemed to have lots of money.

∞ ∞ ∞

The Belt. It was thin and black and made a certain whirring sound as she flung it through the air. Mostly, she used it to cower us into submission, but when that didn't work she'd pull the old "wait 'till ya Daddy gets home!" routine. That always got our immediate attention and was her most powerful ace in the hole. Daddy scared us and frightened Mama, too. Looking back, I feel a profound sense of sadness for Mama - she had no real power of her own.

Sometimes, when Daddy really frightened Mama, she'd take us away in the middle of the day without so much as a note. She always seemed so frantic, like she was ready to fall in a heap and have a good cry. Taking us to Aunt Marian's house,

I tried my hardest to listen to what they talked about as Mama recited her complaints. Somehow, I knew our future was being discussed and I didn't really feel all that secure with Mama's decision-making abilities.

All-too-soon, we'd be back home. Daddy was always disgustingly nice to us the first day or so, but it always changed back to the old way - always. Usually, about the third day, Daddy would come home from the bar in a nasty, obnoxious mood. Mama would meekly announce the menu for that evening, (having spent all of the two dollars he'd given her that morning) all the while keeping her eyes on the floor. "Not that crap, again! Jesus Christ, Flo, what's wrong with ya? When God was givin' out brains, did ya think he said rain?"

∞ ∞ ∞

The next school year in fourth grade, I had a wonderful teacher named Mrs. Frank. She wasn't very pretty on the outside, but she was as beautiful as a magnolia blossom on the inside. She was kind and spoke respectfully to her students, as though we were real people.

One day an announcement pounded from the loud speaker. "ATTENTION! We have just been informed that President Kennedy has been shot." I saw the look of shock on Mrs. Frank's face and knew this was very bad. A sense of deep loss and tragedy filled my body, but I wasn't sure why. Mrs. Frank began to cry and I began to sob, too. Suddenly, other kids began to whimper. It felt like someone I knew personally had died; I felt forlorn and a profound sense of loss.

Mrs. Frank's grief saddened me deeply. I loved her. She was the first person who ever cared to notice that something might be wrong in my home. More than once, she took me aside to ask if I had milk money. When I said no, she'd reach into her purse and give me a buffalo-head nickel and two shiny pennies. That worried me; I didn't think I could pay her back. Daddy would not like the idea of charity. "Don't ya worry, sweetheart," she said, "this will be our 'lil secret". She was soft, never yelled and she really cared about what happened to us. I felt more love in that little classroom than I ever did at home.

Mrs. Frank also noticed that my shoes had holes in the soles. She asked if she could buy me a new pair, but I had to say no. Daddy would have my hide if I let her do something like that. Milk was one thing; he'd never know but something expensive like a new pair of school shoes was out of the question.

The morning after President Kennedy was assassinated Daddy was not feeling well, according to Mama. "Is he hung over?" I asked. "No, I'm afraid he fell an' hit his head on the coffee table an' he's just not right", Mama explained. He hadn't even gone to work because of the fall and he ALWAYS went to work (well, except for the times Mama called in to his boss to say he had a cold when really he just drank too much the night before). I had no idea what "just not right" meant but I could see she was very worried.

We walked into the kitchen and saw Daddy sitting at the table neatly dressed in his khaki work pants and bleached white t-shirt. His hair was combed with a side part and that funny old cowlick held partially in place by Brylcreem pomade. "Well, hey there girls. How y'all doin'?" That was way too weird. Daddy NEVER spoke to us like that. "Here, sit down an' have a piece of ya Mama's banana bread." God and all His saints, was this the calm before the storm? Was he setting us up for the kill? I looked nervously over at Mama and she signaled me to join her in the living room. "Just humor ya Daddy for now. I've got a call into the doctor." I could tell Mama was very concerned because she was very nervous. Daddy was the breadwinner in our family. If he were really sick, what would happen to us? We were totally dependent upon him. I felt a quiver in the air right before all hell broke loose.

That Sunday, we went to Grandma Schroder's house on Tchoupitoulas Street. I hoped our visit meant that Daddy was feeling better. She'd whipped up a batch of steaming white beans and rice, seasoned with fat back and simmered just right. I loved being in the kitchen with Grandma. She was such a good cook - much better than Mama, who never used any seasonings but salt and pepper. There Grandma would stand, her large, German body cozied right up to that old Sears stove, cigarette hanging out the side of her mouth. Sometimes the ashes would get so long, they'd start to bend downward, aimed right toward the boiling pot! I'd nervously warn, "GRANDMA, WATCH OUT, YA ASHES ARE FALLIN' INTO THE BEANS!" She'd laugh freely in that guttural, raspy voice that came from too many years of smoking and hanging out in barrooms and say, "Ain't nothin' to worry 'bout now, Connie. Ya ol' Grandma knows what she's doin'."

When supper was ready, Grandma instructed Catherine and I to fetch Daddy.

Trying to outrun each other into the living room, we saw Daddy lying on the sofa. He was probably exhausted from being so nice while he was "not just right". After all, being mean seemed to come easiest to him.

"Daddy", I said, as I approached him slowly, "Grandma says come an' eat." Daddy replied groggily, "Come on over here. I got something to show ya."

As soon as I got within arm's reach of him, he removed the sofa pillow laying over his midsection. There, standing in all its glory, was his private part! I knew this wasn't right. Daddy said, "Here, dawlin', wanna play with me?" Jesus, Mary, Joseph, he must've done way more damage to his noggin' than Mama knew.

We ran into the kitchen, where Mama was setting the table. "MAMA! GRANDMA! DADDY IS ACTIN' CRAZY AGAIN!" They both ran out of the kitchen so fast I almost got knocked off my feet. Catherine and I followed the women into the living room just in time to hear Grandma scream, "FREDDY! PUT THAT DAMN THING BACK IN YA PANTS RIGHT NOW! WHAT IN THE HELL IS WRONG WITH YA?! GOD DAMN YA, FREDDY!" Grandma yelled at us to go back into the kitchen immediately. We ate in silence as Daddy was put to bed. Our normally unstable family-life took a noticeable turn for the worse that day.

I had trouble falling to sleep that night. I kept remembering how sometimes in the middle of the night I'd wake up and find Daddy in my bed, lying there with his hand across my chest and his leg hoisted up over my lower body. I felt very, very confused whenever that happened. He wasn't there when I fell to sleep, so maybe he and Mama had a fight and she finally kicked him out of the bedroom. But wasn't that what sofas were for? The really weird thing was that he didn't seem to like me all that much when I was awake. Why was it any different at night?

The chaos that accompanied his fall went on for days, then weeks. Daddy was nicer than ever. YEAH! I was liking this, but Mama seemed to worry more and more each day. Finally, when there was no more money for food, she sat down at the kitchen table and began writing a letter. She looked terribly sad as she wrote, but I was too afraid to ask her about the contents.

When she finished the letter, she folded it neatly and put it in an envelope but neglected to address it. I pointed that out, but she said it needed no address. "Ya see," she said, "this note is for our neighbors. I've axed each one to lend us some money 'till ya Daddy gets back on his feet." I felt deep-down sorry for Mama at that very moment. Now she was reduced to begging.

This must be what second-class people have to do to get by. That hurt.

Still deep in contemplation, Mama shoved the letter into my hand, saying, "Now, Connie, ya go to each neighbor an' give them this letter. Hopefully they'll each give ya a few dollars an' then we can go make groceries." I was mortified! "WHAT?!" Did she actually want ME to go begging for her? How could I do that? "Uh-uh, Mama I AIN'T doin' this," I said. "YA do it! Or, make Ricky do it - he's older than me!"

But the discussion was over before it started as I headed out the door. Maybe Mama figured I was the most pathetic looking of all her kids and maybe the neighbors would have more mercy on me.

As I handed the letter to each neighbor, I'd look away pretending not to know of its degrading contents. When I was handed a dollar or two, I'd thank them with fake surprise in my voice. Dammit to hell, who was I kidding? Everybody knew Daddy was a drunk. No matter what Mama said in the letter, they probably all figured Daddy was too hung over to go to work.

After that day, I found it hard to hold my head up around my friends. I figured the parents told the kids and everybody would be talking. Still stinging from shame, I was surprised that any of the neighbor kids still wanted to play with me. Yet one day, when my friends were playing at a neighbor's house, they invited me to join in.

Old Miss Vicky seemed to like kids well enough and would let us play on her porch, which had a fabulous set of stairs. These stairs were special because they were framed by two cement arms that jutted out to the edge of the steps. The arms - or runways as I called them - felt like stages. Once, during an over-vigorous ballerina turn, I lost my footing and careened off the ramp. THUMP! My chunky frame slammed hard on the sidewalk. Complete silence followed by laughter. Jesus H. Christ, I must've looked like a complete idiot! The only self-respecting thing to do was to play dead.

Silence was followed by, "Connie, Connie, can ya hear me? CONNIE! Quick, go get her Mama! I think she's DEAD!" I had to think fast. God knows, I didn't want my mama over there; she might not be wearing her false teeth - and she'd surely have that belt hanging 'round her neck. I began moaning - softly at first, then louder and coarser to make sure they all heard me. I sat up, rubbed my eyes, then my head, and weakly said, "What happened? How'd I get down here? Why y'all lookin' at me like that?" A unified sigh of relief had me thinking my friends cared about me, after all. It was good to have friends.

∞ ∞ ∞

Although Mama didn't speak too often of her troubled childhood, occasionally she'd unexpectedly open up. "My daddy left my mama for a floozy named Vesta when I was only four years old." Grandma Kraemer didn't have enough money to feed Mama and her two brothers and one sister, so she put them to bed very early. By four o'clock, the Kraemer clan was all in bed, stomachs growling. Mama said it was hard to fall to sleep when her stomach hurt so bad. She recalled how Duke, their German Sheppard, made funny noises when he was hungry. Mama said when she did get a little food she always shared it with her beloved pet. Grandma eventually gave their old sidekick away to a better home. Maybe she should've given Mama away, too. Poor Mama. When Mama was really, really mad, she'd curse, saying "GOD DAMN VESTA!" I understood why Mama hated Vesta, but I didn't feel the same; she was always nice to us, never forgetting the kids at Easter and Christmas. Maybe she felt it was disloyal to give Vesta a chance.

Mama loved her mama very much and took us to see her

as often as possible. Visiting Grandma Kraemer in the housing project where poor people lived was always done quietly, but it was fun just the same. Oddly, Grandma never seemed poor to me, but Daddy made fun of her as though living there was a bad thing.

He never came with us; I don't think he liked her very much, though I couldn't understand why. She was so gentle even when she had to be firm. "Now, Connie, ya have to draw straight lines if ya wanna play dots with us. OK, darlin'." Grandma meant what she said; she liked to see all those little boxes drawn neatly, especially if she got to insert her initial. "Take ya time, sugah. I'm in no hurry."

Sometimes, when I was sitting on the floor at her feet, I saw a fuzzy image behind her head. It had a pink tint and felt very loving and reassuring. I'd tease her, saying, "Grandma, ya hair is turning colors again!" She'd rock back and forth laughing joyously from deep within her large, round belly. "Yeah, I do that just for ya, Connie-girl." And somehow, I knew she did.

Grandma Kraemer had a special toy box just for us. We were allowed to play with anything in that box while we were visiting, but the rule was that we had to pick up everything before we left. Even though I hated picking up at home I didn't mind it at Grandma's house.

She was so mushy sweet; I wondered why we didn't escape to her house when Daddy was being cruel. Maybe it's because Grandma Kraemer never cooked. In all the years we visited her, I never once saw her in the kitchen or even smelled food on the stove. It was odd that she was so plump, since she apparently never ate.

On the days when she and Mama didn't put in their false teeth, they could pass for twins. I'd grown accustomed to Grandma's wrinkled gummy smile, but I didn't like it one bit on Mama.

Fishing for something to entertain myself, a *Merlin the Magician* storybook edged itself between my fingers. Funny, I'd never seen it in the toy box before then. I handed the book to Grandma, asking her to tell me about it.

"This then is ya quest," Grandma said in a lowered voice and accent very different from her own. "Ya must travel to the otherworld and retrieve for yaself an amulet of ya personal power. In doing this, ya will face many choices, and ya will be asked to overcome many of ya deepest anxieties and fears. This amulet will forevermore be yours and will aid ya in time of need. It is a powerful amulet and a powerful quest - one which few can complete."

"Tell me more, Grandma!" She so thoroughly sucked me in that I couldn't wait to hear more. My excitement caught Catherine's attention from across the parquet floor. Until that moment, she and Mama were oblivious to what was happening between Grandma and me. She studied me carefully for an elongated moment, and I got fidgety where I sat.

"Very well. To begin ya journey, ya must start where all those who leave this life begin." The pink, fuzzy glow behind Grandma Kraemer had changed to a sharp, luminous blue and it seemed to vibrate as she spoke.

(It never occurred to me that neither Catherine nor Mama could see Grandma's magic. She and I had a special connection but I didn't realize just how unique it was at the time. To this day, she periodically comes to me in dreams to encourage my spiritual psychic path.)

The tranquility we found at her house did not follow us home where Daddy was extra mean to Ricky. Mama's worry increased and she figured she had to get him away from Daddy before something really horrible happened. She and Aunt Marian agreed that Ricky could go live with them for a while - at least until Daddy mellowed out. I was smart enough to know that hell would freeze over before Daddy softened; in my saddened heart, I just knew that Ricky was not coming home ever again. For his own safety, he had to move out and stay away, even though I knew he didn't want to leave Mama, me and Catherine.

We stood on the front porch at eight-thirty that awful, *awful* morning. Dew lingered on the grass as it often did at that time of year and heaviness filled my already-hurting heart. I worshiped my big brother. He protected me from the beast as much as he could and played with me when nobody else would. As Ricky gave Catherine a good-bye hug, my heart pounded so hard I thought I would drop dead right there on the spot. How in the world could I say good-bye? It was insane! This just couldn't be real! I loved my brother so very much and I needed him in my life. I wasn't ready to let him go. When he reached out to me, I fell into his embrace like a limp rag doll. My legs got weak and I thought I was going to faint. God, please don't let this be happening – PLEASE don't take away my brother! God? GOD!

I HATED FRED SCHRODER! Every cell in my body ached over the excruciating loss of my beloved brother, yet I understood it was unavoidable.

As we waved upward toward the bus window, Ricky was hard-pressed to look at us directly. Just like when Daddy came to my room at night, or when my best friend was pummeling me, I "jumped" out. Seeing myself on top of the bus directly over Ricky, I leaned over as far as I could to let him see me. "Hey, Ricky, LOOK, it's ME! Was he pretending not to see me? He wasn't comfortable with that part of who I was, but he sometimes asked me about certain things I did, always followed by feigned disinterest. "I'll come see ya, OK. Soon!" I blew him a big kiss. "I LOVE YA, RICKY!" With that, I returned to stand next to Mama and Catherine. They didn't seem to notice that I was gone. They never noticed, and that was fine by me.

I knew my brother well and behind his brave front, he was also weeping. Even though Ricky was courageous and rarely cried, I saw the pain in his All-American face. We saw him only a few times after that day. Mama talked with Aunt Marian on those rare occasions when we had a working phone and found out that Ricky was enrolled in a new parochial school. I had no idea what that meant but the photograph my aunt sent proved that he had to wear a uniform. Each night, I'd remove his picture from under my pillow and study it very carefully. I could see those powder-blue eyes even in the black and white photo and I could strongly sense that behind that broad, toothy smile there was a deeply saddened and abandoned boy. He missed us as much as we missed him - at least for a while.

Eventually, Aunt Marian and Uncle Joe adopted Ricky. I figured he was better off, but I never stopped missing him. I was madder than hell at Mama for a long time after. Why didn't she stand up to Daddy for Ricky's sake?! Why couldn't she just tell Daddy to be nice to him and let him stay with us, where he belonged?! To this day, there is a gaping hole in my heart where my big brother once lived. In that same yearning heart, however, will always live the glowing image of my truest, and one-and-only hero: Richard Lewis Schroder.

One Friday not long after, as Catherine and I got home from school, I nearly bumped into Daddy standing right at the back door. Even though I thought he'd be happy with Ricky gone, he was angry about something and was bound and determined to take it out on us. "I'm sick an' tired of this filthy pigpen. Y'all get in ya room an' take everything out of there an' put it in a pile in the backyard. DO IT NOW!" I jumped at the deafening tone of his voice. JESUS! Where was Mama? We dutifully began building a pile of beloved toys and prized possessions in the yard just as Daddy demanded. "What ya gonna do, Daddy?" I asked timidly. "None of ya God damn business," he snarled. I was truly scared by then. Sometimes Daddy had a crazed look in his eyes, like a wild animal after its prey. "Hurry the fuck up, I ain't got all day!" He stormed into our room and pulled out the beautiful dollhouse he'd built with his very own hands. We played with our Barbie dolls in that little house that was constructed with so much precision and attention to detail.

With the last toy - Catherine's treasured stuffed monkey - perched at the very top of the heap, Daddy began squirting lighter fluid from top to bottom. We huddled together crying frantically. Daddy intended to "clean" out the house by torching all of our toys. We begged him to spare the dollhouse. "Let us give it to Carol. Ya like Carol, 'member Daddy? Please!" Astonishingly, he agreed as he pushed it over near the back steps. That old familiar feeling of deep despair poured over me like so many times before when I knew there wasn't a damn thing I could do to stop the craziness.

WHERE WAS MAMA? The heat from melting plastic burned my face. And even though the smoke stung my eyes, I couldn't stop staring into the blaze. Was I being hypnotized by the fire or was it Daddy's rage? At that moment, I didn't even care if he threw me into the blaze along with my half-bald teddy bear. I didn't want to live the life chosen for me by my family. I was only beginning to understand that Daddy only got power if I gave in to him. I'd rather be hung by the neck and have my fingernails pulled out one-by-one than to submit to that monster. I'd show him one day. Yeah, I surely would. I tucked the thought of this day into my mind, along with so many other daytime-nightmares I'd endured. The tables would be turned one day and he'd get to feel what it was like to be me.

That weekend we found out why Daddy was in such a hurry to clean house. Mama woke us up in the middle of the night. "Get up y'all, we're movin' tonight." WHAT? This was the first I'd heard of it. We hadn't even packed. As I stumbled out of bed, I bumped into three large cardboard boxes - the only possessions Daddy would permit Mama to take.

What about Carol? She'd be terribly worried about me if she came by and saw we were gone. My heart ached. I didn't want to leave my closest friend and I wasn't even permitted to say goodbye. Daddy hadn't made rent again. The property owner was really mad this time and wouldn't wait another day for his money. We'd be long gone before the landlord had his first cup of coffee on Monday morning.

As our old Ford pulled out of the driveway at three AM, my eyes were magnetically pulled up to the stars. I was still in my pajamas and fighting sleep. As I drifted off, I thought about how dead people felt. I'd spoken with people who lived in Heaven and they all seemed to be happy with no worries. For some reason, the dead liked to visit me while I was saying my nightly Jesus, Mary, Josephs. It would be decades before I understood the true nature of my special connection with the deceased.

Maybe God would take me to join the dead of whom I'd become so fond. I didn't see any reason to go on living; after all, Daddy had – and would continue to - take away most of what was so very important to me.

CHAPTER FOUR

Hurricanes and Ant Hills

A pungent odor rolled in along with daybreak along the bayou. As I sat up and rubbed sleep from my eyes, I couldn't believe what I saw. For the love of God, was that a river running right through the middle of town? I was afraid to ask where Daddy had driven but more afraid not to.

Since I had slept during the entire drive, I had no idea how long we'd been on the road, but I sensed it was quite a while. As we drove along Bayou Lafourche, Daddy sang the virtues of our new hometown, Golden Meadow. "It's a damn heaven here. No Niggahs, Spics or Wops to steal from us an' all this fresh air!" I hated it when he talked that way. FRESH AIR MY ASS! All I could smell was nauseating diesel fuel fumes and the overwhelming odor of fish. Tugboats were literally cruising up and down the bayou like it was normal to do such a thing.

We crossed over the bridge to the less populated side of the bayou. I didn't know at that time that the 308 side of the bayou had a bad reputation.

The 101 side was more populated and looked somewhat normal (normal for a town with a bayou running right down the middle). The other side of the bayou had very few homes in certain areas and lots of overgrown weeds. It looked scraggly and a bit creepy because of the thick trees and lack of light. I'd later find out that the 308 side was referred to as *"the other side of the bayou"* largely because of some of the outcasts living there.

The pontoon bridge was slowly moving its main span to make way for the oncoming tugboat. *Miss Ginnie* lumbered through the passageway majestically, causing several cars to form a line behind us. That was actually kind of neat, but I would die before saying so. After all, I was really very mad at Daddy for taking us away from our home and my best friend. I would not give him the satisfaction. No sir-ee bob.

On the other side of the bayou, we turned left on Highway 101 and drove for at least one hundred miles – or maybe it was fifteen. Daddy drove torturously slow, so it took forever to get to our new house. We drove through three towns – Larose, Cut Off and Galliano – to arrive in Golden Meadow. Once in town, I couldn't help but be drawn to the beautiful fields of yellow flowers that ran along the highway. "Goldenrods," Daddy announced proudly and with no prompting. "The town is full of them – everywhere ya go." Yellow was my favorite color; it made me feel bright and cheerful in a way that I never felt at home.

Daddy clicked on the right blinker and turned very sharply into the skinniest street I'd ever seen. "OK, y'all, here's ya new home on Griffin Lane!" It was spittin' distance from the bayou – and all the smells that came with it. As he turned left into the shell driveway, I glanced over toward the porch. Red-ant piles invaded the front yard and the back yard was overtaken by mud mounds. The house was wooden and in dire need of a fresh coat of paint; I prayed the inside looked better. Opening the screen door, which had a long rip running from side to side, Daddy walked in ahead of us. A musty smell let me know that the house had been closed up a while. A thick layer of dust had settled over the dead cockroaches on the kitchen counter; the linoleum tile looked aged, with cracks and pieces missing; the stove was filthy and the oven was much worse; the walls were painted drab gray and the bathroom was very small.

Jesus H. Christ, he didn't actually expect us to live in this joint, did he? He was CRAZY – STARK RAVING MAD! "Mama, tell Daddy we don't wanna live here – we wanna go home! Mama, tell him!" When I looked squarely at Mama's face I saw tears; it was as though her once-blue eyes were now grey. She hated this place as much as we did – maybe more. First Daddy made us get rid of Ricky, and then everything else that we loved. Then he moved us to the end of the world further away from Little Freddie to this God forsaken place. Away from anything familiar, he would have more control than ever.

We had a month to get settled in before school started. There were no curtains on the windows so Mama hung sheets. That was embarrassing; none of the neighbors on the lane used sheets for curtains. Why did Daddy insist on making us live so differently than everybody else? I hated being so unlike normal people.

Three weeks after we moved in Hurricane Betsy headed our way, right on schedule. Hurricane season traditionally begins in August and goes straight through November of each year. Usually, the Bayou Lafourche area experienced two or three hurricanes each season, some much worse than others. Betsy was labeled a category four, with five being the worst and deadliest hurricane ever recorded. We had experienced hurricanes in New Orleans but Golden Meadow was much closer to the Gulf of Mexico and had less to protect it from the ravaging wind and rain. Betsy was causing such a stir in the Gulf that local officials were urging all residents to evacuate. The logical thing to do, Daddy said, was to go further north. His employer, Mr. Shep, from the Larose Shipyard said we could take cover there at the yard. Daddy assured us that the building was two stories and would be safe from flooding.

Before heading fifteen miles north to Larose, we had to hurricane-proof our house. This was pretty much a routine in our lives. We lifted all the furniture onto cinder blocks and made large adhesive tape X's on each window. It was really better to board up your windows, but Daddy seemed to like taking the easy way out.

Traffic was thick as molasses on the slow trek to Larose. People were taking Hurricane Betsy's threat seriously, unlike many prior hurricanes.

When we arrived at the shipyard, Daddy pulled our one bag out of the trunk and led us into the old dusty building. It looked like a hardware store on the first floor, with lots of tools and odds and ends. The second story was very hot and more like Grandma's attic, with things stored in piles. We found a small room where a mattress had been placed on the floor.

Mr. Shep, who was also our landlord, was there with his wife and daughter, Trixy. Trixy suddenly became very quiet and slowly - with much authority - said, "Ya know, there could be a tidal wave come through here." I thought tidal waves only happened out in the ocean, but Trixy surely seemed to know about this sort of stuff. She came from a long line of many generations who had all lived down the bayou their entire lives – they must surely know.

As Mr. Shep and his family left it hit me – why weren't they riding it out here? Was that a sign? Where did they go to stay safe? I sat contemplating the huge wave that could sweep us all out to the Gulf. I didn't know how to swim, for God's sake, and floating on my back - which I could do very well - would probably not save me.

With only catnaps here and there, we didn't really sleep that night. The wind increased to one hundred and ten miles per hour and the metal roof was taking a colossal beating. The power was out and it was hotter than hell. The only light we had was the flame from Daddy's soldering torch, which he used sparingly; we had no idea how long we'd be without electricity and our battery-powered radio was the only contact with the outside. We were, for all practical purposes, on our own.

At two o'clock in the morning and without warning, a sustained gust of wind, howling at approximately one-hundred and forty miles per hour ripped off a section of the roof directly above us. Mama, who was lying between Catherine and me, grasped our hands as she shot up to a seated position. "OH MY GOD, WE'RE DEAD!" We shrieked simultaneously jumping off the mattress. What precisely does one do at the moment of their death?

"JESUS, FREDDY!" Mama screamed. Daddy yelled at Mama to calm down. "SHUT YA TRAP, FLO, ya scarin' the girls." Daddy began investigating the damage and quickly found several buckets to catch the rain that fell through the beaten roof.

Further investigating downstairs, Catherine and I followed closely, feeling safer with him than with Mama. She freaked out so easily, as did Catherine, especially in situations like this. Daddy had absolutely no patience with Mama when she got that way.

Once at the foot of the stairs, we had to step into two inches of water. (Two inches seemed harmless compared to that tidal wave that I was convinced was coming our way.) Daddy got to the front door and tried to open it. The wind was blowing so hard it created pressure on the door and even though he was very strong (he always said so), he couldn't get that old warped door to budge. Within minutes, the rain and wind stopped abruptly.

Trying the door again, Daddy was able to open it without a

struggle. Eerily quiet, the sky was pitch black. Not one animal could be seen or heard – nor humans for that matter. It was like the world had died while we were upstairs and nobody came to tell us; like fallout after a nuclear bomb. Daddy said this was called the "eye" of the storm. He explained that as the wind and rain whips around they form a doughnut shape, with all the activity on the outer edges and all the calm on the inside of the circle. We were at the inside. It could last up to an hour, he said, depending upon the width of the circle.

A little over one hour later, just as Daddy had predicted, the wind and rain picked up. We emptied overflowing buckets frequently before dawn. About five o'clock in the morning, the rain stopped but the wind continued to sing its ghostlike tune. Daddy went downstairs to check out the damage and found that the water had risen at least two or three additional inches.

We stayed at the shipyard for five days after Betsy made landfall. Mr. Shep, who lived north of the shipyard, brought us additional supplies – food, water, ice and batteries for the portable radio. It was still as hot as a freshly tarred roof, but there was no way to get home until the bayou receded enough to clear at least one of the two highways that led to Golden Meadow.

Still without power, and of course no television, the days were dreadfully long. To entertain myself, I took a mental inventory of the items on the shelves downstairs. Since a lot of the merchandise consisted of small parts and pieces, it consumed most of my days. The nights were the longest and hardest. There was nothing cold to drink except what had melted off the large block of ice, and that was not very clean. I used small chips from the block to cool down. For once, I couldn't wait to take a bath.

Finally, when it was OK to leave Larose, we slowly headed back down the bayou.

The closer we got to Griffin Lane, the more destruction reared its ugly head. Water still flowed over the highway, so it was impossible to tell where the street ended and the bayou began. That made me very, very nervous. Not being a swimmer made me fear the water more than most. Tall, thin sticks with neon red tops lined the street to the left between the bayou and us. Daddy said that was to guide us and keep us from accidentally going off the road. The thought of falling into water so dirty you couldn't see through it worried me. Out of habit, I prayed real hard even though I no longer believed God was paying attention.

After driving three hours and eight miles, we literally floated into the parking lot of Galliano Catholic Church. Police cars with flashing lights barricaded the road, even though anybody could see that the road leading into Golden Meadow was flooded. There were several men there with *pirogues* (Cajun canoes), ready to transport those folks who couldn't get home by regular means. We were warned that flooding might prevent us from staying in our homes, but they'd at least take us there to pick up belongings and any other necessities. The church was set up as an evacuation shelter; we could return if need be.

Daddy, however, was dead set on going home – and staying there. A nice man familiar to Daddy helped us into his pirogue. The two men talked and Daddy helped the man paddle. I secretly let my hand dip into the cool water, even though we were specifically warned not to do that.

When we finally got home, the water was higher than expected. It had reached the front porch, which was about three-and-a-half feet. Luckily, it hadn't seeped into the house yet; what little second-hand furniture we had had not been destroyed.

The heat was unbearable and Catherine and I couldn't wait to head out to the snowball stand just beyond the shrimp

46

factory. Wading in waist-deep water, I was very grateful that the stand had a back-up generator. I loved the little yellow building, with all its flavored syrup bottles glistening in the windowsill. The sound of the ice-shaving machine thrilled me; it guaranteed a cooling off – even if only temporarily.

Although I looked forward to a cool treat, I hated walking around that tight curve in the road in front of the seafood factory. Sometimes the workers would sit outside on break or while waiting for the boats to unload. One man in particular scared me. He looked mentally off and I felt wickedness behind that bizarre smile and those yellow, crooked teeth – nobody could convince me differently. Sometimes I got feelings in my gut about people – either good or bad. I could tell when my internal danger sign was lit and this man made it glow. I pulled Catherine along quickly, warning her not to look at the men and to keep walking. It was hard to keep my composure when they began whistling and howling. God, I hated that feeling – I felt like a cow going to slaughter. Some girls just giggled and seemed to like this type of attention, but not me and not from them. Chills ran up and down my spine as I pushed Catherine faster. I didn't want the men to think that we were afraid – that might serve to arouse attention in some weird way. Once we were past the anger zone, my body relaxed.

Soon, Hurricane Betsy was behind us. School started and I was nervous. I didn't know a soul, except Trixy, who really was Catherine's friend. Golden Meadow Upper Elementary was only a few miles from our house, but too far to walk. The first day of school we met the yellow school bus at the front of Griffin Lane. Mr. Leroy, the bus driver, who was a jolly sort, and greeted us with a broad Cajun-style smile. "Hey, cher', how y'all doin' dis mornin'?" No matter what I was feeling, I returned his gracious smile with, "Oh, doin' fine, Mister

Leroy." Mr. Leroy was Mr. Shep's brother and Miss Cheramie's oldest son.

Surviving the first day of school just wore me out. I went to my room right after supper and sprawled out across my bed. I missed Carol. We had been inseparable; now all I could do was wonder how she was and what she was doing. I began talking to her in my mind.

Before I could play with my visions of hanging out with Carol I drifted off to sleep.

CHAPTER FIVE

Hell's Kitchen

Just when I thought we were truly already at the end of the Earth, Daddy announced that we'd be taking a family drive. The washed-out road to Grand Isle (the true end of the line) was by then repaired and drivable and only a forty-five-minute drive from where we lived. Daddy said the locals talked about crabbing down in Grand Isle, and even though I dreaded "family time", the thought of eating hot boiled crabs got my attention. The only thing that I could relate to on the bayou so far was fishing and eating fresh seafood.

We drove right up to the mangled seaweed strewn along the hot sand at the gulf's edge. It was smelly, but more of an outdoors smell than the diesel smell of the bayou. We unloaded the car and Mama set up her bright pink beach chair with a small umbrella. She was very fair skinned and said the sun made her itch. Daddy said it was because of all the nerve medication she was taking, but she pretended not to hear him.

In about three feet of water, Daddy stuck a tall thin pole in the soft gulf bottom, then walked about twenty feet away from that pole and anchored another one. From the two poles he stretched a piece of twine which hovered about one foot above the water. The next step was to tie several pieces of twine, each about three-feet long, at twelve-inch intervals. At the end of each piece Daddy tied a steel nut, explaining that this would add weight to the chicken-neck which was attached. Once everything was in place, we walked back to shore and got a cold drink.

Ten minutes passed and Daddy picked up the scoop net. "Come on y'all; the crabs should have smelled the bait by now." He instructed us to walk very slowly to make sure we didn't scare the crabs, which were hopefully clinging to each of the lines he'd baited. Daddy crept up to the first line nearest to the left pole. "Shhh," he said as he lifted his left index finger to his lips. With the net in his right hand, he began to slowly raise the line with his left hand. As it neared the surface of the water, we could see three fat crabs gnawing at the chicken neck, which had already lost its color. "AAAAEEEE!" I shrieked with joy. Daddy dropped the line and the crabs scurried off. "God dammit! I told ya to keep quiet, didn't I?! Now shut ya damn trap!" I stood in complete silence for what seemed like forever feeling ashamed and scared. I wanted to cry, but fought back the tears. (I hated it when I thought I was doing something good and Daddy yelled at me because of it. Over time I had learned to become very monotone around him – it proved to be safer that way. I learned very young how to disguise my true feelings.) Finally getting the signal to move on to the next line, I put my hand over my mouth in anticipation. If those crabs came back, I surely did not want to scare them off again. Daddy was liable to get so mad that he'd hit me and tear down the whole contraption and take us home.

∞ ∞ ∞

The bell rang loudly three minutes before third period class on a Monday that arrived too quickly. I stood frozen near the cafeteria, possessing no earthly idea which way to go. I despised that feeling, although it was much too familiar – I should've known my way around by then - everybody else did. Suddenly I became aware of a girl standing to my right. I figured I'd better ask for help right then or I'd be late for P.E. class. "Do ya know what time it is?" Before she could answer, I added, "Do ya know where Mr. Cantrelle's class is?" "Yeah, that's where I'm goin'." Wonder why I hadn't noticed her in class?

"My name is Connie, what's ya name?" "Linda," she responded, a bit shyly. She had black curly hair and the whitest teeth I'd ever seen, all showing when she smiled. We walked together quietly, not knowing then that the future would invite us to become the best of friends. She was a Godsend, all right. Linda was quiet, kind, and generous and I felt I'd hit the jackpot that day because until that moment, I hadn't fit into this place one teeny-tiny bit. (As uncomfortable as it was being a misfit, I was used to it. After all, I'd known that feeling all of my life.)

∞ ∞ ∞

Mama was in the change of life when she got pregnant. I was more than shocked about the whole thing; I was convinced Mama and Daddy weren't physically intimate any longer. Mama said she wasn't expecting this sort of thing to happen and I'd be willing to bet that Daddy wasn't either.

During the last month of her pregnancy, she warned me that she had very quick deliveries. Once her water broke Mama needed to get to the hospital immediately; each one of her babies was born within an hour or so once labor started. Daddy was used to this; the morning I called him at work, he came home immediately. Mama's bag was already packed and within thirty minutes they arrived at the hospital. Within sixty minutes, baby Luke made his first appearance. If I could've warned him, I would've told him not to bother. This was not a happy family. Mama was either crying or staring into space and Daddy was either being cruel or was completely toasted. Not much fun to be in the Schroder family, not much fun at all.

Nevertheless, when Luke arrived home swaddled in a yellow cotton blanket, I could barely keep my eyes off him. He was the tiniest and most precious thing I'd ever seen – even with that pointed little head. Mama said they had to use forceps to help him come out and that his head would get rounder as each day passed.

Giving birth really left Mama weak. She wasn't all that healthy to begin with, but now she was way too pale and alarmingly thin. Daddy instructed me to take care of Luke for Mama. I really didn't mind at all. Little Luke was the first thing since Ricky that made me feel like I had a small place in the world. As long as he needed caring for, I had a purpose – a real purpose – for living. I bathed his tiny pink body, prepared his formula, gave him his bottles – day and night – and rocked him in my arms. I loved the way he smelled and his little body felt so very right nestled against me as I sang lullabies from a second-hand record player.

When Luke's small warm face was next to mine, I could hear his thoughts – or maybe it's more accurate to say that I could feel them. He often told me that he loved me, not in words but in the way he felt. His body temperature would rise a little and I could swear that something inside him was vibrating. The first time that I noticed it, I got worried. But as I held him closer, then away a bit so I could get a good look at his irresistible little face, he would present me with a sweet near-angelic smile. Mama would say that he just had gas, but I knew different and so did baby Luke. He silently called me Mama and we decided to keep it our little secret.

He was my baby Luke - until the day they took him away.

Apparently, the pregnancy and birth were more than Mama could take and caused a nervous breakdown. I knew her body couldn't handle the whole thing, but her mind seriously failed too. When Luke was three months old Daddy came into the kitchen with a very serious look on his face. "Connie, ya Aunt Bev an' Uncle Lewis are gonna take Luke to live with them for a while. Ya Mama ain't well and she just can't take care of the baby." I was horrified!

"NO, YA CAN'T TAKE MY BABY AWAY - NO!" My words got lost in the tears and Daddy said again, "Ya Mama can't handle it, Connie. This is the only thing I know to do." I begged, "I'll take care of Luke, Daddy, I can do it. I been doin' it all along, can't ya see that?! Daddy, please, please don't let 'em take away my baby!"

By then I was sobbing from a place so deep, I hadn't known it existed. The excruciating pain of losing Ricky still ripped at my heart. I wanted a brother so badly – in the worst way. Why didn't Daddy want boys? I just couldn't bear to lose another brother - not again! What was wrong with these wretched people, for God's sake - were they ALL nuts? I was just about thirteen and had already shown how capable I was with the baby – I was a damn good mother - way better than *she was*! Couldn't Daddy see that?

I begged God not to let them take baby Luke away from me. It felt like I was in a very small, dark room which was painfully soundproof; nobody seemed to hear a thing I was saying. IF YA TAKE 'WAY LUKE, YOU'LL BE KILLIN' A PART OF ME – CAN'T YA SEE THAT?! No response.

WHY ARE YA GONNA LET SOMEBODY ELSE RAISE OUR BABY WHEN I'M RIGHT HERE TO DO IT?! No response.

CAN'T YA HEAR ME, YA SON-OF-A-BITCH?! No response.

What if I wasn't really talking at all? Maybe the screaming was only in my head. There was no detectable expression on either Mama's or Daddy's faces. HEARTLESS BASTARD! DON'T YA DARE TAKE HIM! HE'S MY BABY!

The next morning at nine o'clock, Aunt Bev and Uncle Lewis pulled into our shell driveway. It was embarrassing to have them see our rundown shack of a house and overgrown yard. But that paled in comparison to what would happen right before my very eyes.

Drew, my first cousin, got out of the compact Chevy first, followed by Aunt Bev and Uncle Lewis. They all smiled, but I didn't feel at all like reciprocating – not one teeny-tiny bit – and I wouldn't do it just to act friendly. I begged Daddy again. "Daddy, I can quit school an' take care of the baby. Mama will be well soon, and then she can take over. I know this will work – ya gotta let me try this – just gimme a chance to prove it, Daddy!" I could hear the sound of desperation in my own voice and I prayed to Almighty God that Daddy could, too. Continuing to ignore me, he brushed past to greet the thieves who would dare to steal my baby. Daddy didn't even like these people – they were Mama's folks and he made no bones about not liking any one of her relatives. Why all of a sudden were they so acceptable? Two-faced bastard!

After a short visit, Mama, in a sleepwalking-like motion, bundled Luke up in his yellow cotton blanket and handed him to Aunt Bev. My heart dropped to my bare feet and I was certain I'd faint right on the spot. I grabbed for him, but Aunt Bev lifted him up above my reach. Not a damn thing I said or did could change Daddy's mind. I felt so incredibly helpless. That was MY baby he was giving away – MY baby brother – MY reason for living! WAS ANYBODY LISTENING TO ME?

In that singular moment I despised Daddy more than I thought humanly possible. What kind of animal was he, for Christ's sake? Cold, heartless devil! Nothing he could ever say or do would make up for such a horrendous act. He'd just given away the only thing -besides Ricky - that I ever really and truly cared about.

That dreary April day my heart bled all over the filthy kitchen floor but nobody saw it. Nobody gave a damn about me. I was nothing in their eyes, and until I got Luke back, I was worthless in my own eyes. If I couldn't get my little sugah back, I may as well be dead.

That night, a feeling of deep gloom and tremendous hopelessness engulfed me. It was hollow and smothering and cold and scorching all at the same time. I lay on my bed looking up at the stars through the torn screen, knowing I needed to go there for a while.

I couldn't bear the pain any longer and I knew the only relief was to go to the place where I'd always been safe. Rest awaited me there, no matter what was happening to my body or my mind. My precious baby Luke was gone, ripped away from me like flesh torn from the bone. Now my only purpose was to get him back – and I WOULD get him back, no matter what. He needed me. He knew how much I really loved him – I told him so all the time with my words, my songs and especially with my mind. Even at just three months old he knew, all right. Luke and I spoke the same language. That's how I knew he felt as lost and scared as me and how desperately he wanted to come home.

I tried my hardest to tell Daddy how frightened Luke was, but he ignored me. God, would I ever be able to trust an adult? They always screwed things up. Just about the time I realized that I loved somebody - or something– it was stolen right out from under me.

As I floated amongst my familiar twinkling friends, I got the instant knowing that even though I was still a kid, I'd always have to take care of myself. Nobody was raising me – I was all alone. As I drifted from star to star absorbing the warm illumination, anxiety left me.

The next morning, Daddy got up and went to work at six-thirty as usual as though nothing out of the norm had happened. Instead of returning in the evening, he came home within an hour-and-a-half. Catherine and I hadn't even left for the bus stop yet. When he walked into the kitchen, he asked Mama if her bag was packed. "Yeah, I'm ready," she said flatly.

When I stepped into the kitchen for coffee, Mama said, "Connie, I'm goin' to the hospital for a while. I don't feel too good an' I need a rest." I wasn't completely sure why she needed a rest, because I did most everything around the house, but I could tell by the way she was dragging that she wasn't right again. Thank God the men with the white jackets didn't come for her like so many times in the past. This time she voluntarily got into the car and submitted herself to heavy-duty drugs and those horrible shock treatments. Poor Mama. She never seemed to be able to hang in there for very long. She was weak by nature, Daddy said, and even though I'd always defended her, I had to agree.

As Daddy pulled out of the driveway, I cried. I couldn't stop no matter how hard I tried, but I refused to let myself sob out loud. My world was like a game of craps. I never knew how the die would fall. So much changed and yet nothing changed all. It was hard to count on anything except that my heart would be broken and there would be loss - over and over again.

Weeks, then months dragged by. Deep down inside I had to admit that I really couldn't come up with a plan to bring my baby home. But, in order to keep hope alive, each day I'd visualize how I'd storm my aunt's and uncle's house and nab Luke. They lived in a suburb of New Orleans, a good two-hour drive from where we lived. I was only a teenager - and a new one at that. When I was being painfully honest with myself, I had to ask what a kid like me could do in such a case as this.

What I could do was talk to Luke every day, telling him how very much I loved him, reassuring him that I was NOT the one who sent him away. It was vitally important to me that he understood. "Luke, this is Connie. Hello my lil' puddin', I miss ya so, so much! I want ya to know that I want ya back home now an' I'm doin' everything I can to get ya back. I'll never give up, Luke, ya hear?" When I got very quiet I could "see" Luke and what was going on around him. I knew our relatives were taking good care of him, but I also knew that they could not love him the way I could. He needed me.

∞ ∞ ∞

In August of that year, I entered seventh grade at Golden Meadow Junior High. It was near the upper elementary and most of the kids who graduated from there went on to junior high in the same town. I suppose I might have been a little excited, but Luke was still gone and that dulled most everything. Linda and I were still the best of friends and never seemed to disagree about anything. Her parents were very kind to me and I loved going to their house. It always felt so normal there, even though Linda and her two sisters – one younger and one older - screamed at each other a lot. That didn't bother me compared to Daddy's yelling.

Mrs. Brabham, Linda's mother, cooked a lot and always had massive amounts of food on the table. They were generous with whatever they had and I always felt cared for in their presence. Mr. Brabham was part owner of an independent grocery store that catered to the local fishermen. He was at the store a lot, and since we lived around the corner, I often saw him on my regular shopping trips.

Daddy gave Mama two dollars every day to shop for meals.

She didn't like to go out very much so she'd send me in her place with an artfully constructed shopping list, calculated to the penny. I really didn't mind because Daddy never took us anywhere and I considered this a social outing. I became friendly with the clerks and bagboys and felt sort of normal while I was there. Mr. Brabham would always give me a smile and a hello from the raised booth where he worked.

The second Saturday in October Aunt Bev and Uncle Lewis were scheduled to bring Luke home. Mama was back with us and feeling somewhat better, but still looked awful. She'd lost even more weight and her face was so drawn that if I squinted, I could see her skeleton. Her eye sockets were sunken and hollow and underlined by dark circles. I knew she still wasn't really well, but Daddy said it was time for her and the baby to come home. He gave me a lecture on how I was to help Mama around the house and with the baby. I should do anything she asked of me - at any time. Didn't he realize that I'd always done those things?

Somehow, Catherine was able to escape his commands due to her iron-poor blood. She may have had Mama and Daddy fooled, but it was no secret to me why she was so anemic. Growing up, Mama would cut her meat into small pieces. Catherine would put the first bite in her mouth and chew a few times, but before swallowing, she'd take another bite and continue chewing. Sometimes that girl would get up to six pieces of beef in her mouth at one time – never swallowing - until finally she looked like a chipmunk! At that point, she had no other choice but to spit it all out. Consequently, Catherine never got much nourishment and as a result, she was never asked to help out very much. Catherine may have been smarter than I thought.

As Aunt Bev got out of the car, I ran to greet her. I quickly asked if I could hold Luke and she lovingly handed him to me.

She really was a sweet person, and I liked Uncle Lewis and Drew, too. They were probably some of the nicest of Mama's relatives. (Even though Aunt Marian let us stay at her house sometimes, she always seemed to have an attitude about us. Maybe because of Daddy, though it seemed like she thought less of Mama than of her other siblings. Daddy always said she was snooty, but maybe that's because she didn't let Daddy tell her what to do. I never could really figure her out. She seemed to hide her true emotions behind a wall, possibly so others would think she was strong when she might really be scared. What if I was like Aunt Marian? That thought was of no comfort.)

Luke didn't seem to know me at first, which was very difficult to digest. How could he forget me? I thought about him every single day and sent so many telepathic messages of love and hope. He probably just needed a little time to recognize me again, Aunt Bev said. After a few hours, Luke did seem to know me as I rocked him, singing his favorite lullaby. Within minutes my little bundle of joy was fast asleep. A gentle humming sound whistled through his tiny round nose. Was it possible that everything would be better now that he was home with me, where he belonged? I dared only to hold this thought for a moment or two.

True to form, Mama made many requests of me in the following months. "Mop the kitchen floor, do the dishes, then feed the baby, Connie. Change the baby, fold the clothes, makes the baby's bottles." There was no end to the chores Mama wanted done. I felt like nothing more than a slave to Mama and always on edge around Daddy, whose moods were as erratic as Mama's in a different way.

I taught myself to predict his moods by the way he drove onto the shell driveway. Too fast and he'd be in a foul mood and wouldn't let me go anywhere. He'd probably find a reason to yell and curse and maybe even hit me if he picked up on my thoughts about him.

You see, I communicated with Daddy through my mind, too. I told him to go to hell more times than I can count and I'll bet he knew it each time. If he turned into the driveway very slowly, he'd gone past the point of vicious straight to drowsy. If I made him something to eat, he'd go directly to bed afterward.

Timing was everything with Daddy, and I got pretty good at it. I learned to observe his movements down to the tiniest details. I was convinced that it meant my safety – maybe even my life.

Assuming the role Ricky once held, I felt a very strong responsibility to protect the rest of the family from Daddy's rage. It was my turn to be the buffer. Of course, I could only do so much, but I never stopped trying. Mama and Catherine were so very alike, both weak and frail. They never stood up to Daddy and always seemed so scared. And, Luke, well he was just an innocent little baby. I was the only one who could do it.

Thank God for Linda. She was the only one who seemed to have a lick of sense. Even so, I couldn't tell her about all of the awful things happening inside our four walls. I didn't want to scare her off. Linda was my best friend – really my only friend - and I couldn't afford to lose my connection with her. I needed her so I could stay sane, to have a real opportunity to see how other people lived and how people actually loved and respected each other. Even then, and without knowing the words for it, I understood that Linda was my lifeline.

I prayed the house would not scare her off. I realize speaking this way about a house sounds crazy, but from the moment I stepped foot into that place I got really bad vibes. It was as though it was a living thing and had needs. I can't explain it but I was sure that the old house had seen - and maybe caused - many tragedies. I wondered if I was crazy to "know" those things.

∞ ∞ ∞

It was on a Sunday night two months later, while everyone but the house was asleep when lightning struck my brain. The ten o'clock news was on Channel 4. I wasn't particularly interested in world events. Why bother? I never got out of the community. My physical world was very contained; the people on the news were only actors as far as I was concerned.

The last thing I remember before the paramedics arrived is sitting on the sofa eating a roast beef po-boy. I was dressed in Mama's old pink and yellow striped moo-moo with snaps down the front. The ripped corner of the right pocket was held together with a large safety pin. I fantasized about owning a sewing machine - I'd be happy to fix stuff like that - but Daddy said that kind of thing was ridiculous and too damn expensive.

"Come on now, Miss, come with us." "NO!", I screamed. I would not get into an ambulance with those strange men. WHO called them, anyway? And, WHY were they at MY house?

With a paramedic grasping each of my arms, I had difficulty creating enough drag to prevent forward movement. I simply wasn't going with them, no matter how they coaxed me! The moment I caught sight of those flashing red lights, my heart started racing, my head pounded and sweat dripped down my forehead and burned my eyes. I was scared to death – and not even sure of what or why. This was all too reminiscent of the men who took Mama against her will. The two men got me as far as the front porch when I caught a glimpse of Mama standing behind us in the living room. "MAMA, HELP ME! Tell them to STOP!" Daddy was in the kitchen making a sandwich, as though nothing out of the ordinary was happening. "MAMA! I'm NOT gettin' in that damn ambulance!" Catherine was peeking out from the door, looking smaller than ever. She had that deer-in-the-headlights look, which made me even more frightened. It was like a nightmare I couldn't wake up from. What would possess these strangers to tear me from my home? "Ya better let go of my damn arms RIGHT NOW!"

Finally, after so much resistance on my part, Mama told the paramedics to let me be. They both shrugged their shoulders and one said, "Ya sure, ma'am?" Apparently Daddy didn't think they were leaving fast enough. "Get the hell outta my house, God dammit!"

What had happened to me? As the emergency vehicle pulled out of the driveway, I fell on the sofa next to Mama. "What's goin' on, Mama?" My body was shaking uncontrollably and Mama looked real worried, but tried to stay calm. "Connie, ya had a fit an' fell on the floor." Why was she talking like that? "Whatta ya mean – a fit?" "Seizure" she said quickly. I had no idea what she was going on about. I looked to the kitchen for Daddy's further explanation, but he'd already gone back to bed.

"Why did those men wanna take me to the hospital?" I was more confused than ever. What wasn't she telling me? She was clearly covering up something – but what? Catherine ran into the living room as though the boogieman was chasing her. She jumped into the air and landed on the other side of Mama. I felt sorry for her. She was so easily affected.

"Did Daddy hurt ya head, Connie?" Catherine asked. "What?" I was growing anxious with this cat and mouse game. "Ya head, silly. Did Daddy hurt ya when he hit ya?" I had no idea what she was talking about and looked to Mama for clarification. "Don't ya member, Connie?"

Finally, seeing the panic in my eyes, Mama nervously said, "Earlier tonight, ya Daddy got real mad at ya an' hit ya in the head. Don't ya member Connie? Ya didn't clean up the kitchen like he told ya to an' he got real mad. Ya mumbled something under ya breath, an' he thought ya was back-talkin' him. When he yelled at ya 'bout it, ya just turned 'way from him an' that made him real mad."

Catherine nodded her little head the whole time Mama talked, adding, "Then, he ran after ya an' punched ya in the head real, real hard - plenty times. I was real scared an' I cried a lot, huh, Mama, didn't I cry a lot? I kept screamin' at him to stop, but he just kept hittin' ya. Mama, I'm scared!" Mama reached for her and pulled her close. "You go see the doctor tomorrow." And that was that. No more discussion, no consoling, no nothing.

As I let my exhausted body drop into bed, I realized I was on my own. Mama wasn't telling me everything and Daddy acted like nothing out of the ordinary had happened. If he really did beat me, why didn't Mama stop him or call the cops, or at least yell at him. And why on God's green earth couldn't I remember?

The doctor called it epilepsy – too much energy in the brain at one time. The so-called overload caused me to have a grand mal seizure, which resulted in short-term amnesia. It could be hereditary or caused by a blow to the head. Why didn't Mama tell him about Daddy punching me in the head? Was she afraid he'd say that caused the seizure? He gave Mama a prescription for Phenobarbital and told her to give me three pills a day.

I got little white pills and Daddy got off the hook.

I missed school that day and the rest of the week. Mama said I had to rest. When Catherine got home from school, she joined me on the sofa. "Hey, Connie. How ya feelin'?" "OK, I guess." As I answered, I felt weird inside as though I, too, knew something and wasn't letting my very own self in on the secret. "Are ya sick like when ya couldn't see that time?" Catherine sure was an odd duck. In my irritation, I yelled at her. "What are ya yappin' 'bout now?" Catherine began speaking very quickly, as she was prone to do when she was nervous or scared. "Daddy hit ya in the head so many times ya couldn't see that time. 'Member?"

She often got things confused, so I called out to Mama, who was smoking a cigarette at the kitchen table. She smashed the butt into the beanbag ashtray and walked into the living room, sitting at the other end of the sofa.

"Yeah, dawlin' it's true. Daddy hit ya in the head an' ya lost ya sight for hours. Ya wouldn't go to the hospital that time, either." The tone of Mama's voice was unbelievably calm. "What?!" I had absolutely no recollection of any such event. How could I NOT remember that? Mama said the seizures zapped my brain so hard that I forgot stuff.

What else didn't I remember? Who were these people really? Did I even know them? How could I trust them or myself, for that matter? If I couldn't recall things, how could I know what was really happening to me?

I wanted to talk to Linda about the beatings and memory loss, but I was afraid she'd see how really awful my family was and not want to be my friend. I'd told her some things, for instance like Daddy's drinking. But Daddy never misbehaved too badly in front of her, so she never saw him at his worst. My guess is that she probably suspected more than she let on. I didn't want to lose her. Without a doubt, she was my main link to sanity and I vowed not to let Daddy take that away, too.

CHAPTER SIX

The Gatekeeper

My last year of junior high was the best of the worst. I was nominated to be on the newspaper staff by a boy I had a crush on from a distance. Randy was smart, kind and very good-looking. He had a girlfriend who was hard to dislike, though I tried.

Being a new writer on the Golden Meadow Junior High staff was exhilarating. I was writing with a staff of talented kids, most of who were older and seemed to come from good homes. The "good home" thing made me feel even more misplaced than usual, but I tried my best and held my head up high. I was good at that. I could hide things about myself, like humiliation over the poor condition of our home, tremendous embarrassment about my sparse wardrobe of hand-me-down clothes and worn-out shoes, and bruises caused by Daddy's drunken rages. I was a damn good actress, all right.

Daddy was the gatekeeper of the Schroder shack. He doled out only the barest of necessities when it came to our needs. You see, I had two dresses – just two – for most of my last year in junior high. I wore the black-and-white checkered one with the green sash on Monday and the beige A-line on Tuesday.

Each morning I'd iron the dress I was wearing that day. To make matters worse (if that's possible) Catherine had the same black-and-white checkered dress! On more than one occasion I asked Daddy to take me to the department store to buy at least one more dress and his reply was reliably the same: "Ya have too much now! Besides, I don' have the money for that sorta crap." I could never get over the feeling of being thoroughly insignificant to him. I was either a beating post or a no-thing, or someone to climb into bed with when he and Mama had been fighting. I thought fathers were supposed to want what's best for their kids, but it was painfully obvious that my daddy cared only about himself.

For the most part, I was convinced that I would never be able to escape my home. On rainy days I'd lay on my bed crossways, watching the wind blow the shredded plastic curtains aimlessly above me. The overgrown elephant-leaf plants just outside my bedroom window felt like a prison wall. Some days I felt completely trapped and robbed of motivation. The only thing that helped was music. Songs about love triggered my hopelessness and made me think about how weird I sometimes felt around Daddy. "My love for you is way out of line. Better run girl; you're much too young girl." I wondered if Mama ever noticed my pain.

God, I HATED the sickness of that house! Would anybody believe me if I told them that I sensed that the house supported – maybe even fed upon – the brutality taking place inside? I swear I could hear the house thinking and plotting. It was a relentless enemy and I knew, even if nobody else saw or would admit to it, that it was smothering the hopes, wishes and even the life out of me. It sat up and took particular notice when Daddy was drunkest. It feasted upon his darkness – or was it the other way around?

Hardly anyone other than Linda ever came to the house. It was hard enough to let her see how we lived.

∞ ∞ ∞

Summer was approaching and Ricky was coming to visit. I still missed him terribly, but it was not the same as when we were younger. I'd gotten somewhat used to being the oldest kid. The only noticeable prerequisite in filling Ricky's job was that I be willing to be a barrier between Daddy and my younger siblings. As long as I honored my instinctual desire to protect the younger kids, I was a natural for the job.

On June twenty-eighth, Ricky arrived via Greyhound from Aunt Marian's house (his new home). Standing with Mama, Catherine and Luke at the depot, I got butterflies in my stomach as he stepped off the bus. Since the adoption, his new last name was Maysien. It seemed so odd that my very own brother had a different last name, but I didn't blame him one bit for wanting a better life. He was the lucky one and I was happy for him, if not a bit envious.

Ricky was taller and thinner, though he still had that same beautiful smile. His tanned skin made his teeth look even whiter – "Glistenin' pearly whites," I teased him playfully. When I hugged him I noticed that his body was firm, like he'd been exercising. Guess it was all vigorous activity in P.E. class or maybe it was just the loss of "baby fat" (a term used all-too-often to describe me).

I still adored my big brother, but there was an ever-growing difference in the way we related to one another. It was not as free and easy; I found myself having to think of things to say. Maybe my nervousness was due to the fact that I hadn't really gotten to watch him grow up over the last few years. I just didn't know him as well anymore and that made me sad. I felt a burning sensation starting just below my nose and dropping down through my chest. Although I wanted nothing more than to avoid crying, focusing instead on Ricky and what his life had been like since we'd last seen him, a large tear spilled down my face. I felt a suspended sensation, hovering above my family. I observed Mama, Catherine, Luke and Ricky, but I was not an active participant. Nobody noticed. I wasn't sure if that was good or bad, but all I wanted to do was to get back into my body so I could be there fully with Ricky. Usually I found myself jumping out to escape Daddy, but this was completely unexpected and threw me off.

When the numbness dissipated and I was back on solid ground in my body, I began chatting as though Ricky had never moved away. Any talent scout looking for the next young star would have scooped me up on the spot. Since nobody was tuned-in to my feelings - or me - it made it easier to slip right back into the swing of things without missing a beat. Concealing my fear was the safest thing to do. Perhaps I wasn't an A-student, but dammit, I gave a solid performance! (I would spend time later deciding where to display my award.) There were times I was such a good pretender that it made me wonder how much I hid from my very own self.

Take, for instance, the loss of memory after the seizures. I imagined that it was purely due to my extreme cleverness that I managed to erase some of the horrors of my childhood. I didn't feel a seizure coming on, so there was no fear involved. After the seizure, I couldn't remember anything, so no fear on that end either. What an escape artist I was!

At this point Luke was getting bigger and was always a joy to me. We were attached at the hip but Catherine felt quite differently. Her room was always very tidy and off limits. She had a record player and was allowed to play her records pretty loud, which really attracted Luke. He drove Catherine nuts as he sat outside her room and tried to peek under door. It's no wonder they never grew close. I think Catherine felt he was a huge imposition and stole her role as the baby of the family. After all, his birth had a big impact on her life. I truly understood those feelings because I felt the same way when Mama announced her pregnancy. But in my case, as soon as that precious little guy was born, my attitude took a dramatic turn for the better.

When summer came to a close, Ricky got back on the bus. He got to leave our confusion behind. Ultimately, there was no real pleasure in that for Ricky. He was leaving behind people that he loved and felt an obligation toward. Sure, he lived in a clean, safe environment in which he would not be embarrassed to bring new friends. He would have good food at every meal and he'd always have plenty of nice clothes to wear. But none of that could replace us. And Ricky felt none too good about leaving us there in the path of Daddy's rage.

On that awful day several years earlier, as we helped Ricky "run away" from home, he vowed to come back and get us. Although I always believed he meant that with all of his heart, I could tell that the vow was fading. Not because he loved us any less, but because he was becoming entrenched in his new life with these new people who now referred to themselves as "Mother" and "Father".

CHAPTER SEVEN

Always Wear Clean Underwear

South Lafourche High School was perched along the roadside across from Bayou Lafourche. It was modern for its time and boasted air-conditioned classrooms.

It was during my tenth-grade year that girls were finally allowed to wear pants to school. Jeans flattered my figure but I wasn't able to appreciate it one bit. I became aware of my curvy figure at a very early age but only thought it made me look fat; at least that was what Daddy told me. Catherine was always so skinny and I looked like a piglet next to her. I was called "pleasingly plump", but I was convinced that was only a cutesy way of saying I was too heavy.

I especially hated the way I looked in my P.E. shorts outfit, which was a one-piece ordeal that snapped down the front. Maybe the fact that I hated P.E. had something to do with it. I could not understand why high school girls needed to learn to play football. My classmate, Yolanda, was at least six feet tall and had to weigh two hundred and fifty pounds. Why on earth did the teacher tell me to run straight at her with my arms crossing my chest? Me and my one hundred and ten pounds thought much better of that crazy idea and ran as far away from Yolanda as I could – and as fast!

And why in the world did I need to master balancing on my head? Why would it matter if I could conquer a balance beam by jumping and changing the position of my feet in mid-air? I never felt very pretty, but I valued what I owned as a female and I was not about to risk the consequences of my feet missing the five-inch piece of wood upon landing.

Most importantly, I found no redeeming value in sweating. The only connection I ever made between P.E. and my real life was that similar to running in circles during track, my life, too, was a revolving door going nowhere. Why did I even bother getting an education?

Every once in a while, I would permit myself to daydream, imagining that perhaps one day I could create something different and beautiful in my life. Take for instance those random occasions when Daddy was just tipsy enough to talk about building a small place that would serve as a beauty shop, where I could run my own business. (As a child I just loved styling hair, first on my Barbie doll, then on any girl in the neighborhood who would sit still long enough.) Daddy never seemed to take an active interest in me, so I couldn't figure out why he'd noticed that I had a flair for such things. Was it possible that through the fog of his drunken and miserable life he had glimpses of actual reality - of me? I had to be very careful about how much I allowed myself to believe him. He often broke his promises, actually more than he ever kept. Even at an early age I was aware of how badly I wanted to believe him, but I was also able to see the disappointed results over and over again. Sometimes I traded truth for delusion, letting myself believe that Daddy was really going to take me shopping or buy me that sewing machine. It was a game and Daddy played, too. We'd get all the way up to the finish line, and BAM! He'd be a no-show, or tell me I had too many chores to do to be wasting time on silly stuff.

∞ ∞ ∞

Mid-sophomore year, Joseph O'Flaherty, a big Texas boy on the South Lafourche Tarpon junior varsity football team, began subtly flirting with me. I was amazed; I was certainly not one of the popular kids and as far as I could tell, I wasn't even remotely attractive. Why would he pay even the slightest attention to me? There were so many pretty girls in our class – why me?

He was tall and built like a lumberjack, with a barrel chest and broad shoulders. He had red hair, freckles, wore glasses and had the same gap in his front teeth as me. Joseph was well liked and seemed to have a lot of friends. Of course, all the football players had admirers.

The lunch bell rang and I eventually made my way to the cafeteria to find Linda. We had a routine: we would meet near the cafeteria door, make our way through the lunch line, and then find a spot where we could sit together. That day, however, just as we neared the front of the line, Joseph approached us and initiated friendly chatter. It really threw me off balance since I was used to being ignored by boys. Not only was Joseph a boy, he was a football player! Dammit! I had no idea how to respond, so when I eventually opened my mouth to speak, not one thing came out. Nothing.

Linda was generally much quieter and shyer than me but I really needed her to say something. HELP! She immediately read the panic in my eyes and forced a timid 'Hello'. I assumed that Joseph was there to see her. No matter, this was an exciting event, regardless of which one of us he was aiming for. Up until that point neither one of us had any experience with boys to speak of; this was front-page news by our standards.

After what seemed like hours, I finally swallowed enough spit to wet my throat and speak. First I tried smiling, but I'm fairly sure it looked more like straining on the pot. Luckily, Joseph was a good-natured, kind-hearted guy who didn't seem bothered by my lack of conversation skills. He followed us through the food line, piling more on his plate than I'd ever seen one person eat. I managed to comment on his healthy appetite. He laughed freely, saying that strenuous football practice was the cause.

Before the bell rang for class, (dreaded P.E. class) Joseph asked me if I wanted to go to the next pep rally with him. The blood rushed to my head so fast it must have impeded my hearing. I thought he said, "Do ya want to help me with Sally?" My palms were sweaty and I was so nervous that before I had time to think better of it, I blurted out, "Help Sally? Who the hell is Sally?" The complete and utter surprise in his facial expression told me that maybe there was a massive misunderstanding. Lord have mercy! What to do next? God, I wished the floor would open up and let me fall to a swift death. How stupid could I be?! I was such an ass! There was no way in hell I could get out of what I'd said.

Suddenly, he began to laugh, softly at first, then boisterously. "Ya crack me up, Connie! I like that in a girl, yeah, I sure do." Jesus, he thought I said it on purpose! Maybe there was a God and He'd just performed a pure-dee miracle right on the spot, yes indeed! I was so grateful that Joseph didn't see what a moron I was – at least not then and there - that I said an extra Hail Mary an additional 100 Jesus, Mary, Josephs in my prayers that night.

Just as I whispered the last string of thanks before sleep, a raspy demeaning voice in my head – or was it the house – intruded. "You're not good enough for Joseph, or any boy. He will just play with you and then dump you. Do you really

73

believe he could possibly see anything in you? You have nothing to offer. You're fat and ugly and stupid. Who do you think you are? He'll see right through you."

Tightness seized my entire body and I felt paralyzed. The house keenly sensed my attempts at breaking away from its filthy, raw clutch. When I was frightened, humiliated or depressed it gave me more room to move about, even though, ironically, I had no desire to do so. But the minute I felt the slightest bit of hope, it tightened its grip. As I grabbed my chest for relief, I thought better of allowing myself to entertain even the tiniest pleasurable thoughts of Joseph. After all, what possible future could lie ahead for a popular boy and a loser like me? Stay safe. Yep. Only heartache and pain awaited me. What right did I have to venture outside the walls of my prison? The overgrown elephant leaves outside my bedroom window reminded me that there was no escape. And, if I momentarily forgot, Daddy would quickly jog my memory.

He always said I'd never amount to anything and at times like those, I had to admit he was probably right. I didn't know much about anything except that I felt trapped in a life with people who didn't really know or care about me. Oddly, there was slight comfort in the belief that I would not live to see my twentieth birthday. I'd gotten used to believing that I'd have a short life, but I still hoped that I would go to Heaven and not get stuck in Purgatory. I wasn't very sure at all about my destination and God hadn't really let me in on the plan.

Back in school, I tried to redirect my thoughts; home economics class with Miss Chartrain offered a comic relief perfect for forgetting the house. (I would also put off thinking about Joseph if at all possible.) She was painfully frumpy and carried the stigma of 'old maid'. Linda, Debbie Estee, Judy Terrebonne and I sat at the same table. We giggled our way through most of the class each day. Miss Chartrain begged to have fun poked at her. Wearing what appeared to be old leather corrective shoes with rounded toes dotted with small air holes and thick nylon stockings, she looked like the woman who time forgot. If that wasn't bad enough, she stood with her feet turned inward. She held her arms at waist height as she addressed the class, and always either cupped her hands or formed a triangle with her fingertips. Her clothes were miserably outdated, though in surprisingly good condition. Miss Chartrain was always very neat and scrubbed, with only a trace of makeup. Cosmetics, she preached, were to enhance our natural beauty, not to overwhelm it.

Joseph found me at my locker after school on Thursday. He wanted to confirm our 'date' for the next night's school event. By that time, I had decided to give it a shot. I wouldn't have to tell Mama I was meeting a boy; I would simply say I was going with Linda. I agreed to meet him at school at six-thirty, half-an-hour before the rally began. We'd use the time to visit with friends - mostly his. My friends didn't participate in sports.

After meeting up with some of his friends, Joseph-the-football-hero and I headed over to the rally. We chose to sit in the center about midway up. He wore jeans and a red-plaid, long-sleeve shirt. He was a big guy and I felt small in more ways than one sitting next to him. I assumed he came from a normal home, unlike mine. I wanted to be chatty and witty but all I could muster up was something silly like, "So ya like football, huh?" His confused expression quickly changed to a big smile as he let out a laugh from the depths of his barrel chest. "Ya kill me, Connie! I swear, ya hilarious!" I had no idea what he was talking about.

The crowd roared and stood enthusiastically as the cheerleaders did their thing. The kids sitting near us took one step up onto the seat in front of them, giving them a slightly better view. In an effort to fit in, I did the same. I even let myself go and began clapping along with the cheer. The pep squad wound down and the crowd began to sit. Forgetting that I was still standing one level higher, I bent my legs at the knees and let my body fall to a seated position. Instead of landing where I was sitting before the cheer, I ended up falling down to the lower level with everyone's feet. Jesus H. Christ! My skirt was up above my waist and my legs were sprawled all over Kingdom Come. Dear Lord, was I wearing clean underwear?

Nobody noticed at first – except Joseph, that is. Could I have looked more ridiculous or been more humiliated at that moment – a moment that meant so much to me?! Joseph leaned over from his seated position, grabbed me under the arms, and in one quick motion lifted me up to my seat. I'm sure my face was the deepest shade of red humanly possible and all I could do was gawk at him. I mean, what could I even begin to say to explain away my obvious stupidity? I tried so incredibly hard to fight back the tears but couldn't. I jumped up and ran to the aisle, then down to floor level and out of the gym. I wanted to die! How could I have let myself go there with him? Mama and Daddy never let me go anywhere – why in Heaven did they let me go that night? I wasn't ready for a social life or a boyfriend and in a blaze that set my mind on fire I had to admit that I might never be.

"WAIT UP, Connie!" Hearing him call my name just made me run faster, although I didn't know exactly where I was going. I'd gotten a ride with Linda and her mom was supposed to pick us up after the pep rally at nine-thirty. I made it to a small tree out in the front school yard where Linda and I sometimes ate lunch. My sides were aching and I was out of breath. God, I hoped Miss Guilliot was nowhere around. If she'd seen how fast I could run, she'd surely have much higher expectations in P.E. class.

When Joseph drew near he reached for my shoulder.

"What's wrong?" Surely my ears deceived me! Did he not just witness me show my ass to everybody in the gym? Did he fail to notice my granny drawers as I flashed all of Section C? What in the hell was wrong with this boy – was he pure-dee stupid? Maybe that was the attraction: we were both dim-witted.

"LEAVE ME ALONE!" I screamed so hard I was afraid I'd damaged my throat. The startled look on Joseph's face told me I probably had gone too far. (Daddy had that same look when Mama started muttering incomprehensibly. There was always that fleeting moment when I could tell Daddy was trying to figure out how far he'd have to go to shut her up. I could sense it in the way he tilted his head and I could see it in his eyes. Sometimes I knew what Daddy would do before he actually did it. More than some of the time, actually. If I paid attention to him, if I got real quiet and closed my eyes, I could feel what he was feeling. His rage was the most frightening and his deep lack of worthiness was the saddest.)

Finally, Joseph brought me back to Earth by speaking softly and rubbing my right arm. I was such an idiot! As I furiously tried to concoct a way to repair the damage, he whispered in my ear, "Connie, it's alright. Ya safe with me. Forget about it; who cares what they think, anyway? Y'all be fine."

I looked up and tried to focus on his face, but the tears were gushing out with such force it was all but impossible to see a thing. Suddenly, I felt a tender touch on my lips. Was he kissing me? Oh damn, what in the hell? He sensed that I was scared. Without hesitation, he wrapped those big old Texan arms around me and engulfed me in a bear hug that I've never forgotten. How could a night so humiliating end up so sweet? I was confused, thoroughly and dreadfully confused.

Two weeks later, Joseph called me at home. He asked me out on a real date, where he would actually come to my house and meet the folks. HELL NO! No way was I going to let him see where I lived, and worse, meet Mama and Daddy.

But ultimately I conceded, because I was so desperate to feel normal and there seemed no way around having Joseph come to my house. This was my first real date and hopefully Mama and Daddy would at least pretend to be interested in my life, even if it was only for the briefest moment.

Catherine tapped on my door, "Connie, ya date is here! Come out!" As I dashed around furiously searching for my shoes, which were no doubt hidden in the darkest corner of my chaotic closet, I panicked. I had to get to Joseph before Daddy! As I threw open my bedroom door and ran through the kitchen, I could already hear Daddy turning the knob on the front door. Dammit to hell! That wasn't good at all. I knew I could rely on Daddy to say something crude and humiliating. The good news was that he wore an old terry bathrobe which he rarely bothered to wear. The bad news, it was not closed at the front, revealing a t-shirt, which barely covered his swollen beer belly and striped boxer shorts. Damn, damn, damn! Why did he have to do this to me on this very special night? This was my first real date, a pivotal point in a young woman's life - where the hell was Mama and why didn't she stop him from going to the door? She was so weak. So damn weak.

"I come to pick up Connie, Mr. Schroder. My name is Joseph O'Flaherty. Nice to meet ya, sir." As I watched Joseph step into the living room, my heart dropped to my feet. "Oh yeah. Come on in, Joey. Where y'all goin? Now, ya have her home by 11:00, ya hear. Don't ya be late, either, Joey!" Why was Daddy calling him Joey?!

My God, Joseph's big smile was starting to droop already. He was trying so hard, but he never had a chance with Daddy. I quickly brushed by Daddy and greeted Joseph with a shaky smile. "Hey – ya ready to go?" The return smile gave me hope that maybe he wasn't too put off by my freaky family and the pathetic surroundings of my so-called home. Just as we reached the edge of the yard, Daddy yelled, "Now don't go off an' get pregnant, ya hear!" My knees got weak and started to buckle. Luckily I was close enough to the fence to steady myself. I pretended I hadn't heard Daddy's vulgar remark and prayed to God that Joseph was out of earshot. I promised God that if he kept Joseph from hearing Daddy's horrendous remark, I would do anything he asked of me.

As the evening passed, Joseph didn't say a word about my family. I was so relieved and thankful, but a little worried about what God would ask me to do in return. Well, I guess He'd let me know sooner or later. No sense in worrying about it ahead of time.

We ate at the Rex, a popular drive-in burger joint known for a waitress named Bubba, who'd been there for at least thirty years. She was old and still energetic and greeted us with a warm hello while asking us what we wanted. She never wrote anything down, repeating the order out loud only once. Amazingly, Bubba rarely screwed up an order, but if she did, she always tried to blame it on the customer. She wore way too much make-up and didn't apply it very well, but that was Bubba and we all loved her.

As we pulled up in front of my house, I had a nervous feeling in my stomach. I wondered if Joseph was going to kiss me or not – and if he did, I prayed I would know how to kiss him back. I was terribly inexperienced and I was sure he could tell. Though he never much bragged about it, I just assumed he was way more experienced than me.

The kiss was sweet, even though I wasn't sure when I was supposed to put my tongue in his mouth. No matter, somehow we got through it okay. I insisted that he not walk me to the door. Lord knows Daddy would probably be sprawled out half naked on the sofa, and I just couldn't bear to go through another encounter like the one earlier that night.

Three weeks to the day after that date, Joseph broke up with me just before fifth period. I was devastated. We'd gone to two more pep rallies in the meantime and there was absolutely no indication of a pending break-up. Maybe his cool friends made fun of him for dating a weirdo like me. I got off the school bus after school and ran straight to my bedroom where I threw myself cross-wise on the bed and tried to hypnotize myself to sleep.

In a daze, I felt like a little lost child, much younger than my actual years. I saw myself: a tiny white body curled up in the fetal position, floating through the Universe, searching for something to cling to. Once again, I had to face the cold lonely fact that I could never count on anything or anybody but myself. Very few people care enough to stick to their word. Everybody wants to stay safe. Hell, I wanted to stay safe.

At six o'clock the next morning my alarm clock startled me into the reality of my life. The metal bed frame was cold and sharp as it rubbed the back of my knees. My throat was aching as though somebody had tried to strangle me, my mouth was so dry I could barely swallow and my voice was strained. Had I been screaming in my sleep again?

Mama knocked on the door and came in with a scowl on her face. Her mouth looked more crooked than usual and I could feel her dark mood. "It's 'bout damn time ya got up, don't ya think?!" Why had she angrily stormed into my room as though I'd overslept or something? I usually didn't even go into the kitchen until closer to seven o'clock. Suddenly, like a ferocious hurricane over the Gulf of Mexico, I got a stabbing thought about Mama. She always seemed to be mad at me after a night where I had one of my awful nightmares. With no clear details, I tried to tell her about them, but Mama would have nothing to do with it. She'd get very impatient and yell at me. I was certain that there a connection between my nighttime experiences and Mama's mood.

∞ ∞ ∞

Summer break eventually caught up to us and Linda and I had big plans to go to Grand Isle. Debbie Estee's parents owned a camp on the island and were very generous about allowing friends to visit. If I could convince Daddy to let me go, I'd be able to act and feel somewhat normal for the entire weekend. Permission on that scale usually involved a ton of extra chores. So many in fact, that Mama would literally have nothing to do while I was gone.

Chapter Eight

Clandestiny

After lingering too long in the cafeteria, I ran straight to fifth period English class without stopping at my locker. Mrs. Chanielle did not permit tardiness – there was no excuse short of death, she said.

It was during my junior year at South Lafourche High School that I met Marty Guilbeau. He sat across from me in class, to my right and one seat back. I was very aware of his tall and slender frame, dark, wavy shoulder-length hair and beautiful blue-green eyes. He was very bright in English. Mrs. Chanielle really liked him because he always knew the answers and actually did his homework in spite of the fact that he was on the Tarpon football team. (Marty didn't play as much as he wanted to and it really didn't have to do with being inadequate. In the third game of the season he got slammed in the back by a two-hundred- and forty-pound boy. His one-hundred and sixty-five pounds were not enough to protect his kidneys and the impact caused internal bruising. The doctor recommended he sit out the rest of the season. He was very upset about what he called bad luck, but he continued to show up at all of the games in full uniform.)

Just before Mrs. Chanielle asked us to open our literature books, I raised my hand demurely. "Mizuz Chanielle, can I go to my locker an' get my book?" Mrs. Chanielle did not want me to leave the classroom while she was demonstrating some nonsense on the blackboard. Just as she was saying no to me, Marty raised his hand. "Ma'am, I can go get Connie's book for her."

I was shocked! We'd never spoken a word to one another and I didn't think he even knew I was alive. As he walked past my desk, he looked down and gave me a warm, yet nervous smile. My heart began pounding in my chest. *Why* would Marty do this for me? And, how did he know which locker was mine?

Within minutes, he returned to class with my literature book and red notebook. He laid them down on my desk with a soft thud. I looked up quickly, intending to smile as a way of thanking him, but my lower lip began to twitch uncontrollably.

Mrs. Chanielle dismissed us at the end of class in a melodic, high-pitched voice. "Go an' have a wonderful day, pupils!" In the hall just outside the classroom, Marty lightly grabbed my arm. "Hey, Connie." I was so incredibly nervous that I could feel my own heart pleading to be free of my chest. "Would ya like to come to the next football game with me? I'll be sittin' on the sidelines, but we can go to the Safari after the game." Whoa – I never in a million years expected Marty to ask me out. Actually, I never expected any boy to ask me out ever again. I was positive that news of the break-up with Joseph O'Flaherty had spread like wildfire. I had to face the fact that I was a nobody and everybody knew it. "Sure," I said, very nonchalant, trying to act like this sort of thing happened to me on a regular basis.

Friday rolled around and Marty found me in D Hall between sixth and seventh periods. He was out of breath from trying to catch up to me. "Connie – hey, wait up!" My heart began a familiar pounding, but this time it made me nauseous. I had to swallow hard to push the vomit back. God, why did I have to get so damn nervous whenever a boy talked to me? Would it always be like this? In that moment it was like my life flashed before me. I suddenly understood it was easier just to avoid situations like this altogether. I had no real training in conversing with the opposites (the opposite sex). Mama never brought up such topics as the birds and the bees and I wasn't about to ask.

∞ ∞ ∞

(The first time anyone spoke of female development was in the fourth grade when all the girls were called into the auditorium to see a film. Boys were strictly prohibited, which of course meant that several were caught peeking through the blinds at the rear of the large room. It all seemed so clandestine. Even though I had no idea what we were getting ready to witness, I somehow knew that I would be changed forever. It was the hush-hush way in which we were gathered. We were treated special in a way – maybe a little more gently than usual. After we were all seated, the principal - a short bald man in his fifties - made an announcement from the stage, speaking very slowly and deliberately into the microphone. "Attention girls. Today we are going to watch a film 'bout men-stru-a-tion. Ya all about the age when ya bodies begin to change an' we want ya to be ready for that. We have axed the boys to stay outside while we watch this film. This is very private. Ya will get booklets after the film is over."

For forty minutes we sat through all-too graphic descriptions of changing female bodies. It was hugely embarrassing, even with an all-girl audience. My breasts were not even in the developing stages, much less was I near starting my period.

Apparently, however, some girls started their period as young as ten years old. Jesus! I never wanted to start my period. I didn't want to be a woman. I didn't want to have do what it took to get pregnant and have babies. Mostly, I didn't want Daddy knowing anything about my body. Besides, the idea of strapping on a Kotex pad and trying to walk like you didn't have a diaper on made me cringe. Jesus H. Christ!)

My almost non-existent preparation, therefore, did absolutely nothing to calm my nerves as I stared up at Marty. *God, if only ya let me swallow hard enough to keep from puking all over his shoes, I'll do anything ya axe.* I made a lot of deals with God. I tried real hard to keep my end of the bargain, but I hardly ever felt God reciprocated. It took severe concentration to avoid upchucking right on the spot, but this time God must have heard my prayer.

"Can ya be at the stadium at six o'clock tomorrow night? We can meet at the concession stand." "Sure," was all I managed to squeak out, my voice cracking. I was pathetic and for the life of me I could not see why this boy would possibly want to spend time together. He was good-looking; a little shy maybe, but he seemed to have lots of friends

Once school let out I rushed home so I could practice how I'd ask Mama if it was okay to go out on a date. I knew she'd tell me to ask Daddy – she always did – but after the ordeal with Joseph I was really worried about a repeat performance. Showing Daddy that I wanted to go out with a boy was like leading a vulture to a carcass. Getting so worked up going over my request in my head, I became drowsy. Laying back on my bed, I hung my feet over the side; I could have easily kicked off my weather-beaten oxfords but there was something special about being fully clothed while being on my bed. It was delicious in a rebellious sort of way. As I was drifting into the Netherland, I got a vision of Daddy and me alone in a bed.

Nobody was home but us and I didn't like the way Daddy was touching me. I could smell beer on his breath and he felt very heavy.

"Mama, hey," I smiled at her as I brushed away the remnants of my nap. There were times when I looked into her pale blue eyes and swore that I saw depth and clarity, maybe even life brewing. This was probably as good a time as any to ask about my date with Marty.

"Now ya know, Connie, ya have to axe ya Daddy." They liked giving me the run-around for some reason. I thought it was cruel, but maybe neither Mama nor Daddy wanted to take responsibility for something as big as letting their little girl spend time alone with an opposite. Mama was paranoid and Daddy was downright nasty about the whole idea. The older I got, the more obsessed I became about my sense that I would not live past the age of twenty. It would certainly be an end to the miserable humiliation I repeatedly endured.

I arrived at South Lafourche High School stadium at five-forty-five, thanks to Linda and her mama. Good old Mrs. Brabham. She really did try to give her kids the benefit of being a part of society, unlike my anti-social parents.

Linda and I hopped out of the back seat of the Chevy. Mrs. Brabham would likely get a new car from City Chevrolet soon. They didn't seem to keep a car very long before trading it in, unlike Daddy, who kept a vehicle until the undercarriage completely rusted out. (When I sat on the engine cover of that old Econoline van, I could actually see the street below through holes on the passenger-side floorboard.)

Parents unloaded kids at the covered walkway that led into the interior of the school grounds. Walking through the main hall, exiting the school at the rear double-doors leading to the football field, the excitement of the bright field lights raced through my body. There was something very magical about artificial lighting at night - I'd felt that ever since I was a little girl.

Just as we approached the concession stand, I heard my name. "Connie – hey, girl! I been waitin' for ya." Marty looked very handsome and rugged in his football uniform. The shoulder pads made his upper body appear twice his size but also made his head look small. His dark, wavy hair was a bit messed up, giving him an appealingly rugged look. I was pretty sure he wanted me to get an up-close look.

"Hey, Marty!" I sang back. I was trying to capture the moment by taking a mental snapshot. Nobody, including me, would ever believe that I actually had a second chance for a real date with another football player. "Where should we sit?"

Marty was very thoughtful at suggesting the exact row and level we should sit in order to get the best view of the field. Without hesitation, Linda and I followed him. When we arrived at Level B, Marty placed his hand on my arm, saying, "I'll meet ya at the end of the field after the game. Wait for me if I'm not there right away. Sometimes the coach wants to talk to us first before he lets us go." I nodded, acknowledging that I understood, and then smiled broadly. I was finally starting to loosen up a little. I really liked this boy.

After the game I went to the end of the field. Begging Linda to come with me, she would only go as far as the five-yard line. Walking away, she wished me luck, surely assuming that I would need it.

I walked over to the goal post and leaned casually on the red metal pipe, trying my best to look like I belonged in that sort of environment. Despite my best efforts, I'm pretty sure I still looked ridiculously out of place.

Suddenly, like a flash out of nowhere, all the football players came running from the visitor's side of the field, scaring the holy crap out of me. The testosterone was so thick you could cut it with a knife. Marty quickly approached me in a jog. "Hey, Connie. What'd ya think of the game?" Scrambling to find just the right response, all I could say was, "Well, I think ya did real good for the 'lil time ya were in there." He seemed pleased; apparently that was good enough for him. "Wanna go to the Safari for a while?"

Mama told me to come home right after the game, but she didn't really know what time it would be over. She knew I wasn't old enough to get in to the local bars, but she didn't have a clue about how easy it was to get into the Safari.

Once inside, I couldn't help obsess about how strenuous it was trying to be cool. I was basically a recluse by virtue of living with an alcoholic and a schizophrenic. I panicked if someone even knocked at the door, and I'd never answer the phone if I didn't think it was Linda calling.

(When I was young, Daddy forbade me to answer the phone unless he coached me first. Most often it was bill collectors or the landlord. "Tell 'em I ain't home – I'm at work." Desperately wanting to please Daddy, I'd lie each time. He simply didn't permit outsiders into our home. I suspected he didn't want anybody knowing the truth about his awful problem. I didn't want anybody to know, either.)

Live music blasted from the small hut-like stage at the far end of the bar. It was unbearably loud and I really couldn't hear a thing Marty was saying so I nodded and smiled a lot.

Taking a large sip of the Bloody Mary he handed me, I choked and felt a hot vapor come out of my tear ducts as my nose started to run. Marty began slapping me on the back, trying to help, which only embarrassed me more.

Soon, *Stairway to Heaven*, my favorite Led Zeppelin song, began to play and some of the kids headed for the dance floor. I nervously looked up at Marty and prayed he wouldn't ask me to dance. Daddy said that I had two left feet. I'd never danced before - not ever - and I wasn't about to launch my maiden voyage here in front of half of the students from my school. Lucky for me, he didn't ask.

At ten forty-five, I told Marty I needed to head home. Mama said to be home no later than eleven-thirty, thinking surely the game would be over by then. Taking a last swig of his beer, Marty set the long neck on the wooden bar and then grabbed my hand. I liked the feeling of his large hand wrapped around mine. It made me feel safe, and for the first time, like I fit in. Nobody looked at us strangely; we were immediately accepted as a couple. He opened the passenger door to his mama's Monte Carlo and I slid in. Once behind the wheel, Marty signaled me to sit closer. He gave me a wink and a nervous grin.

We crossed over the bayou to the other side, but instead of turning right, he turned left. "Where ya goin', Marty?" "I wanna show ya something" he said sheepishly. "Ya haven't seen my Daddy's sugarcane fields."

It was pitch black out, so I knew it wasn't really a tour he was after. My heart began beating too fast as I anticipated the make-out session just moments away. Up the road a little, Marty turned right into a narrow dirt road that gave access to at least forty acres of sugarcane. About a quarter of a mile in, he stopped the car and turned off the engine. He put the car in park and then turned to me, placing his right arm on the back of my neck. "I had a real good time, tonight, Connie. Did ya?" "Sure, it was fun." My mouth was so dry that my upper lip refused to glide over my teeth as I attempted a smile. I was in the midst of fretting about it when Marty leaned close and lightly kissed me on the lips. I was scared and relieved all at the same time. At least now he couldn't see the ridiculous clown look on my face. His mouth was warm and inviting.

"Stop," I said hoarsely after several minutes. He looked confused. "Okay. What's wrong?" I sat up straighter and felt light-headed. I was suddenly exhausted and drained and felt weird, like maybe I was going to pass out. "I don't feel good, Marty. I need to go home."

Marty looked very worried, which scared me. I tried to picture what he saw when he looked at me, but I was so weak all I could do was put my head back on the seat.

That was the last thing I remember, until Daddy came to the front door. Marty held onto me under my arms and I felt weak at the knees. "Mister Schroder, Connie had a fit." Daddy was standing there in his drawers and a white t-shirt. "Flo, come here quick. Connie had another seizure. Young man, you can go home now."

I was dazed and didn't really understand what was happening; so tired I could barely stand up. Mama somehow got me into my pajamas and helped me into bed. I caught a glimpse of Catherine standing in the doorway between our bedrooms. God she was tiny, and that haunted look on her face was all too familiar. Mama gently kissed me on the forehead. My thoughts were fleeting by now, but I vaguely remember making note of the oddity of Mama's tenderness toward me. She generally saved that for Luke and Catherine. With that final thought dangling on the tip of my brain, I fell into a deep, shadowy sleep.

Three days later, I awoke to Mama spoon-feeding me chicken noodle soup. "Hey, dawlin'. Feelin' better?" Though she looked familiar, I had to strain to recognize her. Did she know how much I hurt all over? Was I bleeding? Could she sense the swirling feeling in my confused mind? If she knew me at all, she'd smell my fear. If she cared at all, she'd calm my frantic nerves. Instead, all she did was lift spoonful after spoonful of hot soup to my dry lips. "Eat now, Connie. Ya havta eat."

Weakly, I pushed her hand away. "Enough. What happened to me?" Somberly, she said, "Ya had another seizure. Marty brought ya home from the football game an' ya were outta it."

"Marty? Who's Marty?" Mama looked more concerned. "Come on now, Connie, ya remember Marty. Ya went to see him play in the football game on Friday night. Ya remember now, don't ya?" I struggled, diving deeper into the caverns of my mind. I swear I could smell the wires burning as I pushed incredibly hard for an image. Suddenly, I caught a very pale sight of him. "Is he tall with dark, curly hair?" "Yeah! That's him!" Mama said, obviously relieved. I got the feeling she knew something that she wasn't sharing.

"What day is this?" I asked, afraid to know how many days had passed in oblivion. "Monday. Ya been sleepin' the whole time. I even had to wake ya up to give ya some water."

She called the doctor. Oh, *hell* no. I didn't like him one teeny-tiny bit. In fact, he gave me the creeps. Mama took me to him once when I had tonsillitis. He made me get undressed from the waist up and gave me a small rag to cover my chest, then told me to lie down on the exam table. When he came back into the room, the first thing he did after feeling the glands under my neck was to quickly remove my modest cover. He began groping and prodding my chest area. Mama was asked to wait in the waiting room; I didn't want to be alone with him. I jumped up to a seated position and asked him what my chest had to do with my sore throat. He gave me some lame excuse and I yelled out that I wanted Mama in the room. That's when he got all cranky and told me to calm down, then begrudgingly went to the door to beckon Mama. On the ride home I told Mama what he'd done, but she just hushed me, saying I was making too big of a deal of it.

On Wednesday, Mama said she'd think about when I could go back to school. She could never make a decision on her own, and if she attempted it, it would take her forever. Mostly she'd turn to Daddy, who would say he didn't care, but then almost always veto her decisions.

CHAPTER NINE

Butcher Knives & Sauerkraut

Marty and I dated all through my junior year. Things were progressing between us and I was sure I was in love. It seemed to us we were at an age to handle all that went along with being a couple, though our parents thought otherwise.

Marty's parents, Mr. and Mrs. Guilbeau, were nice enough - especially his dad. He was a sugarcane farmer and had raised cattle most of his adult life. That man was a hard worker and seemed to love every acre of his flourishing outdoor heaven. Marty's parents welcomed me into their home and always seemed pleased to feed me and include me in family holidays and special occasions. There was a sense of ordinariness at Marty's house that was absent at mine.

Marty's sister, Julia, always said nice things to me and made me feel accepted. She said I was built like a "brick shit house". I smiled and laughed along with her, but I had no earthly idea what that meant. I could only assume that it was good, since she didn't seem to have a mean bone in her body. In fact, she was very sensitive. She struggled with weight and sometimes her family picked at her about what or how much she ate. Even though she shrugged it off, I could tell it hurt her feelings.

Paul was the youngest and Lessie was the oldest. Marty, Paul and Lessie could be very passionate in a debate. Because Julia was much more soft-natured, it was hard on her when her family all talked at the same time.

Lovable and kind, Mr. Guilbeau didn't mean to speak so loudly, but he was losing his ability to hear, which caused him to do just that. This really bugged his wife who, ironically, yelled at him to lower his voice. Mrs. Guilbeau seemed to be happiest when she was yelling and happier yet when she had a point to argue or defend. She appeared to enjoy feeling misunderstood, even though I thought everyone understood her quite well.

When I was around these people I felt good but it also magnified what my family lacked. Mama and Daddy were so numb half the time. The other half of the time, Daddy was cruel and Mama was crying or sleeping. To call what I had in my own home a life was an overstatement. Most days I figured the best that I could hope for was to marry into this family and hope that their love and genuine affection would rub off on me.

One weekend, after I'd done all the chores, I was allowed to go over to Marty's house for lunch. Mrs. Guilbeau was a fantastic cook and I loved everything she whipped up. Her gumbo, fried catfish and dirty rice were among my favorites, although there was surely something magical about her potato salad in the way it was served warm and creamy.

Marty borrowed his Mama's car and picked me up about eleven-thirty. I waited on the porch for him; even though it was already ninety-six degrees outside, it was hotter inside. The window fan made more noise than cool the air, but Daddy hadn't noticed because he worked in an air-conditioned shop.

I was relieved when I saw Marty in Mrs. Guilbeau's car drawing near. I looked forward to a twenty-minute ride in air-conditioning.

Marty stopped the car right in front of our house. It didn't matter how long we'd been together; I was still embarrassed for him to see our crappy surroundings. I felt like our rundown house was a reflection of me, even though I'd done all in my power to make it better. There just wasn't much I could do to improve that falling-down shanty, and Daddy surely didn't give a damn. He just slept there. Because he always met his drinking buddies at the bar, they'd never seen where we lived.

I ran down the steps, yelling to Mama that I was leaving. While I hoped she heard me, I wouldn't linger to find out. I hopped into the car and we drove off. "Hey, Connie!" Marty leaned over and gave me a quick kiss on the lips. "Hey, beb," I said, happy to be rescued from the Schroder slums for a while.

The smell of rich brown gravy greeted us as soon as Marty parked the car under the carport. I loved Mrs. Guilbeau's gravy. She cooked with all sorts of seasonings that Mama had probably never heard of. Anything she conjured up was absolutely delicious - well, except for one particular stew. When it was my turn to serve myself from the large bowl I picked up the ladle and dipped it into the center of the steaming-hot brown liquid, noticing a tapping noise. I knew the ladle hadn't reached the bottom of the bowl because it was Mrs. Guilbeau's largest serving dish and very deep. I stirred the gravy and heard the noise again. By this time the family had gotten awful quiet. I looked up to see Julia trying to hold back a laugh.

"What's this?" I asked. Their silence was laced with a few giggles. I stood up, got a better grip on the large spoon, and dived deeper into the bowl. As though I were crabbing, I made a wide scooping motion and lifted it to see what I'd caught. Sure enough, I snagged a skull of some sort. "AHHHEEEE! What the hell?!" I gasped and quickly let go of the ladle. In horrific laughter, the entire family was stomping their feet and banging the table with open palms. I'd never seen such a thing! Daddy was not a hunter and the sight of animal bones of any kind, short of pork chop, was completely foreign to me. After what seemed liked hours of laughing and making silly comments, the family settled down.

"Connie, cher', that's the skull from the rabbit Mr. Guilbeau killed yesterday". As Mrs. Guilbeau was clueing me in, Mr. Guilbeau reached into the bowl and lifted up the skull. "Look, beb, ya scrape out da meat from the head – it's good, yeah, cher'! Try some." I could feel the blood drain from my face. No way in hell was I going to eat skull meat. I wasn't hungry enough to eat rabbit brains. I politely thanked him and was more than content to have only rice and gravy that day.

After her nap, Mrs. Guilbeau backed out of the carport on her way to Mama Florie's house. "I'll be back in just a 'lil bit. I'm just bringin' some food to my mom." Within a few short moments, the phone rang. Julia answered it quickly, so as not to allow the ring to wake her dad. "Connie, it's ya Mama," she said quietly. I couldn't imagine why she was calling. She'd told me to be home by six o'clock to cook dinner but it was only three-thirty.

"Connie. It's Mama. Ya Daddy just said get home. He wants ya to come home right now, ya hear." "But, Mama," I began, "Mrs. Guilbeau just left to go see Mama Florie an' might not be back right away. There's no way for me to get home." I heard Mama's flat voice relaying the message to Daddy, and then I could hear Daddy screaming at her. "Ya tell her to get her ass home in twenty minutes or her clothes will be out on the street!" As Mama dutifully relayed the message, I interrupted her by pleading for extra time. Once again, Mama dryly reported my dilemma to Daddy which made him angrier. More monotone than before, she said, "Ya Daddy says get home."

In an obvious panic, I hung up the phone. Marty could tell I was upset by the look on my face. There was no way I could be home in twenty minutes. Hell, it would take more than twenty minutes to get there even *if* the car was readily available.

Thirty minutes later, Mrs. Guilbeau pulled into the carport. No sooner than she got out from behind the wheel, Marty and I jumped into the car. As he cranked the engine, he quickly told her we had to leave. I could see a look of sympathy in her eyes. Dammit, the last thing I wanted was to be pitied, let alone by my boyfriend's parents. All I ever wanted was to be an equal and be able to hold my head up.

On the drive home, Marty asked me what my daddy's hurry was all about. I didn't say it to Marty, but my best guess was that Daddy was drunk. When he got like that, Mama knew better than to try to reason with him. She simply obeyed and prayed for the best, which would be that he'd just fall to sleep before casualties began piling up.

We parked in front of my house exactly sixty-three minutes after Mama's call. There, all over the front lawn, was every piece of clothing I owned. Luke met us in the front yard, apparently very shaken. "Connie, Daddy threw ya stuff in the yard. I yelled at him to stop, but he kept doin' it!" Panic was working its way through his body as he shifted weight from leg to leg. His little brown eyes filled with huge tears. As I looked at him standing there, so pale and undersized for his age, my heart beat extra hard. He was my little love since the moment he made his arrival into this demented family. He looked so much like Daddy that sometimes I had to take a double take. I wouldn't hold that against him; after all, he had his own little personality and was already demonstrating more compassion than Daddy had ever shown.

I ran into the house where Daddy was in the kitchen eating something very smelly. "Daddy, why did ya do it?!" I yelled. Cold as ice, he response was eerily casual, "Ya Mama told ya to be home in twenty minutes or ya clothes would be out in the yard. What else ya wanna know?" God, I hated him! He was so unfair and Mama just sat by and allowed this craziness day in and day out. WHAT WAS WRONG WITH THESE PEOPLE?

From the front porch, I waved goodbye to Marty, and all his good intentions. I knew it could get ugly if he tried to defend me - or butt in, as Daddy called it. With a painfully confused look on his face, he made a U-turn in front of our house and headed up the bayou. I went back inside with the anger of a rodeo bull. That son-of-a-bitch was not going to get the best of me no matter how hard he tried! I found him in the kitchen eating sauerkraut and sausage as though nothing out of the ordinary was happening. I stood directly in front of him and began to blast away for the first time ever. (Catherine would tell me years later that I spoke out more than I recall.)

"I'm tired of this crap! I feel like a prisoner in this house! I do all the chores that Mama tells me to do, and then some! I watch Luke, I help Catherine! What else do ya want from me? I hate this place! I feel like I'm in prison here! I HATE YA! I HATE YA!"

Adrenaline surged through me. By that time, I'd surely gotten Daddy's attention. His stare gripped me, and like an ensnared animal, I was experiencing the flight or fight rush. He said nothing for a moment and the silence scared the crap out of me. Suddenly, he lurched forward and swung his right fist, punching me on the left side of my head near the temple. I heard a crunching noise and saw lightening. By now, Catherine, Mama and Luke had gathered in the doorway between the kitchen and the hall. Luke was screaming at the top of his lungs, "STOP IT DADDY, YA GONNA HURT HER!" Catherine was crying loudly and clinging to Mama. Mama was screaming, "Jesus, Freddy STOP IT, YA GONNA KILL HER!"

Breaking free, I ran into my bedroom, which was about the worst choice I could've made. The only door out of my bedroom led to Catherine's bedroom and by now the others were blocking that passage. I tried to jump over my bed but landed across the width of the mattress. Daddy dove after me and landed on top on me, pinning me down with his swollen body. He grabbed my head with both hands and began thrashing it up and down on the metal bed frame. I don't know how many times he cracked my head on the unforgiving metal; everything was a blur and I began to go into shock.

I finally wiggled free and ran back into the kitchen. Crying hysterically, I was only vaguely aware of the distressed pleas in the background. I reached into a kitchen draw and pulled out a large butcher knife. Spinning around on my heels, I held the knife at chest level all the while looking the brown-eyed creature squarely in the face. "Don't ya come one step closer or I'll cut ya fuckin' guts out!"

As I heard the words come out of my own mouth, I was astounded and somewhat alarmed. Even in a defensive rage I knew I would never stab my own daddy. Oh, he deserved it, all right, but I couldn't hurt another human being, not even him, the vilest person I'd ever known. My unwillingness to wound him didn't take away from the fact that we'd all be better off if he was dead. I occasionally prayed for just that, not sure if God approved or not, but knowing something drastic had to be done to stop him in his tracks. Mama surely wasn't going to do anything. She was weak and half-crazy and couldn't be counted on for much of anything. No, the way I saw it, it was up to me to take care of this problem. Daddy became very still and locked his dark and squinted bloodshot eyes on mine. I knew I couldn't flinch or he might grab the knife and cut – or kill - me. He certainly had murder in his eyes and I believed him to be more than capable.

I held the knife with both hands as steady as I could, though I was still heavily shaking. With as much authority as I could muster, and louder than before and in the deepest voice I could manage, I repeated, "Don't move or I'll slice ya fuckin' guts out!" This time Daddy's expression changed, but only slightly. He froze in his tracks, then in a near whisper said, "Get out, now, an' don't ya EVER come back. Go on, I ain't got no use for ya, ya slut."

Still in extreme panic mode, I waited for him to leave the room before I lowered the knife. Intuitively, I knew the fight was over and even though he flinched first, he'd won. He was the adult; it was his house and that was that. Secretly, however, I fostered the fantasy that I'd won the war, even if I lost that battle. He'd never physically hurt or control me again. He might intimidate the outer me, but he would never overtake my mind or my feelings about him. I knew who he really was and he knew it.

I picked up the phone still sobbing, attempting to dial Marty's number. My hands were trembling so severely that I had to rest my right elbow on the table to steady myself. He answered the phone after just one ring, undoubtedly very anxious to hear from me. I was still hyperventilating, but fought to calm down enough to speak. "Can ya come pick me up? Daddy's kickin' me out." My nose was running and my eyes were swollen nearly shut. Mama went into their bedroom and Catherine took Luke into hers. Daddy was in the bathroom and I was left with the humiliating job of scooping all my clothes off the front lawn. Our house faced the main street and I knew many of my classmates would see me scavenging for my own belongings. I HATED Daddy! He ruined everything for everybody any chance he got. He was so miserable that it seemed to be his job to screw up our lives, too. Daddy would surely burn in hell.

I began to feel lightheaded and noticed a relentless throbbing just above my right temple. I reached up and ran my fingers through my blood-crusted hair. Jesus Christ – I was bleeding! I stooped down to pick up my few pairs of underwear that had landed several feet away from the main spattering of clothes. As I spun around to place them in a grocery bag, I felt myself beginning to black out. I fell back on my heels and landed spread eagle on the lawn, which was patchy and yellow from lack of proper attention. My underwear went flying into the air and my head bounced on the firm dirt beneath the grass. There was a black hornet flying overhead, or maybe it was a vulture. I lifted my head slightly and then let it drop. I was spinning out of control fast on my way to the other side of nowhere.

I was falling swiftly into the mouth of a cave; I waved my arms furiously trying to soften my fall. Hitting the ground with a thunderous clap, I lost my breath and gasped for air. I needed help – I was suffocating! Standing a few feet from where I landed was Mama, silently glaring at me; had I done something wrong? Reaching out to her, she stepped further away until she faded from sight. When I came to, I couldn't immediately tell if my vision was real-time, a psychic vision or a delusion.

I'm not sure how much time went by, but Luke was now sitting near me with his right hand gently under my head. He was calling my name over and over while he held a flimsy paper cup filled with tepid water from the hose. "Connie, Connie, *CONNIE*; here drink this. It'll make ya feel better." Sweet little thing. The youngest member in the family yet he had the biggest heart. It was plain to see why I adored this little guy so much, which only made the pain of leaving that much more unbearable. I took a small sip and slowly sat up.

Not wanting to scare Luke, I said as calmly as possible, "Jesus, that sun is so damn hot it made me faint right away." "Naw, that ain't it, Connie," he said in a pint-sized whisper. His two front teeth had fallen out eight months earlier and had not grown back in, making his courageous yet weak and crooked little smile all the more precious - and heartbreaking. Even with thirteen years between us, we equally understood the gravity of the viciousness that had taken place, although neither one of us could bring ourselves to say it. To admit it gave it power. Instead, we sat silently gazing at each other. The tears of an injured spirit welled up and spilled forth. How could I leave this innocent little boy with this depraved monster? How could Mama let this happen? I never thought I'd escape Daddy's grip, and now I was actually being ejected. I didn't have the luxury to celebrate the moment; I had to figure out where I'd live and how I'd be able to keep an eye out for little Luke.

He reached out and laid his tiny pale hand on mine. I turned my palm up and gave his little fingers a squeeze. "Ya know that ya my 'lil love, don't ya?" Luke lovingly helped me gather my clothes and before long we had most everything put into the three medium-sized paper bags. He clung to me when I stood. "Connie, don't go! I miss ya!" He started to cry, softly at first, then in big choppy whimpers. It broke my heart. Daddy ruined everything. He hurt people. He was heartless and all he cared about was his own damn self – if even that. Fine! His whole family would leave him and he'd die alone and lonely and miserable! (If Grandma Schroder were alive, she'd be very, very mad at Daddy. She was a tough old broad, but she didn't take kindly to abusive behavior, especially toward animals or kids.)

I sent Luke inside to get something to eat. I was always trying to fatten his little malnourished frame. Mama didn't seem to notice the dark circles under his eyes or how easily he bruised.

While I sat on the sun-scorched porch waiting for Marty my thoughts swirled like a tornado. I was emotionally distraught and fragile and I was physically injured and fatigued, yet I was so angry I was afraid I'd burst. In an intense flash all my unconscious questions about men came furiously to the fore. My role model – Daddy – was vicious and hurt others. Did all men hurt women? If you're a woman, are you automatically presumed to be weak? Did men keep their promises or did they repeatedly let you down and disappoint you? Were they always so self-centered? Did they always do as they pleased, never stopping to consider how their actions or words might impact others? When confronted about their behavior, did they become defensive, making you feel like you didn't deserve the same respect they so blatantly demanded?

Even though I wanted to believe it was all true because of what had just happened, something was wrong with my theory. Linda's daddy was not like mine; he was kind and extremely generous. He didn't ask for anything; he had a good heart and always wore a smile. I wished he were my daddy. Life would've been so different. I might have grown up to become a completely different person if I were his child.

Living in my reality had caused me to conclude that being a female was no great treat. What with periods and developing breasts and the future potential of having your body contort and convulse through the process of growing an entire human being within, there was not a whole lot to look forward to. And then there was the image of Mama, which worried me considerably. I'd come to fear growing up and took an odd comfort in the fact that I'd probably never live past the age of twenty.

I clearly didn't understand the setup and I was pretty damn sure that Mama was even more clueless. If men were the so-called protectors, then why did they choose to wield their power, maiming the very ones they were supposedly shielding? Was there a clause in the marriage certificate that said something to that effect? Did men ever actually sit down and think about the fact that females were people with real feelings and good strong minds? Shouldn't we be allowed the same rights as men? WHY would there be two sets of rules and WHY did they fall so heavily in favor of the male gender? Dammit to hell, women were people! I. Was. A. Person!

As Marty and I drove back to his parent's home, I had too many questions and no real answers. Even though my limited trust in men had been severely shaken, I was more than grateful that Marty didn't fit into the same category as Daddy. That day, he was my hero again. As much as I hated to admit it, I needed all the help I could get.

I was leaving my mama, little sister and baby brother because Daddy couldn't stand to look at me any longer. Something about me made him real mad, but what? How could Mama say that I was his favorite child of all and stand by and watch him beat me to a pulp? It occurred to me that even though Daddy had always treated me badly, it got much worse when I hit puberty and started dating. I needed answers all right, but something told me that I wouldn't get what I wanted from inside the Schroder house.

CHAPTER TEN

Menthol Madness

When we pulled into the carport, Mrs. Guilbeau was waiting for us. "Ya all right, cher'?" I could see the worry in her eyes and that, in turn, worried me. "Come inside, beb, let's take a look at ya." God, did I look that awful?

I began to cry as I started to share the horror story that was my life.

"I'm sorry I called Marty, Mrs. Guilbeau, but I didn't know who else to call." She was very present and leaned closer. "That's OK, beb. Ya did the right thing. Ya can stay here tonight, then we'll talk 'bout it tomorrow when ya feel better." Deep down, she was a kind-hearted lady who saw a kid in need and decided to reach out. I felt an overwhelming sense of gratitude rise up through my chest, but all I could quietly say was, "thanks." Hardly enough, I knew, but words escaped me as the impact of the earlier events began to take their toll. For a fleeting moment the thought of a father brutalizing his child flashed up on my inner movie screen. I was especially horrified by the large fist being lifted and dropped over and over again in a savage attempt to crush the skull of a child – my skull.

Chills ran up my spine. It was my pathetic life and that was me being catapulted out of it. I should've felt happy.

Julia was also very kind to me and showed me where to find a spare quilt. I rummaged through my paper bags until I found an old pair of pajamas and excused myself to take a bath. I was more battered and bruised than I realized and my body needed deep rest. I felt so alone and helpless, even with all these caring people around me. Mama didn't even try to protect me and I couldn't really shield my little sister and brother. As I lay my head on the goose down pillow just after eight o'clock, I asked God to help me. "I need ya now, God. Not for me, but for my Mama, sister and baby brother. Please don't let Daddy hurt them while I'm gone. They can't fend for themselves an' even though he hurt me bad, I'm not as scared of him as they are. He hears me talkin' to him in my mind an' he knows I know all 'bout him. So, please God, keep 'em safe for me 'till I figure a way to get them outta there. Thank ya, Lord. Amen. Jesus-Mary-Joseph. Jesus-Mary-Joseph. Jesus-Mary-Joseph."

"Breakfast is ready, Connie!" Attempting to perk me up the next morning while trying not to stare at the dark bruises on my neck, Julia's voice was more chipper than usual. I propped up my upper body on my arms and tried to focus my eyes on her. "Oh, hey." My neck was terribly sore, severely strained from Daddy's death grip and all the violent up and down movement as he thrashed me about. When I tried to sit up a stabbing pain seared throughout my upper back. "Ouch, DAMN!" I yelled without thinking. "Oh, Connie are ya hurtin' bad?" "Not too bad", I lied. In order to further fool her, I tried to spring out of bed so as to look fine. The effort nearly made me faint. I fell back onto the bed with a gasp. I was whipped, all right, and everybody could see it. There was no use trying to hide anything.

If it wasn't for my severely wounded pride, I could've come

clean. But admitting defeat was simply not my style. Doing something like that reliably invoked one of two responses from Daddy - either his nostrils flared in the anticipation of further torment and the sense of power he derived from that or he'd get sickeningly sweet and wanted to hug and touch me in ways that repulsed me. I hated his nearness; it was always for his pleasure and never simply to comfort or reassure. He was disgusting in every way, yet he was my daddy and I mourned the loss of what I'd never had.

"Good mornin', beb. How'd ya sleep?" Mrs. Guilbeau was stirring something in a small iron pot at the stove. "Good. I'm a 'lil sore this mornin', but I'll be fine." Marty emerged from the hall wearing tight blue jeans and a t-shirt boasting a large red peace sign with the inscription, *"Make Love, Not War!"* "Hey, Connie. How ya feelin?" Everybody was so concerned about me that it made me feel weird. I didn't like being the center of attention. I had learned to avoid the spotlight, discovering young that it's harder to hit a moving target.

Late Sunday afternoon, Marty, Mrs. Guilbeau and I sat at the kitchen table for a pow-wow. Marty had already told me that his Mama and Daddy said it would be okay for me to stay there with them for a while, so I had some clue as to what would follow.

I thanked Mrs. Guilbeau for offering me a place to stay but worried about my job at the drugstore. I needed it and didn't know how I'd handle transportation.

(Four months earlier, I was at Vegeaux's Drugs after school. Making my customary swing by the pharmacy counter at the rear of the store, I greeted the owner with a smile. "Hey, Mr. Vegeaux, got any job openins' today? Ya know I live next door an' it'd sure be easy for me to get to work!" With an equally warm smile, he replied, "Ya know Connie, for the better part of a year ya been comin' here every day axin' me for a job. Every day, I tell ya the same thing – no openins' today. But, guess what, Connie? Today I can tell ya YEAH, we got an openin'!"

I was used to being told no; it took me a moment to really hear what he was saying. Stopping dead in my tracks I turned slowly to face him. "What did ya say? Did I hear ya right?" With a broader grin than usual, Mr. Vegeaux nodded his head up and down and waved me closer. "Lucinda is quittin' to get married. She'll be leaving in just two weeks. When can ya start?" All the blood rushed to my head. "How 'bout YESTERDAY?!" I was so excited, I almost peed in my pants! I'd been waiting for this job for so long. I didn't have a car yet – I hadn't even gotten my driver's license. A job close to home was my ticket out!)

"Don't worry, cher', between Julia an' me, we'll get ya to the drugstore. Ya can take the bus there after school an' we can pick ya up." Suddenly, I was overwhelmed by emotions. So much had happened and I hadn't had a chance to even think about it all yet. And now this lady was offering me a place to live and helping me figure out how to keep my job – a job that was so vitally important to my prayed-for escape. Tears fell. Marty leaned over and hugged me tight. "Don't worry, beb. Everything's gonna be all right." More than anything in the world, I needed to believe him. After all, what choice did I really have? For now, my fate was in the hands of people that I really didn't even know all that well. Even though they always welcomed me into their home with open arms, I still felt like an outsider. I wasn't socialized like Marty. Daddy's alcoholism was the guardian at the gate and it didn't let others in.

I hardly knew how to accept kindness. I was innately suspicious of seemingly innocent gestures, automatically searching for the hidden strings attached. My mind was strong and I was always probing the inner caverns for the "real" motivation behind friendly offers. Often, I politely refused benevolent gifts figuring it was just easier that way. I didn't like feeling that I owed anyone. It was simpler to keep it clean and anyway, the last thing I needed was to be viewed as a pathetic charity case.

For the next year-and-a-half until I graduated from high school, I lived at Marty's house. Marty was attended Louisiana State University in Baton Rouge and hitched a ride home most weekends.

I missed Marty terribly when he was away. He was my main link to acceptance, love (at least what I thought of as love) and companionship. There was lots of passion between us, making me feel alive. He talked more than any boy I'd ever known – almost as much as his daddy. Sometimes he didn't even stop to inhale. But for the most part I figured his life was way more interesting than mine and besides, I really didn't want to say too much anyway. Nothing fascinating ever happened to me (I had no idea how special it was to speak with the dead, communicate without words and perceive the thoughts of others at that time in my life), so I generally sat by quietly and listened. About the only thing I had to look forward to was graduating from high school, which was only a few short months away.

∞ ∞ ∞

Graduation night was quite a big deal at South Lafourche High School. Our class of 200 was large for our small community. My name was always called after Loretta Schooner's. I had severe butterflies in my stomach; I knew this was an important milestone in my life and I was alone. Marty was in Baton Rouge and couldn't break away because of finals. Sure, Linda was graduating, too, but she'd be with her family who'd be happy to be there with her. This night marked a pattern in my life. I'd always be alone for the big things – whether good or bad. I'd better get used to it, I thought. This is just the way it was and I probably didn't deserve any better than that. Otherwise, why would God put me with this family? As the principal shook my hand and handed me my diploma, I managed a shaky smile. Sadness replaced hopeful pride. I really, really wanted to cry.

Later that night, several of us piled into the car with Debbie Estee and her mama as we set off to once again spend time at their summer camp on Grand Isle. I sat in the back seat next to Linda near the window. Excited chatter filled the air at first but as we drove and the world around us grew darker, a deadening silence fell over the blue Caddy. I leaned against the door with my face pressed against the cool window. It was a crystal clear night and even though I felt painfully alone there was familiarity in the heavens. I knew my life would never be the same. I was officially grown up; eighteen years old and heading off into my own life. But I was nowhere near prepared and I knew it. A surge of nervousness rapidly covered me in sweat, and was accompanied by a dreadful feeling of being incredibly lost as I began to ponder my needs as an independent girl.

I'd have to have a car. The Guilbeaus had generously gotten me to and from work long enough and now that I was out of school, they expected me to take matters into my own hands. I couldn't blame them. They'd really done a lot for me – more than anyone else, except for Linda and her family. My plan was simple. I had three-hundred dollars saved up and I'd intended to go to the bank in a week to ask for a car loan. I still had my part-time job at the drugstore, but I'd need to talk to Mr. Vegeaux about going full-time. I wanted to make enough money to move to Baton Rouge and be near Marty. He had another three years left at LSU and I couldn't bear to be away from him that long. Besides, there was no way for me to advance down the bayou. The weight of adulthood had already begun to pull me down. I needed to make life decisions.

Once vacation was over, Linda would head off to college. I

knew our relationship would change, it couldn't stay the same – too many things were shifting. She'd make new friends – smart people in college – and I probably wouldn't be as interesting to her. They'd be talking about their classes and projects and I wouldn't have anything to contribute. Things were changing, all right, and I felt a deep sadness about it. I was leaving the hell I knew and had no idea of the hell I was headed for.

For that night, I told myself, I'd just enjoy the trip to Grand Isle. We'd play on the beach and compare tan lines. We'd eat fresh seafood until we were over-full and stay up all night talking about everything under the sun. We would sleep late, then get up and go back to the beach and repeat the routine of the day before. Life would be decent for a week; I'd enjoy it while I could. Growing up could wait a little longer.

The heaviness of my future began to lift the next morning as I made a cow belly, burying my feet in the cool wet sand. The salty gulf waves washed over me and for a few fleeting moments I felt normal.

Chapter Eleven

Ride the Wild Pony

"Mr. Bouclé, I wanna borrow money for a car. I have three-hundred dollars for a down payment." He frowned as he looked through thick glasses at my loan application. "Miss Schroder, ya haven't been working at the drugstore long enough to qualify for this loan." He asked if I could get a co-signer. Not wanting to appear unintelligent, I struggled to understand what he was asking me. Sensing my confusion, he said, "That's when ya have somebody else sign their name on the note." My shoulders drooped as the reality of the situation punched me squarely in the gut. Who would do that for me? I wouldn't dare ask the Guilbeaus and Daddy hated me enough to brutally kick me out of the house. I had a snowball's chance in hell of getting a loan.

At five-thirty, after all the cash and the checks were counted and recorded, I picked up snacks and headed over to see Mama and Luke. I made sure Daddy's car wasn't in the driveway before I stepped into the yard; I didn't want any trouble. I was there strictly to see Mama and Luke - maybe Catherine if she was around.

Opening the front door, the smell of garbage slapped me in

the face, causing me to instinctively pull back. The sofa had a pile of laundered clothes on one end and several of Luke's toys on the other. There were more toys on the floor, which I had to weave in and out of to get to the kitchen. The window fan wasn't working and the house was literally sweating. Daddy knew the fan had given out, but he hadn't made time to do the repair. "Here ya go, Luke – just for ya, 'lil puddin'!" Luke ran up to me and threw his skinny little arms around my waist. He was so affectionate and so unlike the rest of the family. He was deep; I knew that about him since he was a toddler. Luke had thoughts that words couldn't yet support and oftentimes I felt what he was thinking. Maybe that's why we connected so well, unlike him and Catherine or Catherine and me, for that matter. I loved that little guy as if he were my own born child; maybe he wished that I was his mama. Mama was so crazy and that wore on him even at such a young age. I understood that more than he knew. Even though we never spoke of it, I let him know through mind signals that he was right about her. It was important that he learn to trust his own intuition. That's why I felt compelled to see him as often as I could. I somehow thought that I could inject a little stability into his life, although my own was in seriously short supply much of the time.

A sense of urgency surrounded my relationship with Luke. Catherine and I always had each other to turn to. Maybe that made the frightening things slightly more endurable, I'm not sure, but Luke didn't have anybody - not really. Catherine was almost twelve years older than him and truth be known, she never seemed to really like him much. He was like an only child because of the age gap and I knew that when I was gone he was very lonely. That was confirmed when his little brown eyes lit up every time I walked into the house. He was my little buddy and I would look out for him as long as I possibly could.

"CONNIE!" He jumped up and down, clinging to my waist.

"Hey there, Luke. How's my 'lil love today?" "YEAH, I'm good now that ya here, Connie!" He was a shiny little jewel amidst the murky everyday existence in the God-forsaken Schroder hellhole. On many occasions, I dreamed of marrying Marty and moving far away with Luke. I'd happily raise him and give him the love I never got. I'd even spoken to Marty about it. Although he didn't see that happening anytime soon, he was in loose agreement. Marty could see how much I worried about the little guy and he said he didn't like to see me so upset.

"Let me sit down with Mama an' talk for a while, okay, Luke?"

"Mama, I went to the bank today an' I talked with Mr. Bouclé 'bout gettin' a loan. He says that I have to have a co-signer." Nodding acknowledgment, Mama may have been smarter than I thought. I expressed my concern about losing my job if I didn't get a car.

We sat there quietly as Mama lit a cigarette. I loved the way menthol smelled and even the way it tasted as it first rolled over your tongue, but ultimately the smoke always overwhelmed the flavor. Her fingernails were nicotine-stained, which didn't seem to bother her.

Not expecting much of a response, I interrogated Mama. I needed to know if she thought there was any chance that Daddy would help me. He'd recently bought a used car for Catherine. It was only a few hundred dollars but that was more than he'd ever spent on me.

Just the thought of being near Daddy in order to ask for help made me want to throw up. After all, my last contact with him was violent in nature and I'm sure he hadn't forgotten that I threatened to rip his guts out. Not the best foundation for a request for assistance.

I lay in bed feeling the gravity of the day pulling on my body and mind. I was always trying to figure things out, having a huge need to understand what was going on around me. Nothing made sense at my house except harshness and nastiness. I needed to bite the bullet and ask Daddy to co-sign. I had to swallow my pride and remember that this was my ticket out. It was a matter of survival and I couldn't let fear or my pride stand in the way. My plan would be as follows: when I got off work the next day I'd go over to the house and wait for Daddy to arrive. I'd hope that he wouldn't be falling-down drunk, but being a bit tipsy wouldn't hurt.

"Hey Daddy." I tried to act cheerful, but the sight of him made my stomach spasm. "Connie. What're doing here?" His voice was quiet yet biting. "I came to play with Luke a while." I knew I didn't sound normal but I was really making a concerted effort. Even though I was a self-proclaimed actress, I'd never been a very successful liar and I was pretty sure Daddy could see right through my fake cheerfulness. I knew that he somehow picked up on my thoughts as I did his.

"Daddy, can I talk to ya 'bout something?" He didn't seem too drunk and that was a good sign. "What is it?" It was then or never. "I'm trying to buy a car an' the man at the bank says I need a co-signer."

Daddy was showing signs of softening up. "How much ya tryin' to borrow? What do I have to do?" I couldn't believe it! I fully expected him to reject me. Maybe he felt guilty for beating me and kicking me out. I fought back my excitement; Daddy frequently took things away from us if he detected an attachment or even the slightest bit of joy. "I have money for a down payment and the man at the bank said he'll go over the loan amount when I come back with a co-signer. Thanks, Daddy. I'll meet ya at Citizens Bank & Trust Wednesday at three-thirty."

Feeling grateful, if not bewildered by what had just happened, I went into the living room where Luke was playing with Cowboys and Indians. Sitting on the floor near him, I picked up a small green horse, trotting it along next to the Cowboy he held.

∞ ∞ ∞

As the proud new owner of an olive green 1972 Ford Pinto, I realized that my first task was to learn to drive. I had my license, but had very little time behind the wheel. Tammy, Linda's older sister, was an extremely patient driving instructor, letting me drive her car at times. I could swerve just inches from the bayou and she'd gently - if not nervously - simply say, "Connie, beb, ya wanna veer just a 'lil to the left."

Once I became more comfortable with my car and my driving skills, I decided to move to Baton Rouge to be near Marty. The only thing holding me to the bayou was Luke and I would be back often to visit him.

With no plans for college, I thought my best chance for success was to move to a larger city with bigger job opportunities. Plus, I really missed Marty. We were a couple, and even though we fought at times, our relationship was the closest thing I had to feeling loved. I had romantic notions of us living together and eventually getting married, although Marty was more tuned in to getting his college degree than marriage. Surely once I was in Baton Rouge with him and we got to spend more time together he'd have a change of heart.

With nothing more than one old beat-up suitcase in the back of my Pinto, I headed out on a journey that would change my life forever. Having said my goodbyes to the Guilbeaus and Linda, my last stop was Mama's house. I dreaded saying goodbye to them; I knew it would break my heart to look into little Luke's face and tell him I was leaving. He became distraught when I moved just a few miles away. This would really upset him. I felt guilty for leaving him. Deep in my heart, I suspected that I was the bravest of them all – not that I was very courageous, but I was forced to take more risks than Mama or Catherine.

Even if Daddy let me move back into the house I wouldn't do it. I'd tasted a bit of freedom and lived around somewhat normal people; I could never go back.

The thought of leaving Mama, Catherine and Luke behind with Daddy made me sick. Literally sick. My stomach churned and my head began to throb. I wanted to be strong for them and I surely didn't want to cry while I was there. They had to believe that I could find a better life, then come back and bring them into something good. Hope was all I could offer my family and I prayed like mad that God would help me make them feel my dedication.

Luke ran to the front door and swung it open. "Hey, Connie-Connie!" I hadn't told him that today was the day I was leaving. Even though I'd been gently priming him with small hints, I hadn't been able to bring myself to do it yet. "Hey, puddin'. How's my fav-o-rite little guy in the whole wide world?"

"Me? I'm good." Luke responded excitedly, and then continued, "Whatcha got for me there, Connie?" He was accustomed to the treats I brought and this day would be no different. "Check my right pocket; dig deep, now punkin'." Buried deep inside my jacket pocket were little treats he loved. "Yippeee! Connie, ya da best!" With his little hands full of goodies, he excitedly jumped up on the sofa so he was eye level with me. He stretched his little neck out and plopped a big loud kiss on my cheek. This was a bit of a ritual between us. He'd stick his tongue out as he kissed me, getting my face wet. Then as any practiced thespian would do, I followed with my lines. "YUK, ya got me all wet, ya 'lil stinker! Whatta ya, a puppy dog? I'm gonna have to *whip* ya *butt* for that!" Running and giggling, he worked himself up so much that he almost always had to go to the bathroom.

God, how was I going to tell this precious little boy that I was leaving and wouldn't be able to see him every day? I said a silent prayer, and called Luke back into the living room. He hopped back up onto the sofa and I put my hands on his slight shoulders.

"Hey, big boy, sit down next to me for a minute, I need to talk to ya." Every muscle in my body tightened as I tried to hold back the tears. "Sugah, today I'm gonna be movin'. I'm goin' to the town where Marty goes to school – ya remember, Baton Rouge." His little smile began to droop and he looked completely confused. "But, Connie, how will I see ya?" Jesus H. Christ, why did everything in my life have to be so damn hard? "Well, I'm gonna be comin' home on the weekends to see ya an' Catherine an' Mama. That's on Saturdays an' Sundays, ya know the days when ya watch cartoons." His little brown eyes began to tear up and his tiny pale pink lips began to quiver as he caught on to what I was saying. I'd fought furiously to keep this little guy when Mama got sick and now I was moving away from him. Pain and confusion swept over me and I began to seriously doubt my own motives for leaving. He threw his blonde head into my lap and grabbed me around the waist. "NO, Connie, ya can't leave! Stay here with us. Maybe Daddy will let ya move back with us. Axe him, Connie. Axe him to let ya come back, PLEASE, Connie! He ain't mad at ya no more."

By then, we were both crying. Dammit, I wanted so badly to remain composed for his sake but nothing I tried seemed to work. Taking several deep breaths, I looked at Mama, who was standing in the doorway between the living room and kitchen. She raised her arm and used her sleeve to wipe away the tears; she would be of no help to me. Her heart was breaking too, though I'm not sure it was at the prospect of losing me but rather, my contribution.

Catherine appeared in the hallway outside of her room. She'd been purposely avoiding me. She also had tears in her eyes and looked frightened. She scared easily and seeing Mama and me sobbing brought her to the brink. "What's goin' on?" Even though she asked the question out loud, she already knew the answer. I'd told her and Mama about the move several weeks ago, explaining that I'd found a widowed lady who was renting a room in her house near the LSU campus.

Mrs. Breck sounded very old on the phone but she also seemed kind. Mama and Catharine didn't have much to say the day I shared my news. I guess they figured I was pretty lucky for getting to break away from Daddy and my dead-end life on the bayou. Maybe they even admired me, but more likely, I figured that they were jealous.

"Luke, would ya like to come visit me in Baton Rouge sometimes an' spend the weekend? We could go see Mike the Tiger at LSU!" He nodded agreement as he rubbed his eyes with his right hand, which was balled into a fist around his thumb. I knew that it was a meek offering and did little to lift his spirits but I wanted him to know that I wasn't leaving him behind. I planned to spend as much time with him as I could. My mothering instincts were on fire and I wanted to grab him and throw him in the car and take him with me. Dammit! I felt like there was a heavy sack of oysters attached to my heart.

Finally, when I could bear it no longer I stood and hugged Mama then Catherine. "Be good, Cat. Please look after Luke for me." I grabbed my purse and slung it over my shoulder. Kneeling in front of Luke, I said, "Listen to me, sugah. I love ya more than all the stars in the sky, more than all the mosquitoes in the swamp, more than all the money in the world, more than ANYTHING, ANYWHERE! Understand? I'll never stop lovin' ya, no matter what! Nuttin' could ever stop me from lovin' ya, honey bunny. Ya my fav-o-rite person in the whole wide world. Ya know that, right?!"

As I spoke Luke ran his small fingers through my long, straight hair. I could sense that he needed to touch me so as not to lose the bond. I desperately wanted life to be different so I wouldn't have to leave him but I saw no other option. I rubbed the peach fuzz on the top of his head, cupping his little face in my hands. "If ya need me, just call out my name – ya know how to do it. I'll hear ya - I promise! Talk to me in your mind like we've been doin' all along 'cause you know I can hear ya, don't ya?" Still crying, Luke said in the smallest voice, "Yeah, I know, Connie. But what if ya busy doing other things an' ya don't hear me? What if ya buyin' groceries or washin' ya clothes?" I was unwavering. "No chance! I've got ya tuned in at the top of my list. Ya come first 'fore anybody else; ya always will! Okay?!" Luke let his small body fall into mine and we hugged for what seemed like hours. I stood up slowly peeling him gently away.

"Okay, time for me to get my 'lil buggy on the road. I'll call ya when I get there." With that, I quickly turned and left. I couldn't bear his heartbreak – or mine - another second. My life was pure-dee hell when I lived there and now I was being crushed from the inside out because I had to leave. My innards were tormented and torn in half. I didn't completely understand the whole thing, but I knew Daddy was at the center of the pain – *all* of our pain. Damn Fred Schroder! He destroyed everyone and everything around him and now he was forcing me away from the person I loved most. He stood at the core of my deepest loss. God, I wished he were dead!

With my little green pony in reverse, I slowly backed out of the driveway. As the shells crunched under my tires, I caught sight of Mama in her striped moo-moo, Catherine in her two-piece aqua shorts set and little Luke in a stained white t-shirt and beige pants. Seeing them standing on the front porch that way was creepily similar to the disturbing day we were forced to say goodbye to Ricky so many years ago - a haunted nightmare that would forever be burned in my mind.

The journey northwest to Baton Rouge along Highway 10 was burdensome that day - yet mindless - and perhaps the longest of my life. Along the twelve-mile span that crossed the swamp my attention was subtly drawn to the right where Spanish moss hung from gnarled cypress trees. The gray trunks towered up without a leaf for seventy or eighty feet and lulled me into memories of tales about sightings of swamp monsters. The trees grew close together at the top shutting out the light and presented a forbidding appearance. The primitive beauty rose from the water; the sweet smell of wild azaleas filled the air.

Reaching over the front seat to retrieve my map, I focused on finding my new home. Mrs. Breck would be waiting and probably be a little anxious about meeting her newest tenant. At only eighteen years old, this would be my third home.

CHAPTER TWELVE

Home Away from Home

"Hello, ya must be Constance. Come on in." Mrs. Breck was warm and welcoming as she held the screen door for me. Her short, slightly hunched-over frame and uneven stride told me she'd lived many years and been around the block more than a few times.

I followed Mrs. Breck into the kitchen where she poured a tall glass of ice-cold lemonade. Within seconds, condensation began to form outside the etched tumbler.

Taking long slow sips, she reminded me of the rent and then recited the rules. Sixty dollars a month was a lot of money to me, but I counted on getting a better paying job now that I was in the big city. "Ya can use the kitchen anytime ya want, but clean up after yaself. Be in by eleven o'clock at night and *no opposites* in ya room."

I had an immediate reaction to her regulations, especially the no boys thing, but I would wait until another day to discuss it with her. The fact that I didn't have the money for my own apartment meant that living with Mrs. Breck was my safest bet for now. After all, this was my virgin run in the big city.

The bedroom seemed fine enough. The cherry wood

furniture was dark and not exactly cheerful, but it was heads and shoulders above anything I'd ever had. The mattress was hard and I had trouble falling asleep the first night. Try as I might to convince myself that this was the adventure of a lifetime, I didn't feel one bit settled. I missed Luke terribly, and even Mama and Catherine. Closing my eyes, I called out to Luke.

"Hey, Luke, can ya hear me? This is Connie." I became perfectly still and laser-focused. Suddenly, I saw his little face as clear as day. His broad, toothless smile gave me a great lift. "How ya doin', punkin'?" In my own voice, but in his words, I heard, "I'm okay, Connie. When ya comin' home? I miss ya!" Before I could answer, a deep drowsiness washed over me and sleep abruptly seized my thoughts. As I released myself into rest, I once again saw Luke, but this time in what felt like a movie. Because he was looking away, I feared he thought I was leaving him behind for good.

Then suddenly, "Ya know what he does, don't ya?" Luke transmitted in a low, raspy tone. "Yeah, I know," I responded hesitantly. I was tempted to evade the issue, but like a magnet to metal, I was drawn to the truth. More than words were transferred back and forth when we met in this dreamy state. I saw lifetimes in those tiny brown eyes and somehow knew that I had always been with him.

"He don't let Mama see. He thinks she's stupid an' won't ever know." Luke was wise beyond his years; I knew that from the moment I first held him. He knew about things that happened before his birth – things that I had to be reminded of. Mama appeared in my vision. She was dragging her cracked heels and wearing the same moo-moo she'd worn for too many days. She glanced at us and then turned away almost as if she hadn't seen us at all. Catherine then appeared trying hard to stay close to Mama. Finally catching up, she tugged at the back of Mama's nightdress causing her to stop dead in her tracks. Instantly, Mama's expressionless face came to life. She smiled warmly and leaned over, kissing Catherine on the top of her head. Her shiny mahogany hair glistened in the sunlight. In a most triumphant manner, Catherine cooed. Mama tended to her needs very thoughtfully, continuing to ignore Luke and me. It was quite a sight to see Mama so alive, given that she was heavily drugged most of the time. It was rather apparent that Mama had eyes only for Catherine and that her mission, if she even had one, was to protect her youngest daughter. She adored Luke, as well, but not when he was with me.

Luke and I silently vowed to keep an eternal connection, in spite of whatever obstacles life sent our way.

∞ ∞ ∞

Up until this point, my experience with job-hunting had been extremely limited. Back home I'd been diligent in asking Mr. Vegeaux for a job at the drugstore, but that was different. By the time he agreed to hire me, I felt like I knew him. I'd been a regular customer for over a year, so he had a preview of my reliability. But going into strange businesses where I didn't know a soul, well that was entirely different and very daunting. Nevertheless, I put on my nicest outfit, a hand-me-down from Linda, and headed out the door.

Two days later, the phone rang bright and early at eight o'clock. I was awake but still lounging lazily in bed. The woman from the department store was calling with good news.

"Hello, this is Constance." My heart was pounding in my throat and I was sure she could hear it through the phone. "Constance, we'd like ya to come in tomorrow morning at nine o'clock for training. Are ya available?" Did she just ask me if I was available? Hell yeah, I was way more than available!

"Did ya get the job, Constance?" Mrs. Breck asked in an

uplifted voice, in a pitch much higher than usual. "I think so! Yep, I surely think so!" I grabbed her hands and began to spin her around as though we were a dynamic, multi-colored top. *"Whee!* Good for ya, Constance!" She sounded girlishly happy and for that moment, I was, too. I'd come to the big city and gotten a decent job – hell, a downright good job. Daddy never thought I'd amount to much, but I was on my way. He was wrong about me and it bothered me that I longed for him to see that.

I could barely wait to tell Marty my good news. In my mind, getting a good job brought us one step closer to getting married, or at the very least, to living together. Until then, I'd always lived under someone else's roof, and I couldn't wait to have my own place with the freedom to move about as I pleased. There, I envisioned myself feeling safe from Daddy's violent rage and surprise attacks. Mama's depression wouldn't reach me in my own place, either. But, no matter how happy I might be I *would always* miss my little Luke.

At six o'clock sharp, Marty pulled up in front of Mrs. Breck's house. A warm air stream met me as I stepped out onto the porch, where the fragrance of a nearby rose bush filled my senses. Glancing over at Mrs. Henry's house across the street, I noticed movement in the living room curtains where, no doubt, she was peeking again. With a mock-friendly gesture, I waved.

I hated being peeked at in such a sneaky way. I often had that feeling back home and it gave me the creeps.

Chapter Thirteen

The Devil in the Details

Saturday nights with Marty could be lots of fun, especially at the submarine races (a term jokingly used by students as an excuse to park and make out). The lake was nearby and convenient. Cars filled with love-struck teenagers were parked neatly around the perimeter. An unspoken code prevailed; we made room for as many cars as possible. Love was in bloom and often the kids had nowhere else to express themselves in that way. After a short time, the car windows were so steamed up that we all had our own private, little space. Ah, the joy of young love.

Marty was very passionate with all that Cajun blood. From what his daddy had told him, there was still a lot of fire in the stove between him and his wife. Marty figured it was passed down through genetics. His daddy's own family of fourteen proved his theory; something was always stirring in those Cajun jeans.

But his passion for me was often outweighed by Marty's need to be social. I continued to tell myself that he needed an outlet from the mounting pressure of school. He had a few good friends in his program and they loved to hang out, hunt and drink beer. Maybe he felt trapped or didn't feel he had enough time to do all of the things he wanted to do. Whatever it was, it caused friction between us.

Marty's college scholarship was awarded by a local family and granted a certain amount of money each semester - provided he met certain scholastic requirements.

I saved up a little extra money and used that for a deposit on my first apartment. I invited Marty to live with me but he had to live on campus to meet scholarship requirements. After a week of searching, I found an efficiency apartment near campus, which was basically one large room, with the exception of a tiny bathroom. No matter, I quickly made it my home and found many clever ways to create separate spaces within my own four walls of freedom. I loved it; every inch of it was mine and nobody would be leering at me or telling me what I could or couldn't do. It was another very important milestone in my life and I knew it.

Marty began sleeping over more and more and it was good for a time. I cleaned out the top dresser drawer for him, where he left a few of his personal belongings. When his mama and daddy came to visit we took his things out of the apartment, not wanting them to discover our secret. As for my mama and daddy, they never came to visit and didn't seem to care what I was doing.

I continued to visit Mama, Catherine and Luke as promised and I was always so happy to see my little guy. As he got a little older, he tried to act cool when I visited. But, without fail, and as if he could sense my arrival before I came into view on Highway One, he'd be standing on the front porch as I pulled my car into the shell driveway. Right thumb hanging from his pants pocket with his left arm hung freely to his side, he could hardly contain a smile. Jumping out of the car and zipping up the steps, I'd grab him under the arms and swing him around over and over until he began to giggle loudly. "Hey, punkin'!" With a loud smack, I'd plant a big kiss on one cheek, then the other and finally on his forehead.

Luke should have been more tanned; it was summer. Often there were no other kids his age around so he played alone, entertaining himself as much as possible. He planted a garden and by the time I arrived on that particular visit, the okra was in full bloom. Some of the plants had huge pods hanging from the stems. When I inquired whether okra was more tender if picked smaller, he had a firm answer. "Connie, look. This makes so much sense if ya just listen to me, okay? If the okra gets big like this, Mama can make more gumbo with it. Ya see? Ya can't make as much with the small okras, so I grow 'em big for Mama." It made perfect sense to Luke, and that's all that mattered. Already, he was concerned about stretching food rations. He grabbed my hand and led me over to the row of corn stalks. "See this, Connie? This is my yella corn on the cob. When it gets ready, I'll pick 'em for Mama. She don't wear her false teeth all the time so I cut the kernels off the cob for her." He touched me to my depths with his concern about Mama's wellbeing. Daddy didn't seem to care if Mama lived or died, but Mama was the center of Luke's Universe. That worried me.

(Sometimes when Daddy was really drunk and on a rampage, Mama got the courage to call the police. Bayou policeman loved to use their sirens and lights, even in non-emergency situations. One, sometimes two, green and whites swiftly pulled into our shabby front yard. As young as fourteen years old, I would wait for them on the front porch while Catherine and Luke hid in the back bedroom closet. My heart yearned to be there in the closet to console them but I felt I needed to be sure they found our house. By the time the police arrived Daddy was usually in bed pretending to be asleep and

Mama was crying in her rocking chair. The responsibility to greet the authorities was all mine.

Leading two officers into the living room, one man spoke. "What seems to be the problem, Miss? Where's Mr. Schroder?" Mama had too much time to think, even in her semi-hysteria. She began to feel the threat that accompanied what happened after Daddy was released from jail. "Aw, nuttin', really. Freddy come home drunk an' got a 'lil rough." It was humiliating that the local police knew my daddy by name. Jesus H. Christ, could anything be more embarrassing? Since our house was on the main road, everyone driving up or down the bayou could plainly see our troubles. Nothing was private in a small town.

I was old enough to understand that if they took Daddy away there would be a price to pay. Not only would we be eating mayonnaise sandwiches if he was gone too long but he would be fit to be tied when he was released. That was absolutely the worst part.

Once, when the policemen did bother to take Daddy to jail, they gave him a ride home early the next morning. Smelling badly, he walked through the front door saying nothing as he headed for the kitchen. Opening the icebox door, he peered aimlessly. Not finding what he wanted, he slammed the door then took a seat in a wobbly chair at the kitchen table. In continued deadly silence, he lit a cigarette and took long, deep drags. The look of disgust on his face made me want to puke. We'd done nothing wrong, absolutely nothing. In his mind, however, we had dared to call attention to his violent behavior and that was a major infraction. It was always about Daddy. Try not to upset Daddy, don't wake Daddy, make sure supper is on the table for Daddy. Daddy, Daddy, DADDY!)

Just as with Mama and Daddy, the arguments grew between Marty and me. Some days we just couldn't agree on anything.

In spite of our obvious and growing incompatibility, I still believed we belonged together. After all, he really was my first (and only) true love. At least, I wanted to believe it was love. And so, during his third year at LSU, we decided to get married. Maybe I should say that *I decided* we should get married. We would save money and be happy, wouldn't we?

When I told Mama about our plan to marry, she pulled me aside for one of her serious talks. "Connie, I wanna talk to ya for a minute." Mama's tone was very serious, like she had something of grave importance on her mind. It was hard to tell what Mama spent her days thinking about. So often, a blank stare stole the woman inside. "Come ya weddin' night, Marty's gonna 'spect some blood." I was embarrassed and afraid to ask where this talk was headed, but too curious to let it drop. Pausing long enough to allow her words to push through, she continued, "Well, on ya weddin' night, when ya intimate for the first time, something called the hymen breaks. That's all. There's a 'lil blood an' maybe a 'lil pain, but then it's fine. Well, ya won't experience that 'cause its already broken."

Mama didn't know that Marty and I had already been together that way; before I could ask her to go on, she spoke. "When ya was a 'lil girl, ya Daddy axed ya to help him off with his boots. Ya stood in front of him with ya back to him and grabbed one of his feet while he pushed against ya butt with the other one. After ya got the first boot off, ya fell on top of the other one. The sleeve of the boot went right up 'tween ya legs an' caused ya pain. That night, I noticed a 'lil blood in ya undies. So, ya hymen was broken then, Connie. Nuttin' to worry 'bout."

Was she saying that my virginity was damaged at a very early age? I'd never given any thought to the whole thing before then but it was true that I did not bleed the first time.

Marty's very startled response when I later shared the story stopped me dead in my tracks. "That's, funny, cause ya told me that ya mama said that ya wouldn't bleed on ya weddin' night 'cause ya hurt yaself riding a boy's bike." I was really confused. I'd experienced some memory loss with the seizures, and I didn't remember that conversation at all. "Yeah, ya mama already had this talk with ya, don't ya remember?" No, I surely did not recall. I wanted to ask Mama more but it was such an uncomfortable topic that I just let it drop.

In spite of his obvious reluctance, we went forward with the ceremony. I made my wedding dress, a short white cotton A-line with a flowered ribbon under the bust. Marty's family attended the service at the campus chapel but Mama and Daddy didn't bother. And, even though Catherine was there with Luke, I had mixed feelings about the absence of my parents. As in the past, I feared what their presence might mean. Thinking of Daddy's drunkenness and possible crude remarks or Mama's psychotic episodes gave me the chills. I was much safer if they stayed away. Still, a tiny part of me wanted them to share my big day.

Marty and I repeatedly referred to our honeymoon as a vacation; after all, we'd been living together for a while and there didn't really seem to be anything to get overly excited about. Sure, I was happy that we were finally married, but I couldn't escape that nagging little voice that told me our relationship would not improve all by itself. In fact, if I were brutally honest with myself in the quietest of moments, I'd have to admit that things would probably get worse.

We qualified for subsidized housing on campus and I loved it. Even though it really was nothing more than a small cement cube, it had separate rooms unlike my previous studio apartment. Two miniscule bedrooms formed the rear wall, with a tiny kitchen and living room near the entrance. The walls were painted cinder block and the floor were cement covered with hard linoleum. We had an end unit, directly across from train tracks, which suited us just fine. We enjoyed having no neighbor on one side.

I often didn't get home until nearly ten o'clock on the days I worked the evening shift. I was always pure-dee exhausted by that time. Phenobarbital - prescribed for epileptic seizures - made me tired most of the time. I went to bed tired and woke up the same way. Marty became very hurt, especially when I was too fatigued to be intimate. He took it personally and thought I just didn't want to be with him. I knew my body couldn't do one more thing that required even the slightest drop of energy but deep down inside I also had to admit that it didn't feel right with Marty anymore. We'd only been married a short period of time; how could I feel that way? He must not have truly understood what was going on with me, even though he was told about the side effects of the medication. Just a few months in and our marriage was already on the rocks.

The heat and high humidity only fueled our agitation with one another. Without air conditioning we often had trouble staying inside during the day and at night we were forced to use an old noisy box fan to stir the hot air. Often times, I went to bed before Marty while he watched TV in the tiny living room only steps away. Trying my hardest to fall asleep before he came to bed, I hoped he would get the clue that I just couldn't exert myself. Too often however, our connection (or lack of it) disintegrated into quarrels.

I quickly learned that there was no sanctity in marriage, only constant arguments. I had not escaped the horror of the Schroders; I didn't understand why it had insisted on following me like a dark thundercloud.

CHAPTER FOURTEEN

Payback Hell

During our fourth year of marriage I left Marty.

He became increasingly frustrated with me; my fatigue had created numerous problems, some too big to correct. I simply could no longer be with him. I knew that I had to leave yet going filled me with a deep sense of loss. There would be a hole in my heart in which my relationship with Marty once lived.

Even though he appeared shocked when I announced my plans, I knew this was the precise moment he'd dreaded for some time. The very thing Marty wanted - a loving relationship – had become elusive. I wanted the same thing and yet couldn't manage it, either. He begged me not to go. It broke my heart but I knew nothing would change if I stayed. He implored my forgiveness, but by then, my desire to try again had waned.

Unbeknownst to him I'd found a small apartment in another part of town. I was serious this time and he knew it. I felt numb as I packed a bag of only the most necessary items. "I'll be back for my other things later." With that, I turned and walked out of the most painful relationship I could imagine, outside of living at home with Daddy, that is. I had to prove my courage by leaving.

Tears clouded my vision as I tossed my duffle bag into the car. Don't look back, I told myself - *don't look back!* As desperately as I wanted to keep my eyes straight ahead, I quickly glanced into my side mirror. What I saw took years to dissolve; a tall, skinny man-boy with shoulders drooping, head slightly bent and tears streaming down his face. He was the shell of a wounded young man who'd just lost his first love.

I desperately tried not to feel sorry for Marty. Even with all failed attempts at happiness, I ached for his pain. Yet I needed all the steam I could muster to go through with the separation. I had things to do - big things - like setting up my new place and getting my life in order. But mostly, I had to heal.

The imbalance created by being thrown out of my childhood home had not be corrected by marrying Marty. Because he was so different from Daddy in so many ways, I truly thought my spirit would be resurrected.

(When Daddy was mad enough to hit me, it didn't seem to bother him that I was his own flesh and blood. His piercing brown eyes were emotionless and fixed on the target of his fury - which was almost exclusively me. He never cried and no sign of pain ever shown on his face. His movements were robotic and stiff.

Remembering Catherine's comment about the time Daddy viciously "punched me in the head repeatedly until I temporarily lost my sight", I was struck by what felt like the degree of bad luck in my life. It would take many years to come to understand my role in each relationship and that luck – good or bad – had played no part.)

My new home was situated right next to a food store and I liked the ease with which I could walk over to pick up small items. Within days of moving in, I met the day manager, who was always very polite to me. We chatted a bit more each time I placed my items on the counter and I began to find him interesting. He had long curly brown hair, a mustache and large beard and seemed to be somewhat older than me. He was from New York City, which may as well have been another country as far as my almost non-existent life travels were concerned. I was intrigued by his accent and loved hearing him speak.

After knowing him for a few months, I finally gathered the courage to invite him to dinner. I'd been to the store, chatted with him a bit and then left. It was a cold afternoon and I was cooking chili when I got the idea to call him with an invitation. I was lonely and had been refusing Marty's calls.

"Quinton, this is Connie. How ya doin'?" Instead of giving him a chance to respond, I quickly continued, "Hey, I'm makin' a big pot of chili; wanna come have some with me when ya get off?" The pause made my heart race. I was not accustomed to asking men out and it was very possible he'd say no. How embarrassing would that be? I thought he liked me by the way he always took time to chat, but then he was friendly with everybody.

"Hi, Connie! Well, sure, I can come over later. I get off at seven tonight. Is that okay?" I couldn't believe my ears! He said YES, and it was pretty damn easy. Well, well, well.

Hanging up the phone, I was filled with anxious excitement. I told myself that I wasn't looking for a boyfriend but I had to admit there was a void in my life. I wanted to be appreciated by someone, maybe even loved. I needed to put my failed relationship with Marty behind me and making new friends would help me do just that.

The doorbell rang and my heart jumped up into my throat. I never had visitors; I normally didn't want them. That day was to be different. It was the new me. I took one last look in the mirror and then opened the door. "Hi," Quinton said in a very cheery tone. He handed me a bottle of wine and a loaf of freshly baked French bread. "I thought this might go well with the chili; hope it's okay." His manners impressed me. I wasn't used to it, but I could really grow to like it.

Placing the bread on the counter I reached for two glasses in the upper cabinet. Suddenly, I realized I didn't own wine glasses. The best I could produce were two similar, six-ounce juice glasses.

"Sorry," I said with a frown on my face. With a large, friendly grin, Quinton teased, "Aw, it's okay, wine tastes the same no matter what ya drink it from." I was relieved by his casual attitude. Quinton's disarmingly easy manner invited me to relax a little, but just a little. Although I was still very nervous being around a man I didn't know all that well, I was grateful for his presence.

As the evening went on, we exchanged life stories and I found out more about the person sitting across from me. We ate slowly as I found out that he'd been married once many years ago in New York. As suspected, he was older than me but even more than I figured. Almost twenty years my senior, he had a kindly disposition toward my current situation. He didn't say a negative word about Marty, instinctively knowing when it was better to listen than to speak.

Compared to my youth and the time I spent with Marty, Quinton seemed so normal. I gently asked why a guy his age worked at a convenience store. I silently mused that, even in my early twenties, I'd gotten fairly good jobs with decent salaries. After getting to know him a little better, I could tell he was very intelligent and had street smarts. Being a manager at a convenience store would not likely offer him the opportunity to live up to his full potential.

His answer made sense. He'd only just moved to Baton Rouge from New York City. He needed a job right away to cover his basic living expenses. He'd found a nice apartment and got a roommate immediately. Now, he said, with rent paid he'd applied for the type of job that would make full use of his credentials. We all have to do what we have to do, he said.

∞ ∞ ∞

The following Monday was a big day at work for me. My new boss, Bill Johnson, was a chubby unattractive man with a slight bit of red hair and thick freckles across the bridge of his nose. He invited me to go into New Orleans to take a tour of the brand new, yet-to-be-opened Superdome, somehow making it seem pertinent to my job. It was the talk of the town; a giant dome that sat thousands of people and had artificial turf on the playing field - an exciting addition for fans of Big Easy sports of all kinds. I was eager to see it before the general public, as though somehow that made me special. He suggested that I ride with him since it would be a quick trip.

At the end of the tour, Bill thanked the guide and ushered me back to his car, an older Lincoln. "Ya hungry?" I was starting to feel weak but more from the excitement from the new experience than from hunger. When I was having an extreme experience of any kind – happiness, anger or discovery – I seemed to get weak. "Blood sugah" - that's what Linda's older sis said. I promised myself I would try to find a book about the topic, but for now, food would do the trick.

Bill spun the shiny steering wheel with one gliding movement and headed further into downtown New Orleans. "Have ya ever eaten' at the Royal Sonesta on Bourbon Street?" The only thing I knew about the Royal Sonesta, I responded, was that it was a fancy hotel in town. By the time he'd told me about a few of the meals he'd enjoyed at that fine establishment we pulled into valet parking directly in front of the hotel entrance. With full authority he politely, yet firmly, commanded the young man to park his car. He walked over to open my door and grabbed my arm, which made me feel weird. I didn't know

Bill all that well and I immediately realized by the way the hair stood up on the back of my neck that I didn't like his touch. We were seated rather quickly.

"Connie, what would ya like to drink? I think I'll have a rum and coke." I wasn't a drinker, so I asked for a diet cola. "What!" Bill scowled at me. "No! Come on, let's kick back a little and have a *real* drink!" I wasn't prepared to booze it up with Bill, that was for sure but I figured having one drink would be the courteous thing to do. I'd had gin and tonic once a few years ago and remembered that it was sweet, something I could easily nurse throughout lunch.

Our meal was delivered and Bill ordered drink after drink, not only for himself but also for me. I kept saying no but continued to sip on them. By the time lunch was over I was dizzier than a loon and I was afraid that I wouldn't be able to walk a straight line. Bill, paying close attention to that fact, suggested we get a room so I could lie down a while – at least until I was no longer feeling so woozy. Even in an intoxicated state I was able to recognize what was going on.

"No thanks, I just wanna go home. Take me home, please." I felt anxious. Even somewhat drunk, I didn't like where this was heading. If Bill got me into a room there'd be no telling what could happen. He persisted a bit more but finally gave up. I acted as though I'd never expected any other outcome.

Dizzy, I laid my head back. Abruptly, I felt his hands on my breasts and tried to push him away but my arms felt glued to the seat. I tried to yell but nothing came out. Everything was swirling so fast; panic coursed through me as I contemplated jumping out of the car. Just as suddenly as it happened, it stopped. I lifted my head to see Bill driving with both hands on the steering wheel. Had he really touched me or was I hallucinating? Had I had another prophetic vision?

Back at Bill's office, I got out of the car so fast it startled him.

"Well, gotta get goin'. Thanks." I slammed the door incredibly hard, trying to deliver a serious message. For the time being, and in the interest of job security, I thought I should convey my anger without words. As I walked to my door, I promised myself that I would immediately begin looking for another job.

Over the next several weeks I saw Quinton more frequently. We went to the movies and dinner. We were both on a budget but it didn't matter; we always had fun together. He liked to cook the food of his heritage and I liked to eat it. Mama Rispoli taught him well and I secretly thanked her each time he laid a steaming-hot plateful of Italian food in front of me. I enjoyed eating more than ever before. Mrs. Guilbeau was a fantastic cook but her crankiness sometimes lingered in the kitchen, sometimes taking the sweetness out of the meal. The love that Quinton stirred into his food nourished my heart and my soul. Even though I'd never felt that sort of warmness, I knew it must be a good thing - maybe even love.

Marty continued to call me, but a little less often. Once upon a time I had loved him very much but our constant bickering eventually tainted my already-contaminated perception of love. He continually asked me if I was dating; I hesitated answering directly. I didn't want to hurt him yet I needed him to know it was over between us. I was pretty sure that I could never live with him again.

With the wind howling more than usual, I told Marty about Quinton over the phone. We'd become friends, I said. Sure, I was lonely, and I didn't intend to live like a hermit.

"He's just usin' ya! Can't ya see that, Connie?!" With all that I'd just shared with him, it floored me that he chose to go to that place. "What?! Did ya hear anything I just said?" Marty was persistent. "Yeah, I heard ya, all right. But, I'm tellin' ya Connie, he just wants one thing an' ya just plain stupid if ya can't see that!"

With that, I gently laid the receiver back in its cradle. I could hear Marty's protests even with the final click. The physical space between us was just what I needed. I was free and I felt better every minute we were apart. Actually, way better than I'd ever felt in my entire life.

He didn't call again for eight weeks.

Life was easy with Quinton. There was no competitiveness between us. We were so much more compatible than Marty and I had ever been, even with the age difference. I began to calm down around Quinton. The more I could come to rely on his steady disposition, the more I could relax and just be myself. Granted, I was still trying to figure out just who that was, but with Quinton there was no hurry. He never thought poorly of me for trying.

Living with more abandon than I'd known before, my spirit soared. My relationship with Quinton grew and deepened as we continued to enjoy each other. Nothing was too taboo to discuss as we reveled in togetherness. Quinton's own free spirit rejoiced when we flew. I thought of Marty less and less.

Marty called unexpectedly one night while Quinton was at my place. I almost didn't answer the phone, figuring it was him, but since Mama lived out of town I felt obliged to take the call. "Hello?" I said hesitantly. "Connie, this is Marty. Whatcha doin'? I need to talk to ya about something." My body tensed as I struggled to find the right thing to say. Sensing whom I was speaking with, Quinton reached over and gently rubbed my arm. Bless his heart for being so incredibly understanding. "Marty, I'm busy now, I can't talk." Now it was Marty who was anxious.

"Listen, I want ya to give me another chance, Connie. I love ya, girl, an' I never meant ya no harm. I know I acted bad an' I can't take that back, but I *swear* I'll treat ya good from now on." How many times had I heard that? Dammit, why did he insist on getting me back when he seemed so dissatisfied while I was with him? Some things never changed, like Daddy's drinking or Mama's breakdowns. Jesus H. Christ, I wanted transformation in my life and as near as I could tell, *I had* changed. Maybe that's part of the reason why Marty seemed more concerned each time I spoke with him. He likely sensed that the more I shifted, the less I'd want him in my life. He was dead right about that.

"He can't love ya the way I love ya an' *ya know that!* He's just usin' ya!" His voice was strained and high-pitched. Quinton once again reassured me by lightly squeezing my arm. "Listen, Marty, I don't wanna go back. I can't go back."

His heavy sigh gave away his frustration. It had been almost eleven months since I left Marty; Quinton and I had been seeing each other for nearly six months. I could survive without Marty and I'd proven that to myself, even if he wanted me to believe otherwise. Quinton's gentle kindness was more than enough to help me see that there was life after Marty.

CHAPTER FIFTEEN

The Tears that Water the Garden

"Marty, what're ya doin'?" I was anxious about making the call. I didn't want to reconcile with him but I was worried about him after our last conversation.

Instead of a further talk by phone he asked me to meet him at the Brasserie Pub near campus. As much as I didn't want to admit to it, I guess I really did want to see him again. He was my first love and there was no denying that it was powerful. It usually hit me when I was alone and mostly as I was trying to fall to sleep. A deep, aching sensation filled with the most intense loneliness would engulf me, leaving no room for reason. I couldn't get the sound of Marty's pleas out of my head. I had cried so much in my life; I was used to the sound of my own pain. But hearing the raw soreness of Marty's wounded heart tore me up. I couldn't deny the guilt and I wasn't so sure that I should try.

Feeling agitated by the constraint of my heavy coat, I clumsily tripped over a brass spittoon near the entrance. It was late Saturday afternoon and the place was packed. Marty caught me by my shoulders and attentively asked if I was all right. Honestly, I didn't know what to say to him even after all that had happened since I left him. Of course, most of what had happened for me was that I met and became very fond of another man. He surely didn't want to hear about that.

"So how's ya boyfriend?" In shock, my eyes traveled up the entire height of his lanky body. "What?" "How's ya boyfriend?" Still fumbling for the right words, I said, "Aw, Marty, I didn't come here to talk about that. I just came to see how ya doin'." His movements were steady as he carefully replied, "Well, that's what I need to know 'bout, Connie. Are ya in love with this guy?" Feeling ridiculous for not preparing myself, I wished I were anywhere but there.

"Look, Marty, I told ya the truth, but I never planned on givin' ya details. That's my business an' ya know it." My resistance didn't slow him down. The way his nostrils flared told me that he was on a mission. As his impatience grew, my refusal to go along with his line of questioning did, as well. It seemed ridiculous talking about Quinton with Marty.

"Connie, I need to know if there's a chance with ya or not. If there ain't a chance, then I'm gonna start datin' again myself." I was actually relieved to hear him say that. The thought of him with another woman made me shudder a little, but I sensed that my support was the only way he'd back off. I was wrong; my outward lack of jealousy seemed to confound Marty. If I'd shown any upset over his comment, he may have felt there was a slight glimmer of hope so I was very careful and conscious of every word I said. My feeble plan failed miserably.

"Dammit Connie, I can't believe it's all over between us. Just give me one more chance. I *swear*, I'll make it right." It was hard for me to look directly into his eyes. What I saw chipped away at something I'd buried years before, long before I even met him. Maybe his pain was stirring a resurrection in me. But of what? It had a haunted feeling, all cold and jagged. It was a hollow place, a frightening, lonely spot and a place familiar to me somehow. The sockets that cradled his large blue eyes seemed to open up. What surrounded his eyeballs scared the crap out of me. It was vague and abstract, yet very vivid, but I could not grab words for the vision. I felt Daddy and Mama there. Chills traveled the length of my spine - three times, maybe more.

I attempted to move away from Marty but my feet felt glued to the wood floor. I tried again – nothing. My throat was so dry it began to throb. I had to tell myself to swallow. Needing more than anything to pull away from Marty's glare, I tried to will myself out of the room. If I could just jump out of my body, this would be over and done with. Unfortunately, my will simply could not overcome the moment.

God, I wished Quinton were there with me; I felt safe with him. He'd planted a garden where my thoughts and feelings flourished and I adored him for that. He was so much smarter than me and I was blooming under the gentle rain of his love. I'd never experienced anything remotely close to that before. I'd made headway since Quinton came into my life and I wasn't about to give that up.

"Connie!" I vaguely heard my name being called and it seemed to pull me forward. "Connie, are ya alright? What's wrong with ya?" I blinked several times, as if to wash the windshield of my mind. Marty's outline was fuzzy but finally grew clearer. Reaching up to rub my eyes, I asked, "What's goin' on?" Looking completely baffled, he said, "I don't know. One minute ya standin' here talkin' to me, then ya faded out. Like when ya had those seizures." I had trouble keeping up with his words. He pulled a barstool closer to me and helped me sit.

I needed to lie down. Marty offered to drive me but I refused. All I wanted was to be in my bed – alone. Marty's expression told me that he was genuinely concerned about me

143

so I agreed to let him follow me home. Once secure in my own place, I fell into bed. I was so tired I could barely keep my eyes open. Managing to crawl under the blankets, I fell into a deep sleep that would last over thirteen hours.

I may have continued to sleep if the phone hadn't rung. "Hello?" I must've sounded like I was hung over. "Connie, I was worried about ya!" Quinton, who generally had a happy upbeat tone, sounded very serious. "I've been calling ya all morning. Connie, I was *WORRIED* about ya!" I was trying hard to pull my thoughts back into focus so I could respond to Quinton in a reasonable way. I surely didn't want him to worry about me, but I had trouble sounding normal – even I could tell that.

"What's wrong, Connie? I've been calling ya since eight this morning. Were ya up late last night?" I struggled to remember the evening before. "No, I don't think so." This confused him even more. "What do ya mean, ya don't think so? Connie, can I come over right now? I need to see ya to make sure ya all right."

It felt like something had crawled up inside me and died. I must have been as still as a corpse while I slept; the way I laid down was exactly the way I woke up. My hair was plastered straight up on my right side and black mascara was smeared at the corner of my right eye. With little time to freshen up, I brushed my teeth, tried to flatten my hair with a wet comb and wiped the mascara from under my eyes.

As I gazed through the peephole, I saw Quinton fidgeting outside my door. He usually made a silly face, knowing I always looked before opening my door. No sooner than I greeted him, he rushed in closing the door behind him. "Let me look at ya." I'd never seen him so serious before that moment. "Aw, Quinton, I'm okay - really." My weak voice and low energy were not convincing and we both knew it.

"What the hell happened to ya?!" Quinton rarely, maybe

never, took such a tone with me, but now he insisted upon an answer. He had the look of a concerned parent. His words came out so forcefully that I instinctively leaned away.

Realizing he may have come on too strong, Quinton immediately softened. He guided me to the kitchen table, saying, "Honey, sit here with me and tell me what happened last night. I need to know, okay." His gentle way always made me feel safe and I was happy to tell him anything he wanted to know. "Well, I went to talk to Marty at the Brasserie Pub yesterday. He'd been soundin' so bad lately, I needed to make sure he was all right. Ya understand?" Without waiting for Quinton's response, I continued. "He axed me 'bout ya an' tried to tell me that all ya want is to have sex with me – that's all! I was shocked that he even axed an' it threw me off."

By now, Quinton's face was solemn. My guess was that he never expected me to see Marty, at least not without telling him first. As he attempted to hide his disappointment, he tried to keep the focus on what I was saying. I went on, "Then, all of a sudden, I felt like something started to suck me into, well, like a cave. But, I *know* that's impossible, Quinton. *I know that.* But before I knew it, I was in this place that was dark an' cold."

No doubt, Quinton had trouble understanding my story but he also knew I was not one to tell tall tales. My life had been very solemn and he knew that. Hell, I didn't have to make up anything; my own past could have been a best-selling horror story.

"Connie, slow down a little. I'm with ya, honey, but I need to make real sure I hear everything ya saying. I *want* to understand what happened." The pitch of his voice rose slightly as he emphasized his desire to truly comprehend my experience. Nobody had ever cared for me like that. He was a jewel and at that time in my life he shown brighter than anybody or anything else.

"Here let's put this blanket around ya shoulders; ya shivering." I was suddenly very, very cold, yet he noticed before I did. Reaching to pull the bedspread tighter around my shoulders, I continued. "I swear, Quinton, it was like I was sucked right into Marty's eyes. I KNOW that sounds crazy, but it's TRUE! It's like all of his pain tried to jump inside of me."

I wasn't even scratching the surface of what I'd really experienced but there just weren't words for it. How in the world could I explain something so crazy? And how could Quinton understand it even if I could find the precise words? Feeling extremely drained, I slumped forward. I was afraid that I might fall right off the chair. Quinton reached for me by my shoulders and helped me to bed. I could see the concerned look on his face but I didn't have the energy to say even one consoling word. I was used to being the one who looked after others – Mama, Catherine, and then Luke. It was a completely new experience to be cared for so lovingly.

Two days later, I awoke to the morning sun beaming through the elevated window in my bedroom. As soon as I became cognizant of the day, I jumped out of bed with nothing more than the fuel of a pounding heart. How on earth had I slept so long? Jesus, what would my boss say about me simply not showing up for work without even so much a phone call? DAMMIT! I was in big trouble and my first response was that I would surely lose my job. What about the rent, my car payment and the utility bills? JESUS, I was in trouble and besides myself.

The phone rang. The high-pitched shrill nearly made me jump out of my skin. What if it were my boss? Oh God, what would I tell him? I wouldn't blame him for firing me. Who'd want an employee who sleeps for two days straight with no regard for anything else?

"Hello?" I said as meekly as humanly possible. "Connie? How are ya feeling?" THANK GOD, it was Quinton. "QUINTON!

146

I've been sleepin' for two whole days without gettin' up once. I didn't go to work or do anything!" He could hear the panic in my voice and immediately responded. "Honey, don't worry, I called ya boss and told him ya had an awful flu and that because of a fever ya were sleeping non-stop." Then with a slight chuckle, he added, "He was glad that ya stayed away because he certainly didn't want to catch what ya had." Still running off pure adrenaline, I was trying to calm down. Thank God and all the angels above for Quinton. Maybe *he* was one of those guardian angels I'd always prayed to but hadn't met.

Hours turned into days and days turned into weeks. The terrifying event at the Brasserie Pub seemed to blur into the batch of all the other dreadful things I'd experienced during the previous years of my life. Marty began calling more often. I wanted with all my heart and soul to be free of him, but each time he called I felt his gut-wrenching agony. No longer able to hold up under such pain, I finally agreed to go back to him. It was not a happy decision and it did not warrant a celebration. I was in love with Quinton, a good and gentle man. But I did not know how to live a happy life while Marty was so miserable. *Yes*, he brought about his own pain and that was clear to see. But each time he expressed his love for me and the mournful regret of pushing me away, I broke down a little more. Finally, during a late-night phone conversation I told Marty that I would return to him.

Tortured by my own decision and the thought of having to tell Quinton, I lost sleep night after night. Sure, Marty was happy; he would get what he wanted but I would have to give up what I had found. Yet the compulsion to return to my marriage was so strong that I was willing to give up my love for another. With no knowledge of how to separate guilt from love I made my way to Quinton's apartment to tell him of my decision.

Knowing my tears were a dead giveaway, I hurriedly wiped my face with the back of my hand. I'd mentioned Marty's calls to Quinton and no doubt he could see my resistance had worn thin.

"Can I come in?" My voice was thin. Quinton smiled broadly. "Connie, hi! Sure come in, baby." He gently laid his arm across my shoulders as we walked side by side into the living room. I was acutely aware of every sound, like the way the olive shag carpet crunched under our feet and even the subtle sound of our shallow breathing. I was sure that he could hear my heart pounding. We sat on the sofa, very near each other.

"Quinton, I have to tell ya something." My voice was trembling and the words came out all crackly. Before I could get out another word, I saw a huge tear roll down the left side of his face. "Oh my God, Quinton, please don't cry, *please!*" My heart was crumbling into a million pieces yet I had to say what needed saying. I sat on the floor in front of him as he remained on the sofa. "Ya know that I love ya more than I ever loved another man, don't ya? Ya been so kind an' good to me – always. Ya show me that ya love me in so many ways." He was fully crying now, not even trying to hide his pain. He covered his eyes with his large hands as if maybe it would all just go away. I was no stranger to that sort of wish.

"Quinton, I just can't stand Marty's pain. We were married for four years. Maybe that's too much to throw away. I know I don't love him the way I love ya, Quinton, but I can't stand it anymore. Maybe if I go back I'll come to see that it won't work for sure. Then I can leave for good. If ya still wanna be with me, then we can be together. I know this all sounds crazy but I can't take the guilt any more, Quinton, I *just can't take it!* Can ya understand?"

Though I was not sure that he could decipher my words

through my sobs, I knew Quinton was not the kind of man to stand in my way. I was terrified that I might be losing the greatest gift I'd ever been given. If there was a God, He delivered Quinton to me. How, then, could I give him back? Was I mentally insane? I was so confused; it tormented me to sit before Quinton's agony. I rose to my knees and wrapped my arms around his trembling body. This gentle giant had a broken heart and *I* was the cause. I hated myself! I'd never intended to hurt him; in fact, I wanted to be with him for the rest of my life. He was my kind guide, a precious man who thought enough of me to hold my needs and desires in a place of real importance. I was coldhearted and I was vividly aware that I might never forgive myself for hurting this beautiful soul. If I could just get the sound of Marty's pleas out of my head, I might be able to stay with Quinton. I *would* stay with Quinton. Sadly, I could not erase the sights that, like angry ghosts, haunted me for a very long time to come. I was a weak person and I let my pity for Marty steal away my love for Quinton. And now, Quinton would have to suffer for my cowardice.

Maybe I didn't truly deserve a good man like him and I told Quinton so. "NO, THAT'S NOT TRUE, CONNIE! *DON'T SAY THAT!*" He was so adamant, but why? I wished he would get mad at me and kick me out. I didn't deserve his love. I hurt him. I despised myself! I *was* worthless and I would *never* amount to anything just as Daddy told me over and over.

We held each other for what seemed like hours, crying, sometimes deeply and other times, softly. Saying goodbye was agonizing. I'd already lost two very important males in my life – but that was Daddy's doing. Ricky's absence was never overcome and having baby Luke ripped away from me left an indelible mark on my heart.

And now, because of my own decision, I was releasing Quinton. How could I have fallen so low? I wanted to stay away from Marty, I truly did. Yet it was like a gigantic magnet pulling me back to him. I fought it for as long as I could, telling myself that I'd done the right thing. But by then, my resolve was weakening.

"Connie, are ya completely sure that this is what ya want?" He choked the words out one at a time and very slowly. "Jesus, Quinton. I don't know! I know how I feel 'bout ya. I know how guilty I feel 'bout Marty. I might still love him, but not the same way I love ya. I don't know if ya can love two people at one time. I'm not even sure what love is. But I do know how I feel when I'm with ya. I always feel safe an' good inside. I haven't felt that way with him."

As I spoke, I was acutely aware of my own words. I was admitting that I wasn't even sure if I loved Marty and that guilt was the driving force for the reconciliation. While I understood that maybe I truly didn't comprehend the true meaning of love, I was aware that I'd never felt better than when I was with Quinton. Dammit! I wanted out of my own body so badly that I feared my skin would rip.

CHAPTER SIXTEEN

Expired Rabbit

As I knocked on Marty's door, a million thoughts raced through my exhausted mind. I hadn't slept the night before as a feeling of uncertainty churned and rolled deep inside.

"Connie!" He was clearly happy to see me, obviously way more than the other way around. I knew one thing for sure - my pity for Marty was so strong that it flat-out stole me away from Quinton.

"Marty, I've come home." The intensity of the realization that I no longer had anything to look forward to; the knowledge that every day would be exactly like the one before; the fact that part of my spirit had to die in order to tolerate my life, well, that washed over me like boiling oil. I felt weak at the knees and had to sit.

Jumping out of my body was the only way to get through the day; leaving was the only way to stay.

From above, I witnessed the exchange. Marty sat down next to me and put his lanky arm around me. He was happy, for sure. Seeing the paleness in my cheeks he wanted to comfort me, but didn't ask why I was so ashen. My pain seemed to of no concern to him, until, of course it drove me away. Then it became his mission to retrieve what he'd lost.

My heart ached. Just like when I left Marty, I felt an overbearing amount of guilt for leaving Quinton, knowing how much pain it caused. I didn't dare call him though I had to fight myself to abstain. I wasn't sure Quinton would even want to talk to me and I couldn't blame him if he didn't. The risk he took on love - on me - had paid off, but only for a while. He was so happy when we were together. Quinton's eyes shone and he opened his heart to me in a way that I'd never experienced. God, I missed him more than words could say. Sometimes, when Marty caught me teary-eyed I'd brush it off to something silly. I couldn't tell him how I really felt. He probably knew but we never talked about it - unless he was feeling particularly insecure - then he'd throw it in my face. I always responded in the same way, reassuring Marty that I loved *him* and that's why I came home. But each argument chipped away at my resolve - and my will to stay. I couldn't deny it; I was miserable. I promised myself that I'd give serious thought to leaving again *for good*. I couldn't imagine spending my entire life with Marty, no more than I'd ever been able to swallow the hopeless thought of living with Mama and Daddy. Comparing the two, I had to admit that I'd spent most of my life feeling hopeless - until Quinton. He changed everything for me and I missed him terribly. More than ever, I needed him.

Ten months after my return, I awoke feeling very nauseous in the middle of the night. Rising from bed in the darkness, I began to feel woozy within seconds of standing. Because I couldn't see my surroundings, I instinctively reached out to find something to support my body. The wall was right in front of me but I was disoriented. I could feel the blood draining from my head and realized I was going to faint. Standing as close to the wall as possible, gravity pulled my body to the floor with a hard thump. A sharp pain stabbed at the base of my spine just before I lost consciousness; I had no idea how long I was out. Grogginess clouded my brain as I tried to wake up. Marty didn't stir.

Lifting my body cautiously, I hobbled to Marty's side of the bed. Shaking him gently at first, then harder when he didn't respond, I called his name. In an irritated daze, he asked, "What's the matter, Connie?" I felt a sharp pain in my back.

I couldn't hold back the tears. I was frightened. I'd never experienced such a thing and I was afraid something was terribly wrong.

Restlessness set in as I laid next to Marty. The fainting scared me and I told him so. In his typical manner, he just brushed it off as nothing and resumed sleeping while I was stuck in painful darkness with nothing but fearful thoughts circling my head. Once again, I was trapped in a shadowy corner and it was to be a long, lonely night.

A week later, I couldn't help but notice that my period was late. The prospect of pregnancy left me weak.

I continued to think of Quinton often but tried to push those thoughts away. Nothing had really changed between Marty and me. I had recurrent nightmares, different sagas, but always filled with deep regret.

I mailed a urine specimen to a local lab. Sherry and Matt, the couple who lived next door, were visiting on the day I was to call for the results. I suppose I should've waited until they had gone but I couldn't stand the suspense. Marty was talking with them in the dining room while I dialed the number in the living room. I quietly and mannerly gave my name and waited nervously while the nurse checked the records.

"Mrs. Guilbeau," the all-too-chipper voice began. "It shows here that the rabbit died." Dead silence. I wasn't exactly sure what that meant. "What?" My voice cracked even though I tried hard to sound calm. "Ya pregnant, Mrs. Guilbeau." Nobody called me that. My body went cold. How could this possibly be happening? I was not ready to be a mama. I'd always been deathly afraid of anything medical and I feared I wouldn't do well with labor and childbirth. Sherry, trying to eavesdrop the entire time I was on the phone, looked at me with great curiosity. "Well?" she said as I laid the receiver back into the cradle. I could barely say it out loud - that would make it true. "WELL?" She couldn't wait to hear what she already suspected.

"Yep, we're gonna have a baby." Marty stopped talking instantly and glared at me. I couldn't tell if he was happy or mad. Matt looked at Marty, Marty looked at me and Sherry looked at Matt. More unbearable silence and then, "YAHOO!" He jumped in the air, kicking his heels. Matt stood and slapped him on the back, yelling his congratulations. Sherry's hearty giggle was infectious but her heartfelt hug was only slightly reassuring. Everyone seemed happy but me. It's not that I wouldn't adore a baby of my own. I already knew of my capacity to love an infant from my days with little Luke. I couldn't have loved him more if he were my natural-born child; that wasn't my quandary. The hitch was that I now felt more cornered than before; our marriage was on shaky ground and in no way were we prepared to be parents.

I called Mama the next day to share our news. She didn't waste much time telling me that she'd had very quick labors with each of her five pregnancies. "Once I have two labor pains, I get ya daddy to bring me to the hospital. He learned over the years to listen to me an' he knows to come home from work right away so that I don't have that baby right there on the kitchen floor." She let out a joyless laugh and I heard her take a long deep drag on her cigarette.

Fatigue and lower back pain plagued me during the first three months of pregnancy but I somehow escaped morning sickness. The only time I thought I might throw up was early on when I decided I should drink milk. Mind you, I never drank it, but motherhood urged me to be aware of what I was putting into my system. Dry heaves left a mark on my mind; I would have to get extra calcium some other way.

Though I didn't even look pregnant until my sixth month, I felt pregnant the entire time. I loved having larger breasts except that the swelling was painful at times. The skin covering my stomach was taught and shiny. Sherry repeatedly and with great urgency advised me to use cocoa butter to avoid stretch marks. She seemed mighty wise about pregnancy for a woman who'd not experienced it herself. But it always sounded right, so if I could do what she suggested, I did. I gave up smoking and drinking coffee. It wasn't as difficult as I feared; my baby's health made the sacrifice completely worth it. I'd smoked for at least ten years off and on but I couldn't bear the thought of smoke filling up the tiny lungs of my unborn child. No, he needed every advantage possible before he ever took his first breath. Having Marty and me for parents would be challenge enough.

When it came time to be seen by a physician, I met Dr. Patricia Gilmore, who practiced at Earl K. Long Hospital. She was a gentle young woman in her early thirties. "Call me Patricia," she invited during my first exam. She was in her last year as an intern and I felt very lucky to be assigned to her. She was so caring and easy to be around, although her tight schedule didn't allow her the time she really wanted with each patient. She continued to assure me that the pregnancy was moving along fine and that baby was healthy and growing appropriately. I got over my embarrassment of having to go to the charity hospital because of Patricia. She assured me that teaching hospitals had some of the finest physicians around. I believed in - and trusted - her.

Everyone told me that I would have a boy but I didn't need their input to know it was true. I could feel his little body as the months wore on and I knew by his strong kicks that this was no girl. I bought a baby name book and poured over it every day. After saying out loud many name combinations, I hit upon the name 'Tyler'. Tyler Guilbeau. Ty Guilbeau. Mr. Tyler Guilbeau. Yes, it has a nice ring. Then, a middle name. Scott? No, we knew a Scott and didn't particularly like him. Drew? Nope. Douglas. Hmm. Tyler Douglas Guilbeau. Yes. YES! We both liked the name and decided right then and there that our son had a name!

Ty would be a good boy and someday, a great man.

CHAPTER SEVENTEEN

Death Do Us Part

By the time I got the call, Mama and Luke were no longer living with Daddy. Six months prior, and after twenty-seven years of marriage, Mama walked into the kitchen to discover seven-year-old Luke standing on the counter holding the pistol Daddy had hidden on the shelf above the kitchen cabinets. Close to what felt like a heart attack, she reminded Daddy of how she'd made him swear that he would *never* have a gun in the house. After grumbling blatant disregard for her request, he hesitantly agreed but simply hid the gun rather than getting rid of it. That was Daddy, all right. He really didn't give a damn about what Mama wanted.

Luke had done exactly what Mama predicted. He was a climber and staying on the ground never suited him much. She knew that if Daddy hid a gun in the house that Luke would find it. Mama was dead right – as usual. She often seemed to know about things before they happened. After what Mama considered an alarmingly close call, she left Daddy.

After decades of life together, she'd finally gotten up enough nerve to walk out. She and Luke found a small house on the west bank of New Orleans, close to Grandma Kramer.

Being closer to her mother made Mama feel better almost immediately.

∞ ∞ ∞

My relationship with Marty was still strained but in one of our friendlier moments we decided to go on a vacation. We didn't have much money but we convinced ourselves that getting away would do us good. Still in the very early stages of pregnancy, the doctor said it would be okay to go on a road trip. The Smokey Mountains in Tennessee called to Marty; he was Nature's son and loved the mountains. The flatlands of Louisiana could get a bit boring at times and the possibility of cool air and caverns to explore lured us from our home.

Vacation ended one week later and we headed back to Louisiana in our small Chevy. Exhausted, we checked into a motel for the night. The room was old and musty but it was cheap and we were so tired it made very little difference to us. A lamp was clamped onto the bed much like the one Daddy had always read from. He spent many nights reading Westerns as Mama slept next to him. He never seemed concerned that the light might bother her; he probably relied on the fact that her medications rendered her impervious.

The lamp gave me the willies and I told Marty so. Even the bed reminded me of Daddy with its old scratched headboard. Finally falling into an exhausted sleep, I was drawn into a place that had no walls, floor or ceiling. There was nothing but an old bathtub. I was standing at least twenty feet away and felt strangely compelled to go closer.

Drawing nearer, a rich crimson color stood out dramatically against the white porcelain. My eyes were magnetically glued to the tub. Resisting the last few steps, I could not deny what I saw. There, floating face down in a pool of blood was Daddy! OH GOD! What was he doing in my dream that way?

I was mesmerized and repulsed by what I saw. Horrified, I literally forced myself awake. As I dragged myself back into consciousness, I felt dampness on the pillow.

"Marty, wake up!" He stirred. The ticking clock on the nightstand told me that we hadn't been asleep too long.

"What, beb?" Normally, he was groggier than this when he first woke. "Marty, I had a terrible dream 'bout Daddy!" The panic in my voice pulled him all the way into wakefulness. "Come on, Connie. Whatever it is, it's just a dream." He reached over and placed his arm over me.

"NO! It was more than a dream! I saw Daddy face down in a pool of blood! It was SO real, Marty! Let's get outta here. I don't wanna stay here!" Surprisingly, he accommodated my wish without much of a fuss. "Okay, beb, if ya feel that strong 'bout it. But, ya know it's just a dream." On the verge of tears, I jumped out of bed and threw on the same clothes I'd worn the day before. I didn't want to spend one more minute in that horrible room with visions of my dead father.

I didn't talk to Daddy often but when I did, he was always the same nasty alcoholic he'd always been. He'd grown even more pathetic since Mama left him. I actually felt sorry for him living in his one-room shop behind the ice factory. He became even more of a loner, with trips only to the bar and the grocery store.

Climbing into the little station wagon at three in the morning, I was glad to get away from that pit of a hotel. Marty was already calculating how much earlier we'd be getting home.

One month to the day after we returned from Tennessee, I got an early-morning call from Mama. I usually called her; she had so little money that making long distance calls was normally out of the question. I was put on mild alarm as soon as I heard her voice. "Connie, this is Mama. I need to tell ya something. I got a call this mornin'. They found ya daddy dead." The words hung thick in the air. Had I heard her correctly? Did she say *Daddy. Was. Dead? DADDY WAS DEAD!*

"What? Mama, slow down. Tell me again." Mama repeated herself and I heard it clearly that time. "How, when, where?" A nervous excitement shot through my body, rendering me curious as to the feeling. Daddy was an awful black cloud hanging over the Schroder family. He'd done awful things to us when we were kids and secretly at first, then not so privately, I wished for the day of his death. I figured the rest of my family felt much the same, even if Mama always pooh-poohed me when I dared to say it out loud. "Naw, Connie, ya know ya Daddy loves ya most of all." She always floored me with that statement. Did she really believe that? Her words were made of wishful thinking or maybe just plain lies.

Pulling into Mama's short driveway I noticed weeds threatening to overtake the yard. The landlord promised Mama that he'd send someone over to cut her grass on a regular basis, but had fallen short on his word. Seeing the shaggy yard brought me back to the awful conditions Daddy imposed upon us growing up. Mama met me at the door with Luke right behind her. "Where's Marty?" Mama asked immediately, before saying hello.

Luke pushed ahead of Mama, shoving the squeaky screen door wide open and running out to meet me. The door slammed loudly, startling Mama. "Come on in dawlin'," she said in a quiet voice. She seemed oddly calm and I was glad about that. Mama had loved Daddy undeservedly even though he'd mistreated her throughout their entire marriage.

She poured two cups of coffee and put the cream and sugar between us on her small kitchen table. Spinning around in her chair she reached for an unopened pack of cigarettes lying on the counter just behind her. Tapping the top of the pack on her hand, she began to speak. "They found ya Daddy dead in his shop yesterday. They say he had a heart attack an' fell on the floor. When he fell over, he landed on a motor that he was rewirin' an' that cut his throat an' he bled to death."

Mama spoke robotically at first, and then with a little more emotion as her eyes began to tear. "They say he'd been dead for a couple days an' that it wasn't 'till the Cheramie boy went to pick up a motor that he was discovered. He heard the radio playin' and knocked an' knocked but ya Daddy didn't answer. He smelled a foul odor an' that's when he got worried an' got Mr. Estee to open the door. Ya Daddy was lyin' on the floor. They could tell by the look of things that he had been dead a while."

The information was swimming around in my head as I tried to make sense of it all. We all knew that Daddy was in very poor health. Hell, he drank like a fish, ate poorly and smoked like a chimney. How could he live a full life that way? No matter, it was still a shock to hear that it had actually happened. Daddy was dead. The man that had terrorized, beaten and abused me in every way was actually dead. Gone on to another place, most likely Hell. At least he wouldn't be here on Earth to haunt us anymore. "Thank ya, Lord." As I said those words, a pang of grief overtook me. What in the world? Why would I feel any grief over his death? He lived too long as far as I was concerned, so why in the world would I feel pain at his passing?

"Hey, Mama," I began, "was there blood on the floor where they found Daddy?" Suddenly, the dream was in front of me: Daddy floating face down in a bathtub full of blood. "Oh, yeah. Lots of it; he was floatin' in a pool of his own blood."

Jesus H. Christ! I was freaked out. Something weird was happening to me. Why would I see a vision of Daddy's death? I wasn't close to him at all, so why me? Admittedly, things like this had happened before – strange things – but never to this degree. I sort of knew that things would happen before they actually did, but it was never anything so serious. It could be that the car in front of me was going to have a blowout, or that there would be a wreck a few miles ahead, but never anything so serious as a death. Jesus! I wasn't so sure I liked this thing that was happening to me. I would really try hard to stop it from happening again. Somehow, I decided, I would try to block it whatever "it" was.

Obituaries
Schroder, Frederick James
February 13, 1978

Frederick James Schroder, an electrician, died February 13, 1978 of heart failure. He was pronounced dead on the scene in Golden Meadow, La. He was 53. Mr. Schroder was born in New Orleans and lived in Golden Meadow for the past eleven years. Survivors include two sons, Luke and Freddie Schroder; two daughters, Catherine Schroder and Connie Schroder Guilbeau; one brother, Ronald Schroder. A service and burial will be held Friday at noon at the Cut-Off Catholic Church on Highway One.

The obituary didn't mention Mama or Ricky. Ricky had been long gone and Mama and Daddy were separated. I felt bad for Mama. I'd always felt bad for Mama.

The funeral was grim; a priest said a few graveside words about a man he'd never met. There was no gravestone for Daddy; the Veteran's Administration would eventually pay for a modest grave marker but the bureaucracy slowed the process. Mama, Catherine, Luke, Marty and I stood silently as a prayer was said for Daddy. I felt so mixed up inside. A man who by all means would be characterized as an animal had played much too big of a role in my life. Even after he threw me out as a young teen I was not free of him. The anger and deep disappointment stayed with me like a menacing flu bug that just wouldn't let go. It followed me into my jobs, my relationships with other family members and most noticeably, my marriage. Why did I hold onto the fantasy that the most important man in my life would one day wake up and realize that I was a truly good girl? That I was smart and clever and had a big heart? That I was to be protected - not battered? That I was worth loving?

There was no way that I could answer my own questions in that moment and maybe I never would, but that dismal day was the first time that I so vividly took notice of the inquiry. I would look for answers, I vowed. I had no choice. The invisible link between Daddy and me must be broken. I didn't want to live with one foot in his grave.

CHAPTER EIGHTEEN

A Promise Made is a Promise Broken

Near midnight, I turned over in bed to discover I was lying in wetness. Disoriented and somewhat alarmed, I sat up slowly. Swinging my legs over the side of the bed, I held onto the headboard for support. Warm liquid ran down my legs. Hobbling to the bathroom, I placed a large towel between my legs. The fluid was clear – thank God. The sight of blood at that point couldn't have meant anything good.

"Marty, wake up." I shook him lightly so as not to startle him from a deep sleep, but he didn't respond. Shaking him harder, and deepening the tone of my voice, I spoke louder.

"MARTY!" Clearly irritated, he snarled, "WHAT?!" My hormones were on overdrive and his response brought tears to my eyes. "I think my water broke." Sitting up and looking much more like a grouchy old man than his mere twenty-five years, he said, "Whatta ya mean, ya *THINK* ya water broke? Don't ya know?"

No, I did not know for sure, dammit! "I think we need to go to the hospital now, Marty." He was wearing on my nerves, after all I was the one who was getting ready to go into God knows how much pain and try to shoot a baby out into the world. *"Let's go NOW!"*

The nurse in admitting was kind but firm with too many formal questions. "Didja water break? Didja see the mucus plug? Have ya had any contractions yet? If so, how far apart?" JESUS! Trying to answer her questions as fast as she spit them out made me nauseous.

I lowered myself into the wheelchair and felt afraid as the nurse wheeled me down a long dull hallway. The smells were disgusting. Too much antiseptic to cover the urine and other bodily fluid odors made me gag. Since day one of my pregnancy, I was overly sensitive to certain odors.

"How ya feelin', dawlin'?" Up until then, I'd felt fine, except for my frazzled nerves. I had feared this moment for the entire nine months. Even though Mama said she had her babies quickly, I wasn't at ease with the process. I'd made Dr. Patricia promise me that she would administer an epidural to numb the pain. Even that scared me, since I'd heard that the process called for a very long needle injected into your spine. There was no getting out of pain and by then, I just wanted to get it over with.

Still in no pain at that moment, I was beginning to feel better about the upcoming event. Lying back in my bed I used my arms to prop my head on top of the flat pillow. The nurse, seeing my comfortable pose, asked again how I was doing She warned me that the wheels of progress were turning and that I'd begin to feel the pain soon enough. What in the hell did that mean? Was she trying to scare me? Maybe I wasn't like all the others. Within moments, I understood that she knew what she was talking about.

Balled up in the fetal position, I yelled before I could control it. "DAMMIT!" The contractions were already ten minutes apart just forty-five minutes after arriving. "Ya already dilated at four centimeters. Dats good." The contractions were fierce and as soon as each one passed, I was extremely thirsty. The best the nurse could offer was a wet towel for my face. Drinking might cause me to vomit, she said.

Twenty minutes later, when the doctor examined me she discovered that I was dilated eight centimeters. With precision and authority, she ordered the staff to get me ready for delivery. In a panic, I quickly reminded her of her promise to administer the epidural but because of my rapid dilatation it was no longer an option. I would have to deliver naturally - a concept I'd NEVER considered.

"WHAT?!" I was mortified. This was not the deal we made. I did not, *under any circumstances,* want to experience this birth without drugs - and she knew that. I could tell that I sounded like a scared kid, but I didn't give a damn about that. "We need ya to help push this baby out and if I give ya an epidural at this point ya won't be able to help." JESUS! I was really, *really* screwed. The moment that I'd feared most since the second I discovered that I was pregnant was rapidly approaching. My one and only safety net was the anesthesia and now that was taken away. (A friend had suggested that my fear of childbirth seemed extreme.) *OH GOD, HELP ME!*

Trying to stay calm as they quickly wheeled me into the icy cold delivery room, I felt more on my own than ever. Nobody could really help a person through a moment like this. Sure, there were doctors and nurses and I had friends, but nobody could do for me what I had to do right then and there. I prayed for courage, safety and protection - from a place deeper than I knew existed.

God frequently turned a deaf ear to me, in fact I'd gotten somewhat used to being ignored, but surely He wouldn't do that to me. Not with a baby coming into the world.

In between contractions, I laid back to rest. Suddenly, I thought I saw my dad. The shock of seeing him had less to do with the fact that he was dead and more to do with the nature of our sick relationship. Why was he there? What did he want? Oh God, will you keep me safe from him *this time?*

Within minutes of my brief conversation with The Man Upstairs, Dr. Patricia yelled, "PUSH!" Bearing down and trying to remember how in the hell she told me to breathe, I felt like I had a serious case of constipation. *"PUSH!"* The nurse held my hand and assured me that everything was fine. "Go ahead an' push, sugah." She seemed somehow softer now, making me feel more at ease. Salty sweat dripping into my eyes made me squeeze them shut. I couldn't worry about that now, I had a baby to spit out. "Ya doing fine, Connie. Relax and breathe." Dr. Patricia had a sweet way about her and I guessed that I probably felt safer with her than just about anybody else under these circumstances. I knew I'd only feel safe with a lady doctor, especially at such a time. I would never let a strange man touch me down there.

Needing to catch my breath, I prayed for just a few seconds of rest. The sweet sound of my doctor's melodic voice drew my attention to the foot of the bed, where she appeared to be calmly busy. As her right hand drew a what appeared to be a threaded needle up above her head, I asked her how long until the baby would come. I figured it wouldn't be much longer. She smiled a toothy grin and said, "Ya just had a fine baby boy!" She was softly singing rather than speaking the words and I wasn't sure I heard her correctly. "On ya last push, ya son popped out into the world, showin' us how handsome he is." Still confused, I asked what she was doing. "I had to do an episiotomy to create more passage for the baby. Otherwise, ya would have torn. I'm putting in stitches and don't ya worry; I'm adding a Daddy stitch." I was trying to keep up with what she was saying, but it was all too much.

"Honey, meet ya brand new baby boy!" With that, the nurse laid a tee-tiny pink body across my chest. He was a bit scrawny and had lumpy white liquid over his tiny body, but I never felt such a beautiful presence in all my life! Warm and profoundly deep emotion rose up inside me as I lifted an exhausted hand to touch him. *My baby. My sweet little baby.* I knew in that instant that I would always adore him and take care of him to the best of my ability. Most of all, I knew that I would protect him in a way that Mama had never done for me. Yep, this was my little fella and nobody would ever hurt him - not ever - as long as I was alive.

As the nurse wheeled me into a recovery room, we were met by Marty. He looked tired but very happy. "We have a son, beb. Tyler Douglas weighs seven pounds an' six ounces an' he's twenty inches long!" As my words reached his ears, he jumped into the air, kicking his heels. "YEAH! THANK YA, BEB! THANK YA, THANK YA!!" His joy was surprising; he'd not shown this excitement at any time during the pregnancy. All the same, I felt tremendous relief; maybe we would go home and live happily ever after.

Tyler had to be placed under a special light for a day or so; because I'd developed toxemia shortly before his birth he had yellow jaundice. Not unusual, the doc said, encouraging me not to worry.

"Beb?" The next morning Marty's voice was kinder than usual. "How ya doin' today?" I fought to open my crusty eyes, literally having to pry my eyelids apart with my fingers. I was dog-tired. Giving birth was no easy task, even though my very short labor probably made it appear so. I struggled to perch myself up, leaning against pillows at the head of the bed. My lady parts were really sore. Dr. Patricia said the stitches would take at least ten days to heal. I got the shivers each time I thought about a scalpel cutting me down there. I worried about urinating – would it hurt or cause infection?

With Marty's help, I slowly got out of bed. I was anxious

to go down to the nursery to see our little Ty. It seemed like forever since they'd laid him across my chest and I missed him. Amazing how I could become so attached to a baby that had been unseen for nine months with only one brief face-to-face meeting. On the way to the nursery we passed a weight scale. I'd been told by a few people that I'd probably lose most of my pregnancy weight during the birth. Stepping slowly onto the full-size scale, I was dismayed to discover that I'd only lost ten pounds. That meant I had another fifteen pounds to go to return to pre-pregnancy weight. I'd always been obsessed about my body. (Daddy used to call me fat, and sadly I was too quick to believe him.) Being fifteen-pounds overweight seemed awful to me just then. I felt fat and rather ugly at that moment.

Standing at the large window directly in front of all the newborns, we searched for Ty. Finally, sure that I'd spotted him, I said excitedly, "Look beb, there he is!" We cooed over him for what seemed like hours until a nurse approached. "What's the last name?" Before I could respond, she walked around us and unlocked the nursery door. With a broad warm smile, she leaned over and grabbed a tiny baby wrapped in blue. To my horror, this was *not* the baby that Marty and I had lovingly admired for the last twenty minutes! Oh my God, then *who* had we believed to be our beautiful son? Jesus, I was shaken and felt very foolish as the nurse stepped close to the observation window. Marty discretely whispered his own shock at the mistaken identity. The moment the nurse moved the soft flannel blanket aside revealing his little pink face I knew it was all okay and that I was still in love, truly and forever. Tyler Douglas was perfect in every way - oh, but don't all parents say that about their babies? I'd seen a few homely newborns and overheard others say they'd fill out in time or that little pointed head would round out after a while. I thanked God for letting our baby be so precious.

I stayed in the hospital for two more days. My blood pressure had to be monitored closely. Also, Ty was still being exposed to the special light to eliminate the yellow jaundice. I'd have plenty to do when I get home, so I decided to rest while I could.

Mrs. Guilbeau was waiting at our apartment when we arrived. She'd graciously volunteered to stay with us for the first week of Ty's life. I was very grateful; there were so many things I was unsure about. Feeding – bottle or breast? Burping – when and how? Diaper changes and on and on. Mrs. Guilbeau was very good at all of it and she took care of Ty like a pro. She didn't seem to be afraid to break him like Marty and me. In fact, at times I thought she was a bit too rough, but in my exhaustion, I dared not challenge her.

Mama and Luke arrived as Mrs. Guilbeau was due to leave. Mama was much softer than Marty's mama and when her medications were properly regulated, she could function fairly well. She had not endured the same kind of laborious tasks but she suffered just the same. Living with Daddy was hard work no matter how you sliced it. Mama fed little Ty, speaking softly in his ear. She bathed him, making sure that the water in the kitchen sink was just the right temperature. I'd never seen Mama so gentle. Mrs. Guilbeau plopped him in water that was a bit too cold and, just like a Thanksgiving turkey, he got all goosepimply.

After five days, Mama got very tired. She wasn't used to doing so much on a regular basis. Luke was getting bigger but still tentative about holding little Ty. When he finally bonded with Ty, I could see love and wonder shining through his sweet eyes. He would be a good uncle and I told him that more than once. Yep, Uncle Luke would teach Ty good things and Ty would surely look up to him.

Chapter Nineteen

My Will be Done

Ty was a good baby. He slept hours through the night, seeming bothered only by an occasional intolerance for his baby formula. The doctor advised switching to soymilk which seemed to satisfy him.

When he was three months old, green mucus drained from his ears and caused him great pain. He cried and grabbed at his ears constantly. His pediatrician prescribed an antibiotic and within one week, Ty was feeling better. But less than one month after that, the infection returned. Poor little heart.

Marty's unresponsiveness upset me when the baby's cries woke us up in the middle of the night. His reason for not taking turns to check on Ty was that he had to get up early and go to work. I took four months off after Ty was born and Marty knew I could sleep when the baby slept.

Ty was otherwise a happy, healthy little fellow. He smiled a lot and loved to giggle. His particularly liked it when I blew on his little round stomach. His own belly chuckle had everybody laughing 'till they cried. The only time he was upset was when the ear infection came back.

Finally, his doctor suggested that we consider getting tubes placed in Ty's ears. An easy procedure, he said, done right in his office with no hospital stay necessary. Marty and I decided together that we would go ahead with the tubes. Ty wasn't able to fully rebound from one infection to the next causing the doctor to suspect each occurrence was actually a relapse. With so little experience in such matters, I felt I had no choice but to take the doctor's advice. After all, he was a specialist and surely knew what was best.

On a cold Friday morning, I bundled Ty up in his warmest jacket and we headed off to the pediatrician's office. The front desk nurse was only mildly pleasant. In fact, she made me a little nervous with her starched white uniform and fake stiff smile.

"Mrs. Guilbeau, the doctor will see ya now." She held Ty's medical file in her hand as she pointed to an examination room. Ty seemed to find great joy with the crinkling sound of the protective paper as I gently sat him on the exam table. Ten minutes later, the doctor joined us with an insincere apology for the delay.

"Okay, let's see what we have here, young fella." He spoke while he performed the examination, "I'm going to wrap this sheet around Ty to steady him during the insertion of the tubes. We don't want him squirming around during the procedure, do we?" Was that a real question? *No*, of course we didn't want him squirming around, but tying him down like a wild horse didn't seem right, either. Concerned that Ty would feel pain, I inquired further. "Oh, no. This procedure is relatively painless. He may feel a little discomfort, but the reward greatly outweighs that. In a day or so, ya will begin to notice lots of mucus draining from his ears. That is the fluid that has built up and put pressure on his eardrums. The tubes provide a channel for proper drainage."

It all sounded well and good, but Ty didn't seem all too

impressed. He began screaming as soon as the doctor began wrapping the sheet around his little body, not only horizontally, but also in a vertical crisscross fashion. What the hell? He instructed me to help hold Ty down but the moment my hands felt his trembling fear, I couldn't oblige. Tears were unavoidable. I couldn't stand to see anybody suffer; I could especially feel what Ty felt. I would not let this man – doctor or not – hurt my son. "Stop it! Ya hurting him!" He gave me a dismissive glance. "Mrs. Guilbeau, I assure ya that Ty is in no pain. He is just a bit frightened, that's all. The procedure will take only a few moments to complete, but we *must* keep him absolutely still. Do ya understand?" *YES, I understand. I understand that my baby boy is scared to death and I am standing by allowing it to happen. I understand all right dammit!* Had I said that out loud?

"Mrs. Guilbeau, we can do this procedure or not but in either case, ya need to decide now." Jesus H. Christ! Where was Marty when I needed moral support? "Ty will continue to have ear infections without the help of the tubes. If it continues this way, he may eventually lose a degree of hearing." JESUS! Now, I had to make a split-second decision by myself. "Okay, do it, *but do it fast.* I don't want my child fearful anymore."

With that, the doctor once again instructed me to hold Ty firmly while he used tweezers to pick up the first tube. With no anesthesia, he inserted it into Ty's right ear. Ty screamed like a pissed-off mule, shattering the momentary silence. Then, with the left tube in place, the doctor stood up straight. "There, ya see. Simple and quick." He removed the latex gloves, then curtly said, "Good day, Ma'am."

Five minutes later, the nurse came into the room prepared to unwrap Ty, but I was way ahead of her. I ripped the sheets off of him so fast it would have made her head swim. I couldn't wait to get out of that place and take my baby home. I held him as close as humanly possible all the while whispering a plea for forgiveness. I was no longer sure if I'd done the right thing. When a medical professional tells you what's wrong and then tells you what it takes to set it right, you listen, right? Still, I wasn't at all sure that I'd done the right thing by my little boy. I cuddled him the rest of the day and into the night. I wouldn't even let Marty take him when he got home from work. Ty was exhausted from so much struggling. Rocking him slowly, he slept on me into the night. More than anything in the whole wide world I wanted to reassure him that everything would be all right.

Mama let Daddy hurt me and didn't do a thing to stop him, not one damn thing. When we all acted up (before Luke was born), she purposely told Daddy that it was just me and Ricky, vehemently protecting Catherine. She didn't seem to care what happened to me but I cared with all my heart and soul about what happened to my baby boy. Yes siree, God gave me this precious little baby and I would protect him with all my might.

At one-thirty in the morning, he raised his little head and smiled at me. I was exhausted, but that one little smile revived me straight away. I'd beaten myself up ever since we left the doctor's office. I was an awful mom, I told myself; I let the doctor hurt my child. A horrible mother! But, in that one instant that little baby, smelling sweet of innocence, took my pain away.

Holding him with both hands I whispered into his tiny, sore right ear, "I love ya, my 'lil cher', cher', bea, bea, poo-poo puddin." Softly singing his favorite song, we sat and rocked into the wee hours of the morning. I had only known this feeling once before – with Luke. He was God's gift to our family even if my family was oblivious to that fact. When Daddy sent him to my aunt's and uncle's house I died some inside and feared that I might not ever feel that kind of love again. Sitting there in the quiet of a very long night, I knew that I was wrong.

It is hard to describe the intensity of love that wells up inside of you when you hold your own precious child. The way he smells, the warmth and softness of his tender skin, the roundness of his little head, the tiny little hands and feet - all of those things brought tears of joy to my eyes and fullness into my heart. I realized from my experience at the pediatrician's office that my protective nature was alive and well. I would seriously harm – *or kill* – anybody who hurt my child. God gave Tyler to Marty and me and I would do everything in my power to do him justice. I prayed for guidance.

∞ ∞ ∞

At times, Marty seemed to enjoy Ty quite a bit. He arrived home worn out from work around four-thirty in the afternoon each day. Running a crew of eight to ten men for the city's Parks and Recreation Department was like babysitting a bunch of nitwits, he said. Marty was an educated man now holding a degree in Wildlife and Forestry from LSU, but jobs were scarce at that time so he took what he could get. The pay was minimal, so as planned, I went back to work when Ty was just four months old.

One of the most gut-wrenching, guilt-producing things a woman can experience is to have to leave her baby for the entire day for the first time. I knew that I loved him more than anybody in the world and that even though other people knew how to properly care for children, he would be much happier *and* safer with me. But no amount of self-talk changed the situation - I had to go back to work. The bills were mounting and even though Ty was born in a charity hospital, we still received a bill for six hundred fifty-eight dollars, which may as well have been a million dollars as far as we were concerned.

As Ty continued to grow, the marriage began to further stifle me. I hated the way I felt after a loud argument with Marty and

I especially felt awful when Ty cried out from the craziness we created. He didn't deserve that; he was not the cause. In fact, it was only because of him that we stayed together during the next two-and-a-half years.

By the time Ty was just shy of two years old, Marty's job was taking a toll. He had to be on the job site at seven-thirty so he jumped out of bed at six forty-five, ate a bowl of cereal and was out the door.

I had to be at the biomedical firm (where I was hired as a temporary assistant) by eight o'clock and that meant getting up at five o'clock. There was always plenty to do, even before I got little Ty out of bed.

Eventually, Marty got a job as a quality control technician at a local plastics plant. It was a definite step-up, however, a few months later, his moods began to turn once again. He was often unsatisfied and most times I wasn't even sure why. I could only guess that it was job stress; he wouldn't confide in me. I grew weary.

"Hey, beb." I greeted Marty as he stepped inside. "How was ya day?" Before supper was over Marty had vented quite a bit of work-related frustration. The more he talked, the more upset he became. I wondered out loud if this was just "new job nerves" and encouraged Marty to calm down. Ty was standing just outside the bedroom door.

"Marty, can you keep your voice down?" Worn thin from trying to be attentive for over an hour, I didn't know what else to do as my own voice grew louder. Ty shrieked out and then went silent. No doubt he was overwhelmed from listening to us and trying to tell us stop! Standing like a little lost soldier was my precious baby boy, so bothered by the chaotic discussion between his mama and daddy that he was frozen with fear. I scooped him up and ran into his room closing the door behind me. As we fell into the rocking chair, I held my baby close.

Knowing that I needed to be calm for him, yet still feeling drained, I felt helpless. I was failing at protecting my son from strife. Those kinds of conversations happened frequently in our home and weren't likely to stop. I knew that Ty's happiness depended largely upon my own. He was a sensitive child; I'd known that all along. When I was upset, he was upset. If I were to live up to my promise to Ty to keep him happy and safe, then I must make a drastic decision and I had to make it soon.

∞ ∞ ∞

Life had taken me to a new profession as an administrator at a medical weight loss center. I loved my job and quickly got promoted. In my mind, the better I did out in the world, the more opportunity I would have to leave Marty and make a life for Ty and me.

Louise, a lovely nurse working in the center, was a bit pudgy, cute in her own way and very British. She was a dedicated single mama raising two young girls. Louise was quiet and reserved, only laughing occasionally. I always felt comfortable around Louise; things ran smoothly with her there.

Over time we began to confide in each other. I told her about my marital struggles and she vehemently encouraged me to leave Marty.

Arriving at the center a bit later than usual one morning, I found Louise having a cup of tea before the day started. Obviously dragging, she asked me what was had happened. I tried to cover up my despair but it only emphasized it more. She noticed the dark circles under my eyes and bit her tongue no longer.

In a ridiculous attempt at saving my pride, what was left of it, I said something about crying over a sad movie. But good ol' Louise was having none of that. "That's not it! Did you and your husband fight again?" Tears welled up in my already

177

swollen eyes. I was exhausted and didn't really have enough energy to continue the charade. "Yeah," I said, feeling shamed, hopeless and defeated. "Well, we'll just see about that!" She stood up and threw her chest out as if she'd just taken in a large amount of air. "Connie, I want you to pack a bag and you and Ty come and stay with the girls and me until you can find a place of your own." I was flabbergasted! This woman, whom I'd only known professionally, had just insisted that I stay with her in order to be safe. I wasn't accustomed to that much genuine concern and for a moment I was speechless.

At lunch, she brought it up again and asked me straight out when I'd be coming to her house. It was as if she wasn't going to let me off the hook until I gave her my answer, so I did. "I'll be there Saturday night, when he goes huntin'. He'll be gone 'till Sunday night."

"Don't tell him a thing, Connie. That's the whole point of leaving. He'll likely try to persuade you to stay if you tell him. Don't say a word. Just pack the necessities and come over." I knew Louise was right. I couldn't talk to Marty about this. He'd be very upset and hurt.

Restless, I couldn't sleep. The heat of Marty's body made me sweat. He was out of it as usual and making inconsistent snoring sounds. Knowing that in twenty-four hours I'd be leaving him caused an uneasiness that's hard to describe. My heart was pounding in my throat and I felt a bit dizzy. I tried to convince myself that it was the heat, but truly, I knew better.

I wondered if Mama felt like this when she planned our many escapes when I was young. We usually snuck out while Daddy was at work. I'd like to say that his bark was worse than his bite but that would be a lie. Daddy was a vicious and cruel man, especially toward me. Leaving was the right thing – the only thing – to do.

If Mama could leave Daddy, then I could leave Marty. Only

unlike Mama, and unlike my last attempt, this time I would never go back. Now I had a child to think of. So, I would go. I reassured myself over and over until the sun rose and shone through the dusty bedroom window.

I was up when Marty got out of bed. He was surprised, as Ty was still asleep. "Whatcha doin' up this early, beb?" I had trouble looking at him in the face, so I answered while adding cream to my coffee. "Aw, just couldn't sleep any more, that's all."

Thankfully, he wasn't too interested in me at the moment. He and his buddy, Matt, were not leaving until later that afternoon, but there was lots to do. He loved hunting season and each year he counted the days until he could pull out the hunting gear and head for the woods. Between football and hunting, I can safely say Marty was obsessed. There was no talking to him during a game. I knew not to interrupt his sports time. After many seasons of hunting and football, I began to protest the love affair with hobbies that created the absent husband syndrome. It fell on deaf ears.

What he'd told me while he was at LSU remained intact. "These are the best years of my life. I'm not gonna let ya ruin them. I'm *gonna* hunt an' I'm *gonna* watch football no matter what ya say, so ya may as well drop it. End of story."

Yes, it was truly the end of a story, a ten-year-plus story. Halfway into my twenty-sixth year, I packed a bag. It was nine o'clock in the evening as I gently put Ty in his car seat, careful not to disturb his sweet slumber. Before turning the ignition key, I just sat for a moment. Taking a deep breath, I leaned back in my seat looking up at the night sky. Although I cannot deny that I felt a sense of urgency about leaving, I was captivated by what I saw. It was a perfectly clear night with millions of twinkling stars. Allowing myself the momentary pleasure was risky but I just couldn't help it. Why had I always felt safe with the stars? How could I feel safe because of something so far away? It didn't make sense to me, but then sometimes, for a fleeting second I remembered being up there, and then it did.

Relaxing just a bit, I closed my eyes. Without warning, an unfathomable sense of sadness washed over my entire body. I was cloaked in profound disappointment and guilt. Should I take Ty away from his father like this? How would Marty feel when he came home to an empty house with only a small note telling him that he'd lost his wife and child? I didn't disclose where I'd be, only that I was not trying to keep him from Ty altogether, just until the dust settled. "I'll call ya once I'm in my own place," I'd written. I'd signed it simply, *"Con."*

Still captivated by the stars, I was suddenly free of the gut-wrenching remorse I'd had only moments before. Shaking my head for clarity and then rubbing my moistened eyes, I wondered if I had dozed off for just a moment. Ty, still gently sleeping, was the vision of a little angel. His pink cheeks glowed, lighting up his precious profile, and his tiny nose was shiny from a thin layer of sweat. I smiled his way with a deep knowing that even if he couldn't see me, he could somehow feel me. Not sure where that thought came from, I leaned forward and started the engine. Putting the car into reverse, I slowly backed out of the driveway. It's a shame, I thought, as the headlights lit the area under the carport; we'd only bought the house six months earlier. I loved ownership, even though we were so broke we couldn't afford to buy anything new for our home. Ty loved the yard and Marty talked about fencing in an area for a dog. A boy needs a dog, he said.

In the end, I knew all-too-well that a house was *not* always a home. A house could turn on you in a split second, giving you no warning and no way to protect yourself. You could lose yourself in a house. Walls had a way of caving in, of letting you down and then crushing you when you least expected it. No, I would not miss this house as I had not missed any house that I lived in as a child. I desperately wanted to dig my roots down deep but there had not been the chance.

Turning the corner at Long Shadow Lane, a full circular moon hung directly in front of me. It was so huge, so beautiful and so inviting that I put on the brakes and sat for another moment. "I need to drink this in," I thought out loud, as though this same moon might not be visible where I was going. Leaning forward, I felt sudden warmth envelop my head and neck. Instinctively I placed my right hand on my throat, as I often did when it was sore. A tingling sensation rushed through my hand to my arm and then back up to my forehead and brought me to a place I could not identify. It was so fleeting that I could not recall details, though I tried. This had been a long night and I hadn't even left the neighborhood. I was already drained but I knew that I must keep moving. Don't stop, I ordered myself; keep moving. Although the car was mostly empty, with the exception of one duffle bag, I had not forgotten to pack my greatest strength - *the power of my will*.

Ty was only two-and-a-half years old when I took him from his daddy.

CHAPTER TWENTY

Beware the Bulldozer

Starting over with a child wasn't easy. Any single mom will tell you the days are long and the nights, well they're just way too short.

For three months I kept my whereabouts concealed from Marty. I had a huge responsibility to raise Ty and I could no longer afford to model discontent and unhappiness.

As time went by, Marty seemed less angry and more remorseful. Deep down I always knew he loved me and Ty but we were simply too immature to make a go of our marriage.

I continued to work at the weight loss center and eventually got promoted to District Administrator of five Louisiana centers. Moving back to New Orleans offered a pay raise and a chance to start fresh.

After only a few years, the owner began quietly closing centers; the staff and I became concerned that soon our location would die a similar death - and it did.

Finally getting the news that our center would be closed, I wasn't the least bit surprised. My intuition had been right. I'd already refreshed my resume and set out to find my next career.

Serendipity paid a visit and led me across the highway to a strip mall boasting several boutiques, a deli, a popular restaurant and a modeling school. The school was looking for a sales associate and had just begun the interview process.

Getting the job was easier than keeping it. Irony is a humorous bitch! The first three months were murder; I felt like I'd forgotten everything I'd ever known about proprietary sales. Luckily, at the three-month mark something clicked and I began to bounce back and find my groove.

A year later, the Director got married and left town. I applied for her position and got it. I was the clumsy girl who got called four-eyes as a kid and about as graceful as a one-legged man in a sack race. Suddenly I was running a modeling school. I did well not because I had any earthly concept about the modeling world, but because I genuinely liked dealing with people and getting to know what made them tick.

One Friday while Ty was with Marty I stopped off for Chinese takeout on my way home from work. It was about five-thirty and there was only one diner in the restaurant. I let the host know I was there for my order and he asked me to take a seat. The food was always fresh and I didn't mind waiting.

Suddenly, the only other patron - a handsome, thirty-something blonde man - spoke to me. He complimented my hair, which was very short. Working for a modeling school had its perks; it was fun getting the latest hair, makeup and style advice from the pros. Our conversation was so invigorating that it was a bit inconvenient when the host approached to say my food was ready. As I reluctantly rose from my seat, the intriguing pilot from San Diego asked me for my phone number. He flew into New Orleans twice a month and he wanted to take me to dinner. A bit flustered but excited, I gave him my number and then quickly picked up my food and headed toward the exit. Just as I stepped through the door, the host yelled, "Hey, you didn't pay for your food!" Trying to appear cool was not in the cards and Dennis Beaumont would have great fun reminding me.

It rained the day we were married almost two years later. We said our vows before a justice of the peace in New Orleans with only the closest of friends and family present. Luke, who was nineteen years old by then, offered the adage that getting married on a rainy day meant sunny days thereafter.

A reception dinner for twenty people followed at a popular restaurant nearby. When it was time to cut and share the first piece of wedding cake with one another, Dennis shoved the pastry into my face. Cake went up my nose and into my eyes. I was humiliated while he laughed. Wiping enough frosting out of my eyes to look down the long table at our guests, I noticed that not a soul was laughing. This was an omen, a very bad omen.

Within days Dennis, Ty and I set out on a cross-country journey to what would become our new home in San Diego. I had mixed feelings about going after the what happened at our reception. Maybe I had a poor sense of humor; maybe I was picking up what was to come.

As enamored with southern California as I was, I missed New Orleans. I'd been there my entire life and my mom, sister and three brothers were still back in the city that never slept. Dennis, who flew domestic flights when we married, was soon promoted to an international route. He was away as much – if not more – than he was home. I knew no one and felt very alone at first.

Quickly enough, however, I began to appreciate being woman of the house while he was gone. I wasn't so willing to turn that over when Dennis came home and power struggles began to surface more and more. Trying to find balance caused pressure and many arguments between us.

Because he was aware of my sales background he steadfastly

pushed real estate sales on me. I wouldn't have chosen that field for myself but Dennis was very persistent and not solely because he wanted what was best for me. In fact, I didn't even feel he heard me when I said I didn't want to pursue that path. What he wanted – what every pilot wanted, according to Dennis – was to have a backup revenue plan in the event flying took a hit. Airlines were buying out other airlines and seniority lists were being merged right and left. He was fearful about his future, so off to real estate school I went while he dreamed of buying and flipping houses.

I passed the licensing exam and began working with a real estate brokerage near our home. I stayed with it about a year but liked it less every day. Selling came easy to me, but I didn't like the lack of integrity I saw over and over in my real estate office at that time. It was highly competitive and backbiting.

Quarrels increased and I developed migraine headaches. A huge point of contention was my intuitive nature; he felt very threatened by my 'knowing', although he would die before admitting it. I was not happy. I was in Dennis' world doing the things he enjoyed and doing a job in which he aspired. I regretted my decision to marry him more every day.

Three years into the marriage we decided to go to marriage counseling. It was largely his idea, not because I didn't think we needed the help, but mostly because he wanted to have me "fixed". His career meant everything to him and having what he considered a blemish, such as divorce, on his record was unthinkable. So "we" underwent therapy but in his mind it was strictly for me.

Christian Counseling seemed to fit our needs just right, he proclaimed. He'd been a "practicing" Catholic all of his life and by practicing I mean to say that his dedication seemed rather superficial to me.

Marriage and Family Therapist Anna Norris was a petite

woman, not even five feet tall. She had dark hair and an east coast "no bullshit" attitude. She'd been blind since diabetes stole her eyesight at the age of twenty-one. I sometimes wondered if her glass eyes were prosthetic at all; she was so intuitively observant – it was freaky!

I instantly liked her even though I'd resisted a Christian environment in which to unravel my soul. God had not been overly present in my life. How could I feel any differently then? Scarcity, abuse, shame and guilt followed me around throughout my life. Although I managed to surmount poverty, I'd not been able to get past the rest of what followed me like a shadow.

The Bulldozer. For the next year, when Dennis was in town we sat on her couch as a couple. It wasn't long into the first year that during a one-on-one session Anna told me that she could see that Dennis was a "bulldozer". I was so relieved that I wasn't the only one who saw it. I felt manipulated at every turn. Even going to dinner was an orchestrated act of dominance shrouded in generosity. Anna understood what I meant when I described how what appeared so princely on the surface was really quite manipulative underneath.

Once I came to understand the exhausting dance, and why I had once again attracted a dominate male, I began to stand my ground. Anna encouraged me to create a flash card with the word NO written in bold print. When The Bulldozer tried running me down she suggested I hold up the flash card and ask, "What part of this don't you understand?" Brilliant. Simply brilliant.

During a significant milestone session with Anna, emotional mayhem struck. I remember it like it was yesterday although at this writing it has been over twenty-five years. Anna was seated behind her small desk while we sat opposite her; Dennis was on my left. Even though I don't recall the conversation up to that point I do remember that something she said triggered a shocking response from me, "It's not like I was sexually abused or anything!"

Time stood excruciatingly still. I was frozen for God knows how long when I felt myself split in two. There was the 'me' who'd been sitting there all along and suddenly there was another 'me'. The 'me' sitting farthest from Dennis sat forward with a great deal of fogginess and thought aloud, "Did I just say that?!"

Had an anvil fallen on my head? Anna's voice broke the trance. "I've been wondering when you'd remember." What the HELL?! I was stunned! I became very agitated and demanded she tell me how long she'd known. As a very capable therapist, she'd suspected soon after we met. I demanded to know why she hadn't told me before then. Her model, she declared, was to let the client's own psyche reveal the past when ready. DAMMIT! I was dumbfounded; there I sat for all those sessions, both with and without Dennis present and she knew ALL ALONG?! I felt betrayed by Anna and humiliated that such an immensely disparaging disclosure was happening in front of Dennis, a man I'd had difficulty loving, much less trusting. He'd have a field day with this information; it would validate what he'd always thought and more frequently began to express – *I was broken.*

A large part of me wanted to run from her. But continuing to see to see Anna on my own was with without a doubt one of the wisest life decisions I'd made to that point. I got over my anger toward her, realizing it was really anger directed at an aspect of myself. I grew to respect her beyond words and felt understood and cared for in her presence. Most importantly, she was helping me find answers to as yet unidentified questions, which had floated wordless in my head for years.

Trying to figure out my abuser's identity wasn't necessary – I knew who it was - Anna concurred. My father was the perp. Wasn't it odd, I thought, that for the first thirty-five years of my life I had no idea that I'd been sexually molested as a child. I knew my dad treated me cruelly, and I remembered his late night visits but nothing to the degree of incest. Then, in one encapsulated moment as my world stood perfectly still, I knew. Even without visual memories, I knew.

So many long-unexplained sensations, feelings and fears, which appeared unfounded on the surface, began to make sense over time and with continued talks with Anna.

I was invited to participate in a sexual abuse group led by Anna and a fellow female therapist. During the first meeting, which consisted of twelve women including me, it was very apparent that eating disorders were prevalent amongst those who been sexually abused as children. All of the women were overweight while I was very thin. I attended twice weekly meetings for eight months and got in touch with a great deal of hidden fear and anger.

Each woman had a different story about her life with an abuser. Most offenders were male, but a few were women. Some in the group declared great love and affection for their perpetrator, while others were not shy about expressing hatred.

My story was probably more similar than I could see at the time, but I saw myself as somehow different than many in the group. I was a scrappy survivor - not a helpless victim. Looking back, I understand that it didn't matter what I thought about my past, the truth was in my reactions and behaviors. I began to see more clearly how I handled trying times - medical issues, money problems, relationship upheavals and job challenges - through the filter of fear. It was all I could see and it was written all over me.

During that time, I also attended a twelve-step program for adult children of alcoholics. It was quite a mixed bag.

Some members of the group were friendly, chatty and open while others were very guarded and rarely shared. Dennis had highly encouraged me to join, agreeing with Anna's suggestion. Reluctantly at first, but more enthusiastically later, I began to look forward to the weekly meetings. The social gathering afterward at the neighborhood pizza hang out was an opportunity to discuss things somewhat less depressing than our screwed up lives.

I continued to see Anna as she guided me through the shadowy swamp of physical, sexual, verbal and emotional abuse. The damage had been done – that was crystal clear. Every thought, feeling and belief I held as truth was based on my horrific past; I was drowning in overwhelm.

During the course of a two-month period I had three very disturbing episodes of visual transference. When I looked at Dennis I literally saw the face of my father. At first I dismissed it, thinking there was, after all, a slight resemblance. Two incidents later, I decided to bring it up to Anna. She suggested that when this happened I speak to Dennis - which would cause his voice to shake me out of the daze. I never mentioned it to him; I feared he would add it to his arsenal of "Connie is the cause of our problems" evidence.

The tension grew between us as I swam deeper into the emotional vat of my tortured childhood. The last thing I wanted or needed was sexual contact. Anna carefully explained this to Dennis and he claimed to understand – but really didn't. Shortly after that, we separated and Dennis moved out. It was meant to be a break while I continued therapy. Anna understood the needs of an incest survivor and feeling safe was at the top of the list.

CHAPTER TWENTY-ONE

Jackity-Schmakity

Sitting quietly in the little library where the Adult Children of Alcoholics (ACA) group met, I observed Jack Stewart. He was a quiet man in his thirties, short, had a kind face and was balding. He spoke thoughtfully and made it clear that his number one priority was his young son. He'd been divorced for four years and although he shared custody with ex-wife, she rarely spent time with the boy. Instead, her parents would take him on her weekend; she was free to pop in and out which really upset Jack.

By the time we met, Dennis and I had all but finalized the divorce. Jack I eventually became friends and later, we began to date. He was gentle, which was foreign to me but I liked it. I felt safe in his presence.

In time, we discussed a blended-family future together. We had much in common – one alcoholic parent and the other, a self-centered martyr. I remained in therapy and once we were married, introduced Jack to Anna's amazing therapeutic abilities.

One year into our marriage I began to have lower abdominal

pain. When I visited my ob-gyn for a checkup she revealed what I feared - I was pregnant.

We were both shocked; I was forty years old and on the pill and had been taking Dilantin (anti-seizure medication) for many years.

There was suspicion that it was an ectopic pregnancy. Testing proved that was not the case and yet the cause of severe pain remained undiagnosed. There was great concern about carrying a baby full term; the child would have a one in four chance of being born with severe abnormalities.

I spoke with Jack about the possibility of going forward with the pregnancy (provided it was viable). My pain worsened; I was frightened and didn't know what to do. The risk of serious complications was high. Ultimately, we decided to end the pregnancy. Even though I wasn't completely sure it was the right thing to do, Jack was adamant. He absolutely did not want another child.

Because it was against my gynecologist's religion to do the procedure herself, she referred me to a doctor who would perform a D&C. I'd seen her for years; her refusal to do the procedure increased my feeling of abandonment ten-fold.

Jack and I went to the clinic together but a great emotional distance divided us. There were several younger women in the waiting room and I wondered if they were using this as a regular method of birth control. How out of place I felt.

When my name was called I reluctantly followed the nurse to the exam room. It was cold and drab - or maybe that was just the way I felt inside.

The moment the doctor inserted the medical instrument into my cervix I began to tremble. Crying quickly turned into uncontrollable sobbing. The nurse held my hand as the otherwise stoic doctor stopped to ask if he was hurting me.

I thought I saw compassion in his eyes, but only for a brief moment.

When the procedure was over I got dressed and went to the waiting room to find Jack. Still shaking, I cried all the way home and on and off over the next five years.

Life was not the same between Jack and me after losing the baby. He didn't want to speak of it while I continued to grieve.

It was in those moments after he fell to sleep each night that I cried for her. I felt myself jumping out to the stars again. It was lonely there but I was accustomed to that form of isolation.

During a dream five years after that dreadful day, I was visited by a beautiful baby girl. She was robust with rosy cheeks and blonde curly hair; I knew she was my daughter. She let me hold her, but not too closely. We didn't communicate as I studied her face. A bittersweet feeling washed over me the next morning as I laid still while capturing my experience. A few days later she returned in another dream and this time she was more receptive. She was perfect! Everything about her made me smile so broad that I cried. Speaking telepathically, she asked why I was so sad. I told her that I owed her an apology for being such a coward. I could've – should've – fought harder for her. I succumbed to the pressure to let her go. I told her that I'd not forgiven myself and might never. That's when the most incredible thing happened. Precious "Sarah" (the name I'd always wanted for a daughter) reminded me of a promise I'd made so long ago – one that I'd completely forgotten. She assured me that I was not a coward, but rather a hero. Hero – that was crazy! She repeated herself without using words. "Very long ago you made a solemn promise to never bring a girl into this world. You said you'd stop the chain of sexual abuse of females in your bloodline." She spoke like a wise old soul and that's when I knew that I was communicating with her beautiful spirit. She appeared in physical form simply to make it easier to relate. Sarah was a most magnificent teacher and I will never, ever forget her.

Not long after I communicated with Sarah I purchased a beautiful picture of a sun, moon and stars with a meaningful sentiment. I hung it in our family room for her, offering no explanation to my family. As I placed it on just the right wall, I was struck by the words so beautifully etched on the print. I understood more than ever how true it was that some people stay in our life for but a brief period but make a huge impact. It so quintessentially fit my experience with my baby girl, for whom I still get teary eyed.

No one will tell you that blended families are a cake walk and ours was no exception. Jack's son, Little Jack, was nine years old and Ty, fifteen by then. They had spats but nothing serious.

Jack and I that couldn't agree on house rules for the boys. This ongoing incongruity further chipped away at our partnership. Unable to recover, it was quite apparent that when it came to biological vs. inherited children, feelings about child-rearing run deep.

There were certainly other unresolved issues between us, mostly caused by our unhealed pasts. Therapy helped but did not change our individual behavior patterns.

Just before Thanksgiving we moved to a larger home. It was in a pleasant neighborhood and had plenty of room for a family of four and two cats. I began to reengage with my supernatural experiences. I'd had mystical experiences throughout life starting in early childhood and again when I was married to Dennis (who vehemently discouraged me from believing in that type of "unfounded information"). Not knowing who to discuss such things with, I usually kept it to myself.

Finally, ready to embrace my gifts, I began by self-teaching myself to interpret my dreams. Somehow I knew that my dreams were the gateway to my own magic. During an intense two-year daily dream analysis period I discovered past lives and more about my past in this life. Sleep was the most exhilarating eight hours of any twenty-four-hour period. Each morning I awoke to find out more about myself, my life, my gifts and my hopes and fears. My dreams helped me see where I was stuck but also where I'd made headway.

With Jack's blessing I quit my stressful job, where I cried almost every day the prior three months. Not suiting up and going into an office every day felt very strange, but I loved it - at first. My creativity began to soar as did my newly learned practice of meditation. I was in Heaven! That is, until Jack started to worry about the loss of my income. It became clear quite quickly that he really wasn't okay with my hiatus and my stress quickly returned. I began to feel guilty and also angry.

Within three of weeks of handing in my resignation I jammed my foot into a piece of furniture and broke a toe. The pain was excruciating and resulted in wearing the ever-fashionable boot for six weeks. I secretly wondered if I did this purposely on a sub-conscious level. I couldn't very well go job hunting when it was difficult to walk.

Although Jack was unhappy about the job search delay, he showed compassion for my predicament. With a little breathing space, I began to focus more intently on my psychic gifts.

Like a sponge desperate for water, I read anything pertaining to psychic development, the nature of the Universe, dream interpretation and mediumship. I marveled at how quickly I was absorbing the information for which I thirsted. I wondered where this voracious hunger came from.

Because Jack rose every morning at five o'clock, it was not unusual for me to be awake for a short while before drifting back to sleep. During the brief period of early morning awareness, I began to notice a large crow regularly flying very near our upstairs bedroom window. Enjoying coffee outside later in the morning, I stumbled upon several curious objects placed near one end of our second story deck. I identified bones, teeth and shells and started to believe that (as crazy as it sounded) the crow was delivering these objects as gifts. Even though I was intrigued by the novelty of the stash, I tried not to make too much of it until noticing that there were new items added daily.

During meditation, with which I was becoming more and more comfortable, I received a message indicating that the bird was bringing the objects for me to mark the occasion of my *shamanic initiation*. Even as I said the words aloud to Jack, I realized it sounded out there. But to my great surprise, Jack agreed. He was not a spiritual man and I never dreamed he'd see the deeper meaning in such things. Becoming quiet, he said, "You're gifted, Connie, and the angels are encouraging you." He admitted that he'd actually experienced some paranormal experiences himself and believed it happened to him only because of me. You could've knocked me over with a feather!

I dove into spirituality head first. I loved everything about the unseen world. It was wiser, more beautiful, more loving and kinder than anything I'd seen or experienced in the 3-D world. It was delicious and I couldn't get enough.

I yearned to learn and grow and began to play with the notion of having a mentor. Someone who had all the gifts I had – and more, someone who knew what I knew – and more. Within one hour of declaring my desire to Jack - who was more aware than I'd imagined, yet less enthusiastic than I'd wished - the phone rang. It was Marin Lind, a woman I'd met and worked with in San Diego earlier that same year. She was a Medium from New Orleans who'd come to town to do workshops on Divine Energy. I answered the phone and listened eagerly as she invited me to another workshop in my area. Asking if she mentored others, I could barely contain my excitement when she said yes. I was elated!

Our marital problems had mounted and now I was saying that I wanted to go away to explore my shaman nature – my psychic gifts. Jack couldn't understand the connection between my unhappiness and the disconnect to my divinity. The truth is, I hadn't understood it until the moment I realized how joyous I was at the prospect of developing and furthering my gifts.

On the fifteen-minute drive to the airport to begin my mentorship with Marin, Jack casually mentioned that he was contemplating divorce. God! Even though he'd recently hinted that he wasn't happy, I wondered why was he talking divorce at that moment? We said goodbye at the terminal just before I reluctantly boarded the plane for New Orleans. I was very concerned that if I followed through with the mentorship that my marriage to Jack would die. Something else told me if I *didn't* follow through, a part of me would die.

In spite of my heavy heart, the next two weeks were the most exhilarating of my life. Marin welcomed me into her home in keeping with gracious southern hospitality. (Her home was on fifteen secluded aches on the north shore of Lake Pontchartrain.)

First order of business was to go "make groceries", which meant food shopping. Nourishing ourselves was par for the course, Marin said. So, off we went to return later with fresh organic fruits and vegetables, hearty grains and robust New Orleans coffee. Of course, we did not forget the seafood! Stuffed crabs graced our dinner table that first night. I was back in the bosom of a lush Louisiana and preparing to walk through a gateway so powerful that I would never return to the "me" that had so long ago hijacked my life.

She put me through the paces and began by asking

me to share with her all of the things I wanted to learn. I was prepared – my list had eight requests listed in order of desirability. First on the list was remote viewing. Saying she didn't do that, she was more than willing to hold the space for me to try.

My first full day of training began with a guided meditation. Marin turned the volume down on the stereo so that the planetary sounds CD would assist, but not override, her words. I stretched out on the couch and quickly went into deep relaxation. My many months of meditating in San Diego had helped me find the sweet spot quickly. I didn't realize how yummy that was until Marin explained that some people have difficulty achieving such stillness.

Almost immediately I sensed my spirit lifting out of my body. I actually saw (in my mind's eye) what appeared to be a translucent figure (my etheric body) drifting up and out of my physical body. About that time and unbeknownst to me, Marin's neighbor came by with his trusted companion, Buddy, a black lab.

Busy floating around at ceiling height, I came across a loft. I surveyed the contents, making note of a sewing machine and several other small objects, such as a lamp and a few boxes.

When the meditation was nearing an end, Marin directed me to come back into my body and open my eyes. Returning to a dense body was way more challenging than lifting up. After all, I was very good at leaving my body; I'd been jumping out since early childhood. I couldn't wait to tell Marin about my out-of-body journey! As I described the items I saw, she interrupted me saying those items were not located in her loft. I was disappointed; I saw the objects so clearly. She went on to say that the items I saw would be found in her neighbor's loft; he and his wife split and she left a few things behind. Marin felt that the neighbor and his dog attracted my psychic energy enough to cause me to investigate his home rather than hers. I was amazed at how it all worked - I was hooked!

Needing to stretch my legs a few days after I arrived, I took a walk down a long country lane. Stopping periodically to pick flowers for our supper table, the sight and scent of wildflowers was breathtaking for this city girl.

A mile or so from Marin's house I came upon a lane where treetops met to create a dense canopy. At first, I was delighted; it was hot and sunny and cooling down in the shade felt wonderful. About a quarter of the way into the covered area I began feeling a very odd sense of alarm and got goosebumps from head-to-toe. I began to feel panicky with no visible reason why. When I reached the grove's half-way point, my fear had considerably increased. My attention was drawn to a thicket to my left, which I purposely tried to ignore. But when the pull became too strong, I allowed myself to stop to peer deeply. What I "saw" sent shivers down my spine and for a moment, I froze. My mind was whirling; all I knew was that whatever this thing was, I had to get away quickly. I began to run forward; it seemed a shorter distance than turning back; I had to get away from whatever it was as quickly as possible! But, the entity, which appeared to be a large black panther with an oversized head and tremendous teeth, ran alongside me in the trees the entire way. Its growl was hungry and very angry. Every hair on my body stood to attention.

Finally reaching the other side of the thicket, I bent at the waist to catch my breath. What in the world – *or out of this world* - had I just seen?! Why hadn't Marin warned me? Surely she knew what lurked in that neck of the woods.

Feeling safe was quickly replaced with the reality that I had to pass through the same grove to get back to Marin's house. Dammit! There was no other way. God, don't fail me now! I stood still for a bit longer trying to think, but there really was no way out other than to face the creature again.

Running like the wind (more like a breeze), I felt like an Olympic sprinter, not because I was fast but because I was motivated. I made it to the other side but not without the dark being following me the entire way.

As soon as I emerged from the shadows, the feeling of dread left me. I couldn't wait to get back to discuss this with Marin. She would, no doubt, be able to shed light on what I'd just experienced. To this day, I have never been more frightened by anything I've dealt with in the psychic realm.

That would not, however, be the end of my challenges on the longest walk ever. With about half a mile to go, I received a call from a woman in San Diego. I'd done several complimentary sessions for her (with our last meeting just days before I left to do my mentorship with Marin) while she dealt with a challenging marriage and ensuing break-up. Her primary motive for calling was to tell me how upset she was that I'd seen abuse in her early years. I approached the subject gently and honestly shared the information I "saw". (Since that time, I've come to understand that when I gift sessions, the recipients aren't always yet committed to the work required once information is revealed. The exchange of money for healing abilities creates a balance with one another and the client tends to take it more seriously.) She accused me of falsely creating the scenario because of my own childhood abuse experience. I was mortified! The more she spoke, the more upset I became. I couldn't understand how she could believe such a thing. I'd known her long enough to prove my character and done enough sessions for her to demonstrate my accuracy.

Nothing I said made her feel any better, which made me feel worse. Why had I defended myself? I began to wonder if the Universe was trying to dissuade me from the spiritual journey I'd put into motion. My marriage was about to end, a friend accused me of fabricating details about her past and I'd run into an entity so fierce that I truly didn't know if I'd survive the encounter. By the time I returned to Marin's house I was a big ol' pile of hot mess!

Later that evening we had coffee on the back porch. It was a cool evening and the humidity was low – the kind of nights Louisianans cherish. She spoke softly, "The higher up the mountain, the lonelier it gets." I trusted her completely, but her words did not soothe my battered heart. Did I really want to travel to a place where I lost everyone and everything that mattered? Was the price too high?

As the night wore on, I began to understand what Marin was saying to me. My Soul Contract beckoned me to step into my healing gifts and abilities. I could deny the invitation; it was my prerogative, but would I be any happier rejecting my Divine gifts in order to hang onto people who didn't truly understand me or my soul calling? I didn't have to give it much more thought after that. I knew then - and continue to know - that I'm doing exactly what I was born to do in – and with - this life.

After that fateful day, each moment spent with Marin was more magical than the last. We cooked, ate and explored my psychic abilities together. She did a great deal of energetic clearing on me and methodically explained what she was doing as she encouraged me to stretch my clairvoyant wings.

With each new challenge, I became more enthralled with soul energy. I'd always loved the concept of a soul and recalled falling to sleep many nights (as a child) while reciting a short prayer designed to release trapped souls into heaven. I discovered that I could actually hear the soul's whispers! I wanted to know as much as possible about how I could use that ability to help others heal.

Being psychic in and of itself wasn't the end-all for Marin. She repeatedly stressed the importance of going all the way to the soul in order to effect genuine healing. Recognizing the healer in me, she pointed out that my strengths were patience and focus. Many psychics push an answer quickly so as to appear capable and also to please the client. That was a big no-no and she was quite pleased that I didn't give in to such impetuousness.

Day after day, we worked diligently to unravel the ancient shaman within me. Lying dormant, it had always been there. In fact, as Marin tapped into several of my past lives, she saw me as a witch who'd been killed many times for my magic. It began to make more sense that I'd avoided my gifts until now. She said that the cells don't forget even though the mind has no recollection of past life experiences. I had no trouble believing this as I had recently adopted the concept of reincarnation. This was a saving grace for me as I'd been taught the concept of Heaven and Hell and the "one-shot" story, which had me resigned to the fact that I would surely be surrounded by brimstone and fire for all of eternity.

As departure day grew close, I began to think more of Jack and his threat of divorce. While working with Marin, I was joyful. I didn't want to go back to sadness.

Jack picked me up at the airport and I could feel his decision to leave the marriage in his silence. Once home, I brought up the subject first. Saying nothing had changed in his mind, he added that he was upset that I spent money on a mentorship with Marin. It made me so very sad that he didn't understand how meaningful my spiritual and psychic inheritance was and how joyful I was in the reunion.

After unpacking I joined him in the family room, where he was stoically parked on the couch. Sitting on the floor near him I asked one question. "Would you consider staying if I give up my spiritual quest?" I held my breath while waiting for an answer. After a long pause, his one-word answer, "Maybe", told me that we were done. Lowering my head, I sobbed. It was over. My wounded heart had finally found a path out of the darkness and I couldn't give that up; I'd turned my back on my inner self for forty years and I wouldn't spend one more day denying my deepest needs.

Within a week, Jack announced he'd placed a deposit on an apartment and a few days later he was gone. (Was this karmic payback? It was eerily reminiscent of the first time I left Marty). I was devastated. I cried every morning, every night and off and on during the day. Ty was worried about me and often sat and held my hand. Irish Crème helped, which concerned Ty. I tried to assure him that I poured more than I drank but I could tell by the look on his face that it did nothing to comfort him.

All I wanted to do was crawl in a hole and be alone in my sorrow but having a child gave me a reason to get up and get dressed.

During the first few months of our separation, I repeatedly reminded myself that my pain was caused by my perception. I'd learned this from both Anna and Marin. The ego can keep us trapped in fear but the soul will set us free. I kept thinking of a diamond with its many facets. I told myself that all I needed to do was turn my diamond to get a different perspective. I must've said that to myself fifty times a day. Eventually, my perception - and my outlook - shifted, but it wasn't an easy transition. Losing a ten-year marriage - that I thought would last until death - was very traumatic.

Reflecting on my previous two marriages, I could clearly see the rise and fall of each relationship and began to understand my role in each marriage. I'd divorced my first two husbands but Jack divorced me. That kick in the teeth stayed with me for years - and I'm glad it did.

Chapter Twenty-Two

<hr>

I'm so Dizzy

Continuing my spiritual studies along with psychic development kept me going during the months following my divorce. I knew I had a gift and I felt the urge to fully develop my skills. Taking some time off from work also helped but in order to bring in a steady income, I began working part-time as a real estate assistant.

Practicing my skills was exhilarating and I found a few willing participants in the office. I felt I should charge for my healing sessions and it wasn't long until I had the confidence to do so. I'd noticed that many spiritual healers offered their healing at no charge and wondered why they did so. I surmised that it must be a low self-esteem issue, otherwise they would be proud of their craft and barter for cash as with every other service offered out in the world.

I continued to work with Marin when possible, by phone and occasionally when she was in San Diego. My skills increased rapidly and before long I was doing more private sessions.

There's nothing like jumping in and doing the work. I was highly psychic and I truly embraced that aspect of myself. I had a gift and Marin had lovingly guided me to expand my etheric knowledge and wisdom. The more I sought understanding of the higher realms, the more I received. At first, I wondered if I was making it all up; it was so easy for me. Doubt is a three-dimensional attitude and the antithesis of an infinite Universe.

Late one Spring, I met a massage therapist, Meagan, who split her time between Sandpoint, Idaho and San Diego. She encouraged me to share my gifts with Sandpoint, saying there was a large community of spiritual-minded people in that area. With a little thought, I decided to do it. What did I have to lose? San Diego had been a tough go of it for me. On the heels of my third divorce, I wondered if I was done with southern California – or maybe it was done with me.

Flying into the Spokane International Airport still left a one hour and forty-five-minute drive to Sandpoint. Meagan was quite the go-getter and seemed to have lots of friends in town. The nomad-type, she always looked like a scruffy hippie chick and made her home wherever she landed. Meagan's lifestyle was foreign to me; I was a nester and sleeping somewhere different every few days on an indefinite basis would drive me crazy. Though we were like night and day, I admired her moxie.

A few days and two group sessions later I met Hank Chatman at a local social event in Hope, a very small nearby town. I was exhausted from working with so many people. Because I have the ability to read (intuitively profile) the energy of a person, and any person they speak of, it's likely that I'm reading up to five energies per person in a group setting of ten. That's a great deal of energy running through my body.

After everyone had their fill of pizza and beer Meagan and I headed back to Sandpoint, but not before Hank gave me his phone number. We'd had a friendly conversation when I discovered that he was open to the work I was doing. Although

I always looked for that kind of receptivity in a man, I rarely found it.

Back in town, I fell in love with Sandpoint in the summer. The grass was emerald green (unlike the brown lawns of San Diego), the giant trees were majestic and the sky was spectacular. The people were easy going and quite friendly. Meagan encouraged me to consider moving to her favorite little northwest town, saying that I'd have a larger clientele than in San Diego and as an added bonus, I'd really appreciate the lower cost of living.

Hank and I began to communicate regularly once I returned to San Diego. We had many long and easy conversations often while he sat on his deck under the evening stars, sipping whiskey and smoking a cigar. There was a certain lure about the laid back lifestyle, friendly residents and Hank.

After some time, he invited me for a non-working visit. Hank's home was nestled in a quaint little hillside neighborhood, with a population of around three hundred at the time.

While there, I received a call from my sister informing me that our brother, Ricky, had passed away. He'd been ill with cirrhosis of the liver for some time and had been hospitalized a week earlier. My feelings were so jumbled. I hadn't had a connection with him for most of my adult life, yet I thought of him and certainly missed the Ricky I knew as a child. He was only fifty-three years old. It took me a few days to register that Daddy died at the same age from the same illness.

The funeral was to be the next day and I opted not to attend. I knew that his soul had already ascended and that all that remained was the shell of who he'd been. Instead, I channeled Ricky and had the best conversation we'd ever had.

Over the course of an hour, we communicated about his life, his wife and two daughters and our childhood. I cried during most of our chat, but was able to stay with it. Near the end of our talk, he told my something I wasn't prepared to hear. He said that Mama would join him on the other side within thirty days. She'd been ill and in and out of consciousness due to several strokes. Still, a thirty-day prediction was a bit shocking.

During that visit, Hank and I became closer. He did his best to console me as I tried my best to carry on with our visit. We continued a long-distance friendship until one day he suggested I move to Hope to be with him. It was a tempting invitation. I was still working part-time for realtors and didn't really enjoy it. I wanted to do energy work full-time but hadn't built up enough of a client base at that point. After quite a bit of thought, I decided to go for it. Another leap!

After announcing my decision to Ty, I began packing my belongings and prepared for the second biggest move of my life. I knew I'd miss San Diego and its gorgeous weather, I just didn't know how much. I'd miss Ty terribly as we had always lived near one another – he was my closest family.

Just before leaving San Diego, I received the news that Mama crossed over. It was right at the thirty-day mark, just as Rickey said. Even though she was only seventy-three years old, she'd been old for years due to poor physical and mental health. Mama was finally reunited with her first born child after so many long years of separation.

I don't recall crying over her death. Maybe I was depleted from trying to be supportive of her during the many years of her illness, neediness, meanness and manipulation. She'd been tortured on Earth; I prayed that her passing would allow her to receive the peace and love every soul deserves.

After her death, Mama came to me every night for three months in my dreams. Mostly, she appeared youthful, looking more like a vibrant thirty-something than the haggard woman she'd become. I was intrigued by her age choice; each visit was marked by her bright red lipstick and beautiful, flowing hair. In one dream visit, she was a security guard for a fine department store. I wish I'd known THAT woman. She was smart, witty and talented. R.I.P Flo.

Hank welcomed me and my two cats, Roux and Peeschwank, but quickly became quite protective of his space. He found it very difficult to share his home after living alone for so many years. Instead of bringing some of my furniture and belongings into his space, it was stored in the garage. I needed to see my things to remind me of the comfort of my own nest, but Hank didn't feel comfortable with that. His home was not mine and sadly would never become so.

Our bliss was short-lived. We seemed to disagree on many things and had difficulty finding balance together. The tension expanded to the point where I decided to move out. Hank offered to pay for my moving expenses back to San Diego, but my trust in a higher spiritual guidance told me it wasn't time to move back just yet. I found a nice little apartment in Sandpoint, which was about fifteen miles from Hank's home. I wasn't bringing in income yet and living off my savings caused me concern.

Even though there was a considerable spiritual community in the area, there was also a conservative church on every corner. As a resident, I got an insider's look at another pervasive aspect of the town - money consciousness. It was explained to me that because Sandpoint got so cold each winter many of the businesses closed for several months. Locals conserved their earnings by becoming thrifty. Apparently, my healing service was considered a luxury and my livelihood never really got off the ground.

I'd made my decision to move to Idaho on the promise of a loving partnership, a beautiful sunny region and a substantial spiritual community. At some point, I had to admit that things probably didn't work out with Hank because instead of running toward this new land, I was running from my life in San Diego.

Five months later, I moved out of Hank's home. He once again offered to move me back to San Diego whenever I was ready.

In an effort to get to know the townspeople, I decided to do a talk radio show. Mind you, I'd never done anything like that, but it surely seemed like a great idea. Woman plans, God laughs! I visited the local station and shared my idea with the young manager. Listening thoughtfully, he finally spoke. Their station was known for conservative political and religious talk show formats. He wasn't at all sure that the listeners would respond positively to a psychic medium channeling the dead on air! I assured him that there was a large spiritual population in the area and invited him to "shake things up". The answer was no - *that day*.

Five months later, after regular monthly visits, he succumbed. I was granted a one-hour live talk show per month. Curious (and naïve) about funding, I wondered how much they paid their radio hosts. I quickly found out that not only aren't they paid, but that they must seek financial sponsorship in order to pay for air time.

Eleven months after my first show, which to everyone's surprise, drew more on-air callers than any of their talk shows, my world crashed and spun around in ways I couldn't have imagined. After a long day in Spokane, I came home and had a phone conversation with a San Diego gal pal. At about ten o'clock I went to bed when suddenly I became very dizzy. My only thought was, Oh God, not this again! I was no stranger to vertigo. I'd experienced it twice in San Diego, each time associated with an inner ear infection. Antibiotics seemed to be effective and the longest I'd suffered was twelve hours.

This time was very different and immediately felt more

violent. I laid as still as possible making sure not to move my head. I counted the seconds and prayed it would pass. But, it only got worse. What felt like a giant wind catapulting me out of bed caused me to fly across the room. I hardly noticed hitting my right temple on the corner of the nightstand. It felt as though I had a huge iron ball attached by a chain tossing me an all directions at once. Wherever that ball went my body followed. I couldn't stand; I could barely crawl. Even the slightest movement increased the dizziness and made me want to vomit. It was one of the longest nights of my life, folding into several months.

Two hours into the attack and while lying on the floor in complete darkness, I saw what appeared to be a skeletal face. It was distinct and very close. Without thinking I said aloud, "GO AWAY!" It disappeared momentarily but came back. By then I was sweating profusely and probably going into mild shock – I was in no mood for games. "GO AWAY; I HAVE WORK TO DO!" It once again disappeared. I had no spiritual thoughts and no visions of loved ones appeared before me. All I wanted was to inch closer to the phone to call for help.

After hours of lying in the dark, I was finally able to get to the phone to call the only person I knew in the area other than Hank. Sandra was a young mother who practiced energy work in town. She came over and tried her best to help me in the way she knew how, but it was not enough.

Sandra tried to help me back to bed, but my dead weight was too much to lift. As I laid on the floor I began to hear loud metallic noises in my right ear, which lasted only a few moments before it went completely silent. I knew that I'd lost the hearing in that ear, but I was so focused on getting myself to the hospital that I paid little attention.

I finally succumbed to the dreaded ambulance ride. Ever since I was a child, I'd had a terrible fear around anything associated with doctors or hospitals. I'd seen my frenzied mama taken away by ambulance too many times and my own experiences with doctors left me cold.

As the paramedics wheeled me out to the ambulance I noticed my elderly neighbor standing outside her door. The siren had obviously woken her; I wondered if she was relieved that, for once, it would not be she who would be whisked away.

My blood pressure had risen to one-sixty over one-hundred. After doing an EKG the doctor said it was not my heart. He gave me travel sickness pills and sent me home, urging me to check with my family doctor as soon as possible.

It was a little over a week before I gained full consciousness. I was in and out of awareness and heard what resembled glass chimes and phones ringing throughout that entire time. Sandra came to my home daily to care for me and the cats and to help in any way she could. She went to the grocery store and pharmacy on my behalf; I was extremely grateful.

Sandra eventually called Megan, who came over as soon as she heard. She lovingly massaged my feet and wanted to know if she should call Hank, whom she'd known for many years. We were no longer a couple; I was not his responsibility and I didn't even know if he'd care. It was then that Megan blurted out that for the first seven days she and the others who came by to help thought I might actually die. WOW! If dying felt like what I'd been experiencing it wasn't so bad. I counted the seconds and prayed it would pass, but it only got worse.

Several doctor visits and one MRI later, there was still no diagnosis. All I knew is that it felt like lightning hit my brain. My balance was severely impacted which was obviously connected to the hearing loss. It was recommended that I see a neurologist but I declined. I had my own thoughts about what had happened and scheduled a call with Marin for further insight.

Marin scanned my energy remotely. She quickly yet

thoughtfully offered the following: I'd made a huge energetic shift, the kind that most people literally die in order to achieve. She said she'd only met one other person who'd experienced such a profound transition while still in body. This was not a surprise to me on some level; I'd been working diligently to develop my skills and just as importantly, I'd held a solid intention to serve the highest good with my gifts. I was firmly committed to this path and apparently to assist me with my spiritual goal, Spirit decided to drop-kick my butt!

Incidentally, it was the sixteenth of September when the face of death paid a visit. It didn't escape me that my mother had died one year earlier on the same date. For a fleeting moment I wondered if she had anything to do with my experience. Just as quickly as that thought entered my mind, it left. Maybe I was still giving her too much power. (The sixteenth of September held another significance - it was the day I was diagnosed with frisky cells in my breast.)

Hank found out about what was going on with me through the grapevine. Even though we hadn't spoken in several months, he quietly dropped by and left flowers on my porch. Along with his note of well-wishes there was a check for two-thousand dollars. Anticipating that I'd need a recovery period, he wanted to contribute to my expenses. Grateful that we were now on good terms, I wept from sheer gratefulness and humbly accepted his help.

(The journey back is still in progress; I still have a noticeable hearing loss, which still affects my balance but which I seem to have compensated for fairly well. My close friends know that they need to hold onto me while walking outdoors at night (when there is no horizon to aim for) for fear I will stray off! We have a good laugh about it and keep going.

Since that day my psychic abilities have increased considerably and my commitment to serving humanity grows even stronger. What my right ear does not hear in the physical realm is wildly compensated for in the psychic realm.

Nine months after that fated event I woke up one morning with the words, "You can go home now" floating around in my brain.

I packed my car with my fur babies and as much as I could squeeze into it, then headed back to San Diego. A friend offered me a place to stay until I could find my next home. I wasn't used to taking such help and it was time I learned the fine art of gracious acceptance.

Chapter Twenty-Three

Eye of the Beholder

Not long after my return, I found a quaint old apartment building near the San Diego Zoo, at the edge of Hillcrest. I'd lived in East County for seventeen years before moving to Idaho and I was ready for a change.

It wasn't listed online and had only a small FOR RENT sign posted on the front lawn. I quickly found out that the off-site owner lived in Sandpoint, Idaho. Synchronicity had brought me to my new home. We had a cordial chat and I took occupancy in one month. Even though I was still building my clientele and was concerned that I would have difficulty paying the higher rent, it didn't take me long to come to the conclusion that in this beautiful space I would be busy and prosperous – I would be happy!

It was perfect. Built in the late twenties, the building has character and charm. With only four apartments in this two-story structure, it feels like a house rather than an apartment. My intuition was spot on; within the first week of living here, the phone began to ring more than before and I became busier than I'd been in a while. I felt very grateful - and rewarded - for listening to my higher guidance.

I let Hank know about my move and as promised, he showed up in a U-Haul truck with my furniture. I was home; the familiarity of my belongings made it feel real. It was good to see Hank again; we'd made peace with one another and were grateful for the closure.

Soon after I moved in, I was abruptly awoken in the middle of the night by a thunderous noise. Realizing my bedroom door had slammed, I instinctively jumped out of bed. Checking for an intruder (what in the world would I have done if I'd encountered someone?), I found nothing. Sitting on the edge of my bed, I checked in psychically to see what was going on. Almost instantly, I picked up on the energy of a client I'd seen earlier that day. During her session, I energetically cleared a business partner from her energy field. The partner was psychic and seemed to be alpha. My client became distraught simply talking about her. Stripping her energy from my client had undoubtedly upset the partner. Even though the partner had no conscious knowledge that I had cut the energetic cord, she obviously picked up on a psychic disturbance. The furious slam was her way of letting me know she was very angry. I dealt with her by being bored! In other words, I vibrated the energy of, "be gone, you have no power here!" I never felt her in my home again. That's not to say I haven't had lots of other "visitors" over the years.

Spirits and ghosts often seek me out when they have messages for their loved ones. My stern energetic boundaries, however, make it difficult for them to intrude at will (at least that's what I tell myself). The "uninvited" seem to know that I prefer to speak with them in my dreams as that's when I have the highest degree of spontaneous visitations.

Many years ago our corporate vice-president died unexpectedly. His long-time assistant and I were friends at the time of his passing. There was a company-wide buzz; he was in his early forties and had no worrisome medical history.

The night after he crossed over he appeared to me in a dream. I was in a men's locker room and saw a life-sized painting of a man on the floor. He was dressed in a basketball uniform, had a basketball tucked under one arm and was broadly smiling. We didn't speak with words (as if often the case in my psychic dreams) but communicated telepathically. It was our vice-president and he wanted me to know – and share – that he'd died happy.

Speaking with my friend the next day, she revealed that the vice-president truly loved the sport and was engaged in a game with friends the night he fell dead on the basketball court. Wow! He conveyed so much to me without saying a single word.

∞ ∞ ∞

Once settled in my new home, I began to reflect on my past, especially as it related to men. I'd been raised to believe having a significant other was absolutely necessary to survive. I tried in vain through three marriages to secure the American Dream - to no avail. I'd dated off and on throughout my single years but never seemed to make any progress. Ty felt my frustration saying that he couldn't understand why a "good woman like me couldn't keep a man". Hmm.

I had more work to do with regard to healing my perception of men. How could I have a son and not wholly love and appreciate men? I knew I desperately needed to do this work and so I set out on what I call a *Social Experiment: Searching for the Goodness in Men.*

My goal was to consciously and purposely begin to look for instances where men showed up in ways that I'd not seen before. In order to do that, I had to reprogram my old conscious and subconscious beliefs about men, disassociating myself from people and conversations having to do with male-bashing. No matter what, I would not listen to or make negative male-related comments.

I actually looked for the smallest kindnesses, such as holding the door for me, smiling at me and asking sincerely about my day. These examples all became small but important stepping stones toward a healthier view of the opposites.

I kept a journal and recorded each positive incident as it happened. As the list grew, it made my heart lighter. I didn't date for three years during the initial phase of my Social Experiment because I felt that I really needed the space to heal internally.

(By having the ability to read, clear and heal energy, I was able to learn a great deal about vibration. In 2006 the film, *The Secret*, told the world what I had known for years: we are more than just our physical body. We are pulsating energy in a Universe comprised of energy. Our energy attracts like-energy. This means that whatever vibrates similar to me will appear in my life. If I don't like what I'm attracting, it's a sign to turn inward to inventory and release my deeper negative beliefs.)

When I began to date again, I found the men interesting but not yet at the level of awareness I desired. I was still healing.

Using my dating experiences as a practice field, I exercised expressing myself very clearly, worked at being non-judgmental, was patient and supportive, all the while asking for the same. My commitment was unshakable. This was my salvation and I knew that I needed to free myself from a past where I had been emotionally injured by men. There was no option in my mind – I HAD to discover the best aspects of men and to do that I had to uncover the best aspects of me. I had to release the role of victim! My own woe-is-me mentality had to go bah-bye. I was attracting men who also felt victimized, therefore there could only be one result. We each played roles where we saw the other as perpetrator; we each walked away feeling bruised and emotionally battered. In other words, I caused as much pain as I experienced. It took a very long time for me to consider the damage I'd left in my wake. When I began to broaden my scope of perception, I was taken aback by what I could no longer deny. I had played the roles of both victim and perpetrator; a definite Come-to-Jesus moment.

Mid-2013, I developed a macular hole (a hole in the retina). At the end of a very big week (completing a large energetic space clearing job of a twelve-thousand square foot antique gallery, a large residence and an architectural firm, plus several private sessions) I noticed blurred vision in my right eye. It was very traumatic; little did I know that it would offer me an up-close opportunity to further my Social Experiment by meeting a good man.

Because the sight distortion happened instantly and affected the central vision in my right eye, I immediately made an appointment to see an ophthalmologist. He sent me to a retina expert where I became even more disheartened and fearful. A poor bedside manner would have been a step up; the specialist clearly did not know the meaning of empathy. His observations were negative and sharp. Viewing the photographs of my retina, he said, "Look at this hole; it's only going to grow larger". He told me that surgery was necessary and should happen soon, before I lost the vision in that eye. To add insult to injury, I didn't have vision insurance. No problem, the financial manager said, as she offered me the cash discount cost of fifteen-thousand dollars.

Crying all the way home, I immediately went into fearful little girl mode. I didn't have the available cash for the surgery but I had to have the procedure. I'd already lost most of the hearing in my right ear – which affected my balance - if I didn't have my right eye repaired I feared I'd simply walk in circles!

Trapped in a vortex of fear, I felt weighed down. I had to come up with a plan of action. Action always made me feel better; I tallied up my available credit and prepared myself to pay for the surgery with plastic. Not the best choice but at the time, my only option.

One month later, while still trying to gather my courage to have the procedure, I began to experience light streaks out the corner of the affected eye. It scared me enough to call the doctor's office and schedule an emergency appointment.

Fortunately, my regular doctor wasn't in that day. When I arrived, the nurse told me I'd be seen by another specialist, then leaned forward to whisper, "You'll really like him".

And, so I did. The doctor was a tall, handsome young man with a broad and welcoming smile. He explained everything he did before he did it, which lessened the fear. Viewing the photographs of my retina, he told me that the hole was "dying to close!" Even before he got permission from my doctor to take over my case, and before the finances came up, I knew that HE was my guy.

He explained the procedure saying that a gas bubble would be injected through the eyeball after which I would be required to lay face down for seven days. The patient is allowed to get up for fifteen minutes every hour – that's it. In the prone position, the gas bubble puts pressure on the raised ridges of the injured retina and helps the edges to meet and fuse. Using the example of a draw bridge, he used his fingers to demonstrate the open and closed positions.

"I think we can do your procedure in-office." This wonderful man was trying so hard to help me –*ME!* He continued, "I think we should do it for two-hundred dollars." I began to cry - the ugly cry! Was I hearing this correctly? Had this angel, who'd only worked in this office for a month and a half, found a way to get me what I needed? It was an overwhelming OMG moment.

As before, I cried all the way home, but for very different reasons; I'd experienced a divine intervention.

The now affordable fee did nothing to de-freak the procedure; three needles were inserted into my eyeball to administer gas. Having prepared myself for the recovery period, I'd rented a massage table. I was determined to make a success of the generous gift I'd received.

My beloved four-legged friend, Roux, took it upon himself to lay on the table around the clock with me, leaving only for necessary trips to the litter box and to eat. At the end of the seven days, Roux's right pupil was dilated. After a series of tests, the veterinarian could find no reason for the anomaly, but I knew the cause. My sweet and powerful friend had absorbed my trauma – and not for the first time.

Each of the following exams over the next three weeks showed marked healing. My doc admitted that he'd never done that procedure in-office and was thrilled with the results. He decided to publish the technique; I was as happy for him as for myself. We'd both taken a risk and it paid off beautifully. We maintained positivity throughout the process and made a great team. (When I shared about Roux's pupil, he got goosebumps! He was open to the same magic.)

I had been purposely searching for the goodness in men and I'd witnessed it big time. This man didn't know me, I was not a friend or family, yet he went out of his way to so generously help me get what I needed. I was overwhelmed with sheer gratefulness.

At my last exam, the vision in my right eye was restored to pre-macular hole. We had achieved one hundred percent healing! (As with the hearing loss, I gained magnified psychic abilities after this event.)

I'd held the intention to bear witness to good men; it was an integral part of my path to healing. Extremely joyful that I'd accomplished two milestones during this process; I'd brought forth the opportunity (the macular hole) in order to find good men *and* I'd honored my body's needs by being very diligent in my recovery. I knew that this was more than a physical challenge; it was no mistake that it was the sight in my right eye (and many years earlier, my right ear) which had been impaired. In the study of symbols, the eyes represent perception and the right side of the body speaks to masculine energy, or father.

Healing severe father wounds may take a lifetime – if not many lifetimes – to achieve and is not to be viewed as punishment, but rather a true soul journey. Looking back, I realize that since my "awakening" in my early forties, I can handle most anything as long as I stay connected to Spirit.

CHAPTER TWENTY-FOUR

Magic Carpet

Frisky Cells. I was determined to view these overenthusiastic cells as tutors. They came into my life to teach me something and it was my job to learn. Being thrust into a frightening medical crisis in the fall of 2015 helped me discover a higher level of love than I'd ever known. Family and close friends rallied and stayed by my side. There was always a gentle shoulder to cry on and an ear to listen.

Checking in at the Out Patient Pavilion at nine-fifteen on the morning on the seventeenth of February, 2016, I was working hard to psyche myself up for a lumpectomy. I was a stranger to this level of medical care. My past physical challenges had not warranted attention anywhere near this. A trusted friend and student of mine - in the medical profession herself - volunteered to accompany me. She was familiar with the surroundings and that helped put me at ease.

A few hours after registration, I was injected with a weak radioactive solution near the mass of frisky cells. The solution traveled through the lymphatic system to my sentinel lymph nodes. This was done in preparation for a node biopsy.

As I chatted with the anesthesiologist I felt a bit silly in my hospital socks, gown and cap; it all seemed so impersonal somehow. He left after a brief discussion about my surgery.

Next, my surgeon came to visit; a gentle man quick to smile. According to law, he was to place his initials on the area where he was to perform the surgery. Using a small purple marker, he placed the letters MK on my right breast. Jokingly, I mentioned that I felt it only appropriate to place my initials on him, as well. After a brief pause and expressing that no one had ever requested this before, he grabbed a new marker and rolled up his sleeve. He asked me to write above the scrub line so it wouldn't wash off. Playfully, I added a smiley face and told him that my initials were to remind him that today we were connected. Adding that my initials were also to remind him that all of his focus was to be on me; I was queen for a day. We laughed and it helped to ease my nerves.

(A lumpectomy is a surgical procedure that involves removing a malignant tumor, or lump, and a small portion of the surrounding tissue from the breast.)

The next time I remember seeing my surgeon was during my follow-up visit when we discussed the pathology report. Fortunately, my lymph nodes were clean (no spreading) and the doc was able to obtain clear margins (visible normal tissue or skin margin that is removed with the surgical excision of a tumor). The biopsy indicated Stage II-A (early stage with no lymph involvement). However, one margin was narrower than he would've liked, so a re-excision was scheduled.

This process has triggered a healing crisis for me. Processing a diagnosis like this has multiple layers, but the most significant (for me) are emotional and spiritual.

I easily accepted the first surgery as necessary. Excision, he said during a lengthy evening phone consultation, would further facilitate the expeditious removal of frisky cells. Making it clear to me that "standard of care" dictates that a lumpectomy is *always* paired with radiation, my surgeon said that if that's not the chosen treatment, a mastectomy is recommended. That night, I agreed to have the follow-up treatment. In retrospect, I realize I said yes to please my doctor.

I continued to feel uneasy about the upcoming radiation treatment. I sensed that my physician *had* to say the things he said. He was trained - and now enmeshed - in the world of orthodox medicine. Could he sense the agony I experienced thinking I had to choose between the beliefs of the 3-D world and my innate psychic ability and beloved spiritual principles?

During this same period, a radiology department counselor called to "help me" make a decision about treatment. I shared my thoughts and decisions as I had with my surgeon. She was concerned for me, saying she really wanted to help me make the "right" choice. I believe that she believes radiation is the best option.

Synchronistically, I came across a series of videos called, The Truth About Cancer, created by Ty Bollinger, ten days before my first scheduled radiation treatment. With over one hundred medical and naturopathic doctors, as well as research scientists interviewed, the message was clear - there are numerous ways to naturally heal the body. Orthodox medicine has been treating cancer the same way (surgery, radiation and chemotherapy) for a very long time, with less-than-thrilling results. With no real emphasis placed on nutrition or bolstering the immune system, there were huge holes in their go-to method. Alternatively, everything I heard in the series resonated with me. I pulled away from western medicine several years ago in favor of naturopathic treatment and intuitively knew that the answer to my frisky cell situation was both emotional and natural. I wanted to help my whole body be well as opposed to blocking natural processes or killing healthy cells.

The video series confirmed everything I'd been thinking

and feeling. I called the radiation department to say I needed a time-out and wanted to do more research. I knew I would not actually reschedule but didn't say so because I didn't want to be contacted by the counselor again. I had made my decision and it was based on what I knew to be right for me. (A few weeks earlier I'd had a dream; three spontaneous fires flared up in my house. As quickly as I doused the first fire, two more fires erupted. When I woke, I instantly knew the fires represented radiation and that while the treatment may initially destroy a few rogue frisky cells, I'd have to deal with two more occurrences down the road.)

I felt encouraged after reviewing the results of the Occotype (Genome) DX test with my Oncologist. The test helps doctors determine a woman's likely risk of early-stage, estrogen-receptor-positive breast cancer recurrence. Even though my score was considered low (sixteen), the doctor recommended the long-term use of a hormone-blocking drug. In my opinion, reducing my reoccurrence rate by a mere six percent wasn't worth the risk of side effects. When the doctor mentioned checking liver and bone values after only three months, it further supported my intuition to opt out.

Only one healer, a very gifted student of mine, detected a mass. Her sense was that surgical removal would be all that was necessary.

In all actuality, I believe I was healed on the energetic realm before the tumor was ever removed. When I was first diagnosed, I asked several esteemed spiritually-inclined colleagues and friends to "look in" to determine if they saw frisky cells. None of them (including my mentor and two healers who did not know me personally) saw an imbalance. These incredible healers all have the ability to detect such illness, but could not find a trace of frisky cells in my body. This supports what

I sense to be true; I was already healed in the energetic realm but the tumor would have to be removed at the physical level.

As a healer, I've been blessed to be able to help others heal mentally, physically, emotionally and spiritually. I've seen tangible results time after time and believe wholeheartedly in the positive impact of a belief in a Higher Power or Source Energy. The marriage of eastern and western medicine felt right – to a degree. Even though my surgeon and I disagreed about the viability of radiation, we'd managed to create a harmonic symphony with our deeply held and individual beliefs.

The symbolic part of this leg of my voyage is very attached to healing my emotional heart. The frisky cells showed up to remind me that I was at the end of a very long and arduous family journey. While I'd done immense healing on the emotional and energetic levels, I now had to release the physical manifestation of a lifetime of emotional pain. I sent gratitude to these cells daily, for without them I might've remained idle and not jumped this significant hurdle. I celebrate that discovery! Joyous at the prospect of freedom from what had an intense hold throughout many lifetimes, I'd looked forward to the surgeries as an exorcism of sorts.

Though I've been on a conscious spiritual journey for over twenty years, and have "cut away" (pun intended) much in the way of old wounds and limiting beliefs, refinement continues.

Four days after the re-excision, my surgeon called. He began the conversation in his usual calm manner by inquiring about my progress. After a few moments, he announced, "I have four words for you." I couldn't wait for him to continue. "No more frisky cells!" Exhilarated by his words, I yelled out in joy. We both laughed and with few words communicated the relief we felt. We had teamed up with positive intention and a soul kinship. *We were a glorious success!*

After we said goodbye, I once again pondered the shrouded gift of frisky cells. They were my reminder that there was something left to clear with more to learn.

A watery vision of childhood torture, sexual abuse and the associated ongoing pain reminded me of the jagged road I'd traveled. Raised by narcissistic and rage-filled parents, losing brothers I dearly loved, being permanently thrown out of my home as a young girl *and* being highly sensitive and psychic have shaped me in ways I could not have imagined.

What I've known for many years came back to roost; *a soul whisper can turn into a scream if we do not listen.* I suddenly understood at a higher level why my life had been so hard. Like a bayou and its tributaries, the body IS connected to the mind. Whether conscious or unconscious, one feeds the other. My fear of dying from cancer as a very young girl had simmered until I had an opportunity to be made 'right' by my ego. The physical presence of a tumor reminds me that the power of the mind should never be underestimated. Like a toxic vapor - hard to see but potentially deadly if left unattended - the remnants of abuse were ready to leave me for good.

I'd surrendered to a healing process that was frightening and quite overwhelming at times. Coming to understand my own accountability for my life choices was crucial to making it over this traumatic speed bump.

I suddenly realized that it wasn't about any one day, it's about THIS day. Bad things don't happen because we deserve it, they happen because we vibrate to them. I knew I could change my frequency by making healthier choices on all levels.

I learned that my greatest power is authenticity as I remained true to myself during this particular journey and that my true strength comes not from self-reliance alone but from the love of others and my sincere faith in a Higher Power.

Since the nineties, when I fully embraced my psychic

healing gifts, my resolve to do what I believe I was born to do has been my guiding light – my north star. Attempting to keep my offer mainstream, I made every effort to present what I do and the nature of my gifts as simply as possible, relating it more to science than mysticism. I even shied away from the word "psychic" because there appeared to be many claiming the gift of seeing, hearing and knowing who were not authentically endowed. Once I understood that there will always be "knockoffs", I got back to expressing my work for what it truly is and what I love: soul, spirit and magic.

Continuing to do my sacred work, my commitment remains rock solid – yet fluid. Some of my most trying transformational experiences, especially my recent *Breastcapade*, help me find the song that sung me home.

As my psychic medium gifts perpetually expand, I assist others on their own path to genuine mind, body and spirit wellness. I've long since realized that authentic healing is a foundational progress; life is a spiral with our emotional growth traveling upward. At birth, the spiral is narrow and we are triggered often and intensely by our earliest childhood imprints. These imprints create energetic cords that fuel our pain and unhealthy choices throughout life – that is until the cords are cut. As we heal emotionally, the spiral grows wider; we may still become triggered, but not as often and not as profoundly. The energetic/emotional charge is lessened and we have a much better chance of catching ourselves earlier in the reactionary stage. Over time, our reactions become responses. We become neutralized to people and situations that at one time may have caused considerable pain.

From the soul's perspective, we can see exactly what is needed to heal and grow. I believe we incarnate by choice; leaving a lifetime unhealed requires further investigation and continued opportunities to complete the growth cycle in a new life. Not everyone believes in reincarnation or karma. No matter; we don't have to hold the same beliefs in order to believe that we have a divine right to heal the wounds of the past.

This life offered me a severely emotionally damaged family. Comprised of a violent alcoholic father who hurt me in many ways, a schizophrenic mother who was emotionally void and turned her head the other way, two older brothers – one severely mentally and physically challenged and the other the illegitimate child of my mom's first and only true love, a younger sister who was easily frightened and a psychic baby brother all played a vital role in my pain as well as my healing. At the soul level, I believe we choose our parents, siblings, the locale and the time in which to be born. Whatever needs healing from a prior life gets dumped into this lifetime. The scenario may appear quite different but the lessons – and opportunities to heal – will be the same.

Whether I work with a client for one session, or a long-term mentorship, I hold certain principles very dear. A belief in a Higher Self, Source, God, The Universe; etc., the desire to treat others with loving kindness – *especially* when no outward sign is warranted; the yearning to discover our own limiting beliefs; the wish to release the past by cutting energetic cords that keep us bound to the beliefs and/or destructive behaviors; the longing to recognize that all adult (healthy and unhealthy) relationships (personal and professional) are symptomatic of our childhood imprints and lastly, the aspiration to understand that healing and growing are our responsibility, our life work; it is foundational and lasts a lifetime(s).

∞ ∞ ∞

I'm frequently asked about what I do for a living. The following is a taste of the world in which I live - and -play.

Psychic. As a psychic, most of my work consists of energy work. At the core of my innate gifts, I have the agile ability to decipher and sculpt energy. When I read (channel) for a client, I am tapping into their soul energy. I see the lines between the lines, the words between the words.

People often talk about life purpose or life calling. I have found mine. No one is more delighted than me by the magic that takes place every single time I channel. That's not to say my path has been a straight road. I work at remaining flexible and look at my life as an organic production. Realizing that I have found a way to live in the mundane world by accessing the arcane, I am happy and wrapped in a warm blanket of familiarity and peace.

We are the producer and director of - and actor in - our own screenplay. Think about this. I believe we choose every bit of each lifetime from the other side and in-between lives. Our soul knows what is needed for growth and healing and orchestrates our incarnations to that end. It is a purposeful Universe!

There have many scene changes in my personal production, often quite unannounced and unexpected. When life throws one of those famous curve balls, I turn to my magic carpet. We all have one; the trick is to know when to hop on, sit back and let the flow of life take us where we need to be. My magic carpet has no steering wheel and certainly, no brakes. But I trust it. There are no wrong turns; I am always right where I need to be to learn what I need to learn. Divine timing and order prevail.

Medium. As a Medium, I am able to communicate with the dead. *Mediumship* may sound quite mystical but in all actuality, it is simply the ability to perceive and read the energy of a spirit dwelling in a dimension different from ours. Connecting with the deceased is simply a matter of tapping into soul energy. (This process has served well when assisting the Police Department with disappearance and homicide cold cases.)

Several years ago, I as invited to speak about mediumship to a crime victim support group in San Diego. I was honored to be asked and hoped I could offer comfort when speaking about my ability to connect with deceased loved ones. I was not prepared for the intensity in the room. As surviving individuals quietly entered the room, they placed photos of their murdered loved one on a large table at the head of the room. There I stood between the physical presence of the survivors and the energy of the deceased. It was so overwhelming, I had to take several deep breaths to steady myself.

As an empath, I feel the emotions of others quite deeply, and that day, it was incredibly heavy. My chest hurt and I had to fight back tears. I couldn't let myself think too deeply about the unbearable loss these beautiful souls had endured – until later.

Discovering that many of the cases had gone cold added to the unbelievable burden that hung heavy in the room. I wanted to help.

Saying my goodbyes, I could barely wait to get to my car. As soon as I pulled out of the parking lot, I began to cry. Sobbing all the way home, I knew that I wanted to help the surviving victims of homicidal crimes.

Beyond connecting the survivors with the departed, I was certain I could assist in solving unsolved crimes.

A few years after that, I had the opportunity to work with a cold case detective in San Diego. It was exhilarating! I realized how proficient I am in building psychic profiles from nothing more than the names of suspects and victims. Storylines revealed themselves to me day by day and I was able to offer information that the department had not yet uncovered. Seen from an energetic perspective, each of us are made up of layers of vibrating energy, each of which has their own specific vibration and purpose. This energy holds information about who we are, our choices, feelings, thoughts and past traumas. When I close my eyes with a specific individual in mind, I see pictures and videos as clearly as if sitting in a movie theater. At times, sounds and smells accompany the visual input.

Criminal Cold Cases. For instance, in a 20-year-old cold case, I was given only the victim's name and no other information. As the detective sat across the table from me, I closed my eyes and instantly saw a woman laying on a couch with her arm bent backwards in an awkward position. The arm was bloody and stiff (rigor mortis) and I noticed several stab wounds. Not sure how long I'd been in the dimension of the dead, I opened my eyes to see the detective staring wide-eyed. He was shocked that I'd seen in such precise detail and asked me to continue to work on the case with him. I continued to build psychic profiles as he supplied me with names of the prime suspect and those connected to both the victim and the suspect. It was exhilarating and challenging…*I was hooked!*

(I was recently asked to envision my ideal work day. It took no time to see myself working with the District Attorney's Office in the cold case division. My need to be blissfully challenged is addressed as I share my time doing other rewarding methods of sculpting energy.)

Energetic Space Clearing. When I read a space (energetic space clearing), whether residential or business, I am assessing the energy of not only the physical space, but of the people who currently or formerly occupied the space, as well. It's amazing what a structure can reveal about those (human and nonhuman) who've stepped across the threshold. It's all energy. (When my investigation reveals non-human energy, I often find paranormal activity, unexplained illness, unsolicited anger, insomnia, cravings for sugar and alcohol, nightmares, lost objects and more. Clients may report feeling mildly annoyed or afraid for their life. This negative or dark energy can be cleared safely, restoring the space to optimal balance.)

Cutting Energetic Cords. Working with clients always involves the discovery of subconscious beliefs. This is crucial and without facilitating this process, I could not call myself a *healer* or *mentor*. Once the saboteur – which is often shrouded in the form of the wounded inner child - is discovered, I cut the energetic cords keeping my client connected to the negative flow of old beliefs and trauma. Cutting the cords – sometimes referred to as soul retrieval - is but a piece of the solution when healing a painful past. There is a great deal of education involved when reclaiming one's power. This is where I take a somewhat different path from traditional psychology.

While I love – and utilize - the study of the psyche, I believe there is more to attend to than enlightening the mind when it comes to healing. After years of therapy with Anna, I learned a great deal about how my mind works. I was able to change some of my cognitive behavior but noticed that I continued to be drawn to the same type of unhealthy people and situations due to the vibrational match. In other words, therapy was an extremely valuable tool for having a safe place to express my feelings and helping me become intellectually savvy, but it didn't help me heal at the innermost galaxy of my battered heart. Because we attract life experiences with our emotional vibration, I continued to put myself in harmful situations, even when I knew better. Having knowledge is a far cry from being wise.

Although I will always be grateful for the foundation it provided, I needed more than therapy. That's what led me to Marin and the beginning of my true spiritual expedition.

Each moment is imprinted upon the one that came before as we make our way forward in a reality that spans everything from unbridled pleasure to excruciating trauma. We can change our life - *we have a choice.* Identifying that which brings us unadulterated joy - a reason to rise anew each morning, and the peace to lay our head down each night - is beckoning.

I thank you from the bottom of my heart for witnessing my life through my book. My journey has led me to understand that we truly are all one. The fear in me sees the fear in you; the love in me sees the love in you.

I will continue to travel toward my north star until my last breath – and beyond. If we should cross paths along the way, let us rejoice in knowing that many sacred dominoes fell with precision in order that we might bump into one another. We are soulmates; I suspect I will recognize you by a glimmer in your eye or by the way my cells vibrate when I'm near you. Until then, may your feet know laughter, your voice know kindness and your heart know love.

NOTES ON HEALING YOURSELF

There are many techniques you can use on your own to clear negative energy from your being and your space, as well as shield yourself from the toxic electromagnetic energy of others. Listed below are but a few examples that can assist you in keeping your energy clean and your vibration high. Remember, the higher your vibration, the more love, abundance and well-being you will experience. The opposite is true when your vibration becomes lowered – illness and disease, depression, lack and fear.

You may use my suggestions or any variation that feels right.

Clearing Stagnant/Negative Energy from Your Body:

Visualize a mesh screen under your feet. I see my screen as circular and three feet in circumference. Imagine the screen as its being slowly drawn up towards your head. The goal is to "grab" any energy that does not belong to you or that does not serve your highest good. Inadvertently, the screen will get snagged as it travels along your body. Jiggle the screen until you feel it begin to make upward movement once again. Once you've completed clearing your entire body, toss the remnants into the light. The toxic particles will safely dissipate. Repeat as many times as it takes until the screen moves smoothly and without stopping through your entire body. This can be done daily, especially after you've been around others or as often as you feel necessary.

Epsom Salt Soak. Using four cups of Epsom salt in a warm bath provides a traditional bath for spiritual cleansing. Soak for at least twenty minutes. It has a detoxifying quality that will draw out impurities in the energy bodies. You can substitute sea salt for Epsom salt, which is high in magnesium, easing aches, pains and the muscles.

Clearing Stagnant/Negative Energy from Your Space:

Epsom Salt and rubbing alcohol. Fill a Pyrex custard dish with an inch of Epsom Salt. Add rubbing alcohol (91%), covering the salt by about 1/8 inch. Place the dish on a glass plate and set the mixture in an open area of a room. Using a candle lighter, ignite the mixture making sure you are standing back as you light it. DO NOT MOVE the plate once the mixture is ignited.

The more stagnant or negative energy present, the more erratic the flame and the longer it will burn. Once the fire goes out, let the dish cool before removing. You can repeat the process in multiple areas of the space, making sure the dish has completely cooled prior to rinsing and adding more ingredients. This can be done weekly or as often as you feel necessary.

Palo Santo (a sacred wood; the name literally means holy wood, and it is just that; when it is burned, the smoke is believed to have both medicinal and therapeutic healing power) and Sage.

Burning Palo Santo and sage is one of the oldest and purest methods of cleansing a person, group of people or space. While Native American sage burning is the most commonly recognized form of today, it has nevertheless been a shared practice in other cultures. Burning cleansing rituals can be as elaborate or as simple as you want them to be, but it's of the highest importance that your intention be clear before you begin. If you are burning Palo Santo or Sage to purify a space, or a person (even yourself) then this needs to be clearly planted in your mind before you begin, and while taking the smoke around a home, or through a space.

The process is simple enough. If you have a heavy earthenware pot (something heatproof), place the bundled sage into the pot and light it for a few seconds before extinguishing the flame and letting the smoke billow up. Really dry Sage will catch fire quickly, so watch your fingers.

Focus burning Sage in high traffic areas in and around your space.

Be careful not to breathe in the smoke directly, and not to fill the area too thickly with smoke—this is not a fumigation, just a cleansing, so no need to go overboard. Slowly take the smoke to each area you would like to cleanse. Concentrate on gateway areas, such as windows, doors, closets, as well as hallways. Also concentrate on the corners of a room. Most importantly, use your intuition. If you allow it, your space will usually inform you as to which areas need to be cleansed the most.

You may want to focus on particularly busy areas, both foot traffic wise (kitchen) and mentally (computer workstation). If you have a pet, be sure to sage them (if they allow it) and their sleeping area.

Try burning incense immediately after a saging session. Sage has a more masculine/yang aspect and is nicely coupled by the feminine/yin aspect of incense. Also experiment with bell ringing or hand clapping in between saging and incense burning for a total cleansing effect.

To use your Palo Santo, burn your wood sticks, sitting with and nursing the embers. Let your wood burn for approximately one minute and then blow the flame out. Immerse yourself and fill your room with the sacred smoke. Holding the wood in both hands, visualize and your intentions (or prayers) aloud. Unlike conventional incense, which burns out completely after lighting it, your Palo Santo wood may be relit many, many times. The Palo Santo uses will provide energetic protection, remove any bad energy, uplift your spirit and fill your home with higher vibration.

Forgiveness and Cutting Energetic Cords:

What if RELEASE is a better, more achievable action than forgiveness?

"Since we are forgiven, it's foolish if we cannot forgive." Do you buy this? I don't!

The idea of forgiveness is comforting, but I have found it almost impossible at times to claim true forgiveness. We may think we've forgiven; we may truly want to forgive; we feel better if we have proclaimed forgiveness. But, even when we have done our very best, resentment may still live in our heart, mind AND energetic field as a counterproductive, guilt-producing imprint. Why? Because we have not truly released the situation.

By the way, we can't talk ourselves into forgiveness. My own experience has taught me that I must **cut the energetic cord** (sever my connection to a person, place or situation) to that experience and maybe even to that particular person if I want to be free of the emotional/energetic charge it once held. Only then is the experience and/or person, along with my reaction to it, neutralized. With this action, I can begin to see the higher, soul-inspired reason for the experience and be grateful for the wake-up call to greater insight about myself.

If you are unable to cut the energetic cord, another way to separate yourself energetically from another individual is to **call back your particles**. As you meditate on the other person, simply say, "I call back my particles so that they may be with me in wholeness. I send back your particles so that they may be with you in wholeness. This is done with love and for the highest good of all concerned." Repeat this intention every day for two weeks or until you feel the emotional/energetic connection is broken.

If traditional forgiveness hasn't worked for you, try adopting this perception: "Thank you FOR-GIVING me the opportunity to step into higher awareness." Once we're ready to own our participation in all exchanges, we're ready to step across the threshold into freedom.

Shielding Your Energy:

Visualize a hooded cloak wrapped about your body. Your intention is that only the high vibration of love be allowed to permeate your cloak. Any energy vibrating lower than your own will be reflected back to the sender. Wear your cloak in pubic, even if you're familiar with the group. Anyone can have a bad day and low vibration energy IS transferable. Keep your electromagnetic field clean!

If the above methods do not thoroughly clear your Self or your space, please feel free to contact me for further advice.

Happy healing!

POSTSCRIPT

In 1995 my brother **Freddy** died in his early forties. Still residing in a special-needs home, he developed severe pneumonia and never recovered. I was struck by his beautiful face as he lay content in his coffin. Rest in peace, sweet brother.

In 2003, my beloved brother, **Ricky**, passed away at the age of fifty-three (same age as my father and with the same diagnosis – cirrhosis of the liver). Within two days of his passing, I channeled him; it was by far the best conversation we'd ever had. The last thing he told me was that my mother would join him within thirty days. Rest in peace, my dear hero brother.

My mother, **Florence**, left the planet on September 16, 2003 - one month after Ricky crossed over and just as he'd predicted. I didn't really mourn her crossing; I'd grieved her for so many years. Her weakness on Earth is matched only by her power on the other side. (My Idaho near-death experience happened on September 16, 2004 and the frisky cells revealed themselves on September 16, 2015.) Rest in peace, my "hell on wheels" Mama.

In the fall of 2005, my second husband, **Dennis**, developed a neurological disease which quickly robbed him of his motor skills and his beloved career as a pilot. He was only fifty-eight years old when he crossed over in 2010. Even though we were only married for five years, he had a huge impact on my life. Rest in peace, dear soul friend.

In December of 2015, my beloved eighteen-year old cat

friend, **Roux**, transitioned into a higher realm. He was my "familiar" (a multiple-lifetime companion) and provided grounding and protection as I used my gifts to help others. Roux's magic touched many during his long cat life. I am deeply and forever grateful for his loving presence and unwavering service. We continue to play in the ethers; he will never be forgotten. Rest in peace, my precious Roux-boy.

ABOUT THE AUTHOR

Sitting in as instructor at the floodgates between mystery and answers, Connie reaches into the soul of each individual. She helps others to see their perfect truth by looking into their past, present and future. Cutting through adversity, she sees things as they really are. Connie's highly inspirational and deeply healing work consists of cutting energetic cords that bind us to old and counterproductive ways of being. She is able to detect the soul's whispers and shares messages in a way that is easily understood. Along with maintaining a private *Intuitive Healing* and *Profiling* practice, Connie does *Mediumship* (communicating with the departed), *Energetic Space Clearing* for both business and home and personal *Mentorship*. Offering occasional assistance to *Police Departments*, Connie thoroughly enjoys investigation work. She also hosted *SoulSync Radio*, a regularly scheduled live talk show where she intuitively answered questions for studio guests and callers. Originally from New Orleans, Louisiana, Connie currently resides in San Diego, CA. Visit her website at www.soulsync.com.